IRAN

Helen Loveday

PASSPORT BOOKS
a division of *NTC Publishing Group*
Lincolnwood, Illinois USA

Published by Passport Books in conjunction with
The Guidebook Company Ltd

This edition first published in 1994 by Passport Books, a division of NTC Publishing Group, 4255 W. Touhy Avenue, Lincolnwood (Chicago), Illinois 60646-1975, USA. Originally published by The Guidebook Company Ltd © 1994 Editions Olizane SA, Geneva for the French edition © 1994 The Guidebook Company Ltd, Hong Kong for the English edition. All rights reserved.

ISBN: 0-8442-9457-8
Library of Congress Catalog Card Number: 94-65005

Grateful acknowledgement is made to the authors and publishers for permissions granted:

Serpent's Tail, London for
An Iranian Odyssey by Gohar Kordi © 1991 Gohar Kordi
Serpent's Tail Books are available in the US from Consortium Inc, 1045, Westgate Drive, St Pal, MN fax (612) 221 0124 and in the UK from Plymbridge Distributors, Estover Rd, Plymouth PL6 7PZ

HarperCollins for
In Xanadu by William Dalyrumple © 1990 William Dalyrumple

HarperCollins for
Danziger's Travels: Beyond Forbidden Frontiers by Nick Danziger © 1987 Nick Danziger

Oxford University Press and Peters, Fraser & Dunlop for
The Road to Oxiana by Robert Byron © 1966 The Estate of Robert Byron

Harcourt Brace Jovanovich for
Shah of Shahs by Ryszard Kapuscinski, translated from the Polish by William R Brand and Katarzyna Mroczkowska-Brand © 1985 Harcourt Brace Jovanovich

Editor: Sally-Anne Imémé
Series Editor: Anna Claridge
Illustrations Editor: Caroline Robertson
Map Editor: Tom Le Bas
Design: B/W Graphics
Map Design: Graphic Emotion, Geneva and Image Factory, Hong Kong

Photography by Helen Loveday
Front cover courtesy of Gita Shenasi Cartographic & Geographic Organization (upper left and right, lower left); The Board of Trustees of The Victoria & Albert Museum (lower right)
Additional photography courtesy of Cesare Galli 67; Gita Shenasi Cartographic & Geographic Organization, Tehran 17, 25, 117, 149, 160, 193, 208, 230–231, 234; Robert Harding Photographic Library, London 56–57; The Board of Trustees of The Victoria & Albert Museum 5, 41, 84, 110, 153, 238–239; The Rubaiyat of Omar Khayyám 10, 131–137

Production House: Twin Age Limited, Hong Kong
Printed in Hong Kong

Tile panel, c. 1600, white earthenware with coloured-glaze painted decoration, courtesy of the Board of Trustees of the Victoria & Albert Museum.

Contents

Introduction

For over a decade, the political and social upheaval that Iran has undergone since 1978, reduced Western tourism in that country to a mere trickle. Even today, many people simply do not realize that it is possible to travel in Iran. And yet, for about three years, tourism has been developing at a steady rate and the attraction of Persia's cultural and historical riches is proving stronger in the long run than the preconceived ideas that exist about the Islamic Republic.

Those who knew Iran in the 1960s and 1970s will be struck as soon as they arrive by the most obvious changes that have occurred: the growth in the population, unrestrained urbanization, pollution. In addition, a revolution and ten years of war have inevitably left their mark on the people, although these deeper scars are not always immediately visible. Despite this, the quality of the welcome has lost none of its earlier warmth and modern Iran can be as interesting as ancient Persia.

At the end of the 20th century, fourteen years after the Islamic Revolution, Iran stands at another turning point in its history. This vast country with enormous economic potential—it contains the third largest oil reserves in the world—is on the verge of becoming one of the most powerful states in the Middle-East. Whatever the long-term evolution of its policies, it can no longer be ignored by the West nor by the rest of the world. Let us then learn to know it rather than be afraid of it.

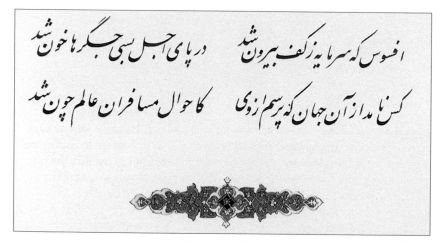

Quatrian from The Rubaiyat of Omar Khayyám

Facts for the Traveller

Since the end of the Iran–Iraq war, and since 1990 in particular, tourism has slowly picked up again in Iran. The great majority of foreign visitors are still Turkish and Pakistani nationals, but the renewed interest in Iran in some European countries and in Japan has lead to a big increase in the number of tourists from those regions too. Even before the 1979 Revolution, Iran was not a destination for mass tourism, and although tourism is tolerated today it should be remembered that a policy of openess to the outside world is still far from unanimously accepted in the government. Outside the main cities, tourists are relatively rarely seen and likely to attract attention, particularly when they arrive by the bus load, with expensive cameras at the ready.

Tourists in Iran have to face certain problems caused by the inadequacy of the infrastructure, and by the strict rules concerning clothing which apply in this Islamic republic. Lack of hotel rooms, especially in the better categories, difficulties in obtaining aeroplane tickets, the unreliability of flight schedules, long distances by road between the main towns, sudden changes in the opening days and times of museums and historical sites, the obligation for women to wear *hejâb* (correct dress for women, either *châdor* or headscarf), and frequent checkpoints on the roads are just some of the problems that can occur.

Expect the unexpected and be ready for delays. Having said that, the situation in Iran is changing very quickly and some of these problems may well be sorted out or at least have improved in the near future.

Climate

The climate of Iran is characterized by large differences in temperature from one season to another and between the north and south of the country. In general, winters are cold, except in the Persian Gulf, and summers very hot, with temperatures regularly reaching over 40° C (100° F). Winters in the mountainous regions are harsh and some areas are cut off by snow for weeks on end. In Azerbaijân and Kordestân in particular, temperatures fall well below 0° C (32° F) between December and February. In summer, however, these regions are less scorchingly hot than the plateau and the plains, where the temperature climbs steadily from spring onwards to reach between 45° C and 50° C (110°–120° F) in summer, most notably in Khuzestân and the central deserts. Khuzestân, which borders on the Persian Gulf, is also extremely humid and travelling there in summer can be an unpleasant experience. Winters, however, are comfortably warm.

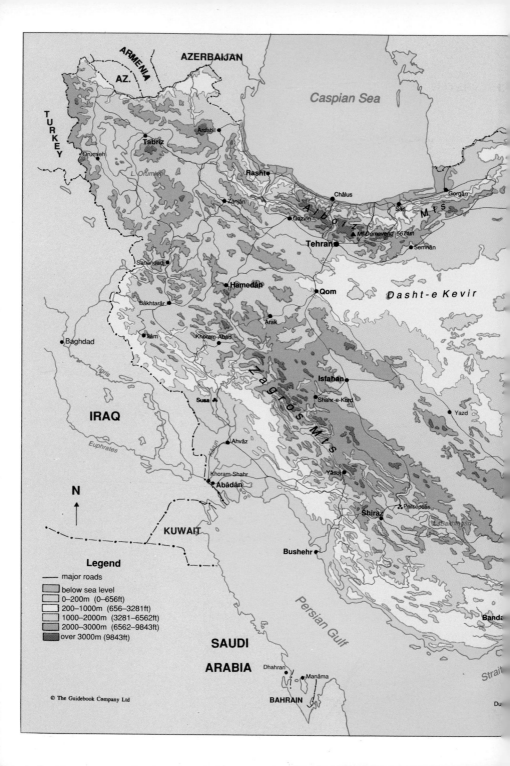

ARMENIA

AZ.

AZERBAIJAN

TURKEY

Caspian Sea

Ardabil

Tabriz

Orúmieh

Rasht

Châlus

Gorgán

L. Orúmieh

Zanján

Sári

Mts

Qazvin

A l b o r z

▲ Mt Damávand 5671m

Tehran

Semnán

Sanandadj

Hamedán

Qom

Dasht-e Kevir

Bákhtarán

Arak

Ílám

Khoram-Abad

Baghdad

Tigris

Z a g r o s   M t s

Isfahan

Susa

Shahr-e-Kord

IRAQ

Yazd

Euphrates

Ahváz

Khoram-Shahr

Yásuj

Abádán

N

Persépolis

Shiraz

L. Bakhtagan

KUWAIT

Bushehr

Legend

— major roads

below sea level

0–200m   (0–656ft)

200–1000m   (656–3281ft)

1000–2000m   (3281–6562ft)

2000–3000m   (6562–9843ft)

over 3000m (9843ft)

SAUDI

ARABIA

Persian Gulf

Band

Dhahran

Manáma

Strai

© The Guidebook Company Ltd

BAHRAIN

Du

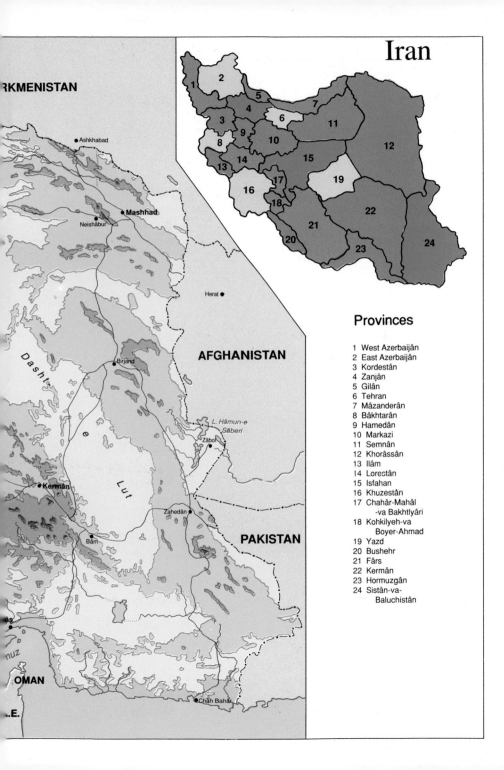

Iran

TRKMENISTAN

Ashkhabad

Neishâbur

Mashhad

Herat

Dasht-e

Birjand

AFGHANISTAN

L. Hâmun-e Sâberi

Zâbol

e

Lut

Kermân

Zahedân

Bâm

PAKISTAN

êş

nuz

OMAN

..E.

Châh Bahâr

Provinces

1 West Azerbaijân
2 East Azerbaijân
3 Kordestân
4 Zanjân
5 Gilân
6 Tehran
7 Mâzanderân
8 Bâkhtarân
9 Hamedân
10 Markazi
11 Semnân
12 Khorâssân
13 Ilâm
14 Lorestân
15 Isfahan
16 Khuzestân
17 Chahâr-Mahâl
    -va Bakhtlyâri
18 Kohkilyeh-va
    Boyer-Ahmad
19 Yazd
20 Bushehr
21 Fârs
22 Kermân
23 Hormuzgân
24 Sistân-va-
    Baluchistân

The coastal zone between the Caspian Sea and the Alborz Range has a high rainfall all year round as the mountains form a natural barrier which prevents clouds from moving inland. Temperatures vary between 7° C (45° F) in winter and 26° C (75° F) in summer, sometimes with high humidity. However, the summer heat is less extreme than further south and many popular resorts have sprung up along the coast.

Spring (April to May) and autumn (mid-September to mid-November) are the most pleasant seasons to visit Iran. The inland regions are generally dry then and comfortably warm, although nights are cool. Showers and storms may occur until June in the mountains in the west and in Tehran, and in the northwest, snow often lies in the mountains until April or May.

Tour Operators

Most Western tourists travelling to Iran today choose to go on an organized tour, either one proposed by a foreign tour operator, or a trip organized directly with an Iranian agency (see below for addresses). Although individual travel is less common than it was fifteen years ago, it is nevertheless perfectly possible and is likely to increase considerably in the years to come. A few foreign travellers have visited Iran with their own car or motorbike; at present, the frontiers with Afghanistan and the Republics of the former-USSR are closed, and the only possible route is therefore from either Turkey or Pakistan (although petrol is exceedingly cheap in Iran, no unleaded petrol is as yet available). The frontier posts on the Turkish border are located at Bâzargân and Seto, in Azerbaijân. The Pakistani border can be crossed at Mirjâve, near Zahedân, in Sistân and Baluchestân Province. Rail links also exist between Tehran and Ankara and between Zâhedân and the Pakistani border.

FOREIGN TOUR OPERATORS
British Museum Tours, 46 Bloomsbury Street, London WC1B 3QQ. Tel 071-323 8895, 071-323 1234; fax 071-436 7315; tlx 28592
Jasmin Tours, High Street, Cookham, Maidenhead, Berks SL6 9SQ. Tel 0628 531121; fax 0628 529444; tlx 846742

For those interested in bird watching and nature:
Birdquest Ltd, Two Jays, Kemple End, Birdy Brow, Stonyhurst, Lancs BB6 9QY. Tel 0254 826317; fax 0254 826780; tlx 635159

LOCAL TOURIST AGENCIES
Certain Iranian tourist agencies can organize tours for one or several people lasting

from a few hours to several weeks (which include all accommodation, transport, and an English-speaking guide). This is a useful solution for those who wish to visit specific sites which may not necessarily be included on more general tours, or for business men who have one or more free days in which to do some sightseeing.
Iran Tourist Co, 257 khiabân-e Motahari, Tehran 15868. Tel 622008, 622040, 623050; fax 626158; tlx 222918. Highly recommended, efficient and helpful.
AITO, Azâdi Grand Hotel, Chamran Expressway, Tehran 19395. Tel 298064, 297021; fax 298072; tlx 212845, 214302
Iran Airtour, 191 khiabân-e Motahari, corner of khiabân-e Dr Mofateh, Tehran. Tel 890298; fax 895884; tlx 213956

Visas

Despite the increase in foreign applications for tourist visas, obtaining a visa can still be a long and complicated business. There are several types of visas: transit visas, valid for one or two weeks; pilgrimage visas; and tourist visas, valid up to a month (it is possible to get an extension once you are in Iran by applying at provincial capital visa offices). Almost all foreign nationals need a visa before they can enter the country; at the moment only Turkish and Japanese nationals are exempt from this rule. American nationals will find it extremely difficult to get a visa unless they have family in Iran. Whatever your nationality, your passport should not contain an Israeli or South African visa.

The visa request must go through one of the embassies of the Islamic Republic of Iran, but the embassy will only be able to issue the visa once it has received an authorization number from the Ministry of Foreign Affairs in Tehran. Apply a good month before your departure date, even if you have joined an organized tour (in which case the travel agency will probably apply for the visa for you. However, you will still have to hand in your passport a month in advance). Passports must be valid for at least six months after the date you leave Iran. If you organize a tour with an Iranian agency, the agency will apply for your visa directly to Tehran; you will have to send your passport to the Iranian embassy in your country once the embassy has received the authorization number from Tehran.

Tourists travelling with a group generally have little trouble obtaining a visa, but individual travellers, particularly young women, may encounter more difficulties and their visa request may even be rejected.

The following are the addresses of some Iranian embassies and consulates:
Australia, 14 Torres St, Red Hill, Manuka, Canberra. Tel (06) 295 2544
Canada, 411, Roosevelt Avenue, 4th floor, Ottawa K2A 3X9. Tel 7290 902

Turkey, Tahran Caddesi 10, Ankara. Tel 1274 320
Consulates: Ankara Caddesi 1-2, Istanbul. Tel 5138 230
Cumhuriyet Caddesi, Kuksay Sitesi 23/25, Erzerum. Tel 13 876
United Kingdom, 27 Prince's Gate, London SW7 1PX. Tel 071-584 8101
Consulate: 50 Kensington Court, London W8 5DD. Tel 071-937 5225
United States, *see* Canada

Getting There

Incoming flights from Europe land at Tehran's Mehrabad airport. The other international airports in Iran (Shiraz, Bandar-e Abbâs, Mashhad, and Isfahan) only take
flights from the Middle East and Pakistan. The number of flights from Europe has
greatly increased in the past two or three years, and several companies have now
resumed direct flights to Tehran: British Airways (from London), Lufthansa (Frankfurt), Alitalia, Air France, KLM (Amsterdam), Swissair (Zürich) and Austrian Air-
lines. The national company, Iran Air, also has direct flights from London, Frankfurt,
Geneva, Rome, Paris and Vienna. Note that alcoholic beverages are not served on Iran
Air, and that women have to wear clothing in accordance with Islamic rules once in
the aeroplane.

Iran Air flights also exist between Tehran and Damascus, Dubai, Sharjah, Karachi
and Istanbul. Other connections are possible between the United Arab Emirates and
Shiraz, Isfahan, Mashhad and Bandar-e Abbâs.

Customs

It is strictly forbidden to import alcohol, drugs and pornographic material into Iran.
Be careful with foreign journals and newspapers which may be confiscated, particularly if they contain pictures of women wearing makeup or without a headscarf. A
reasonable amount of jewellery for personal use, a camera and five rolls of film, a pair
of binoculars and a walkman can be taken into the country without any problem as
long as you leave with them again. The exact number of films taken in per person is
rarely checked but be aware that there is an official limit of five rolls.

Most of the souvenirs bought in Iran may be exported, except for carpets, antiques, gold and silver, precious stones, and food products. In the case of the latter,
the rule is rarely enforced although caviar and large quantities of pistachios can be
difficult to get past customs. The export of carpets and antiques, on the other hand, is
very strictly controlled and can be done only if you are in possession of the right

Bakhtiari Mountains, Chehel Kords area

documents. It is recommended to buy these items in shops that have an export licence and can take care of shipping them abroad.

Getting Around

By Air

Iran has a surface area almost three times that of France and distances between towns are often very great. The quickest way of getting around is by plane. Iran Air operates scheduled flights between all the major towns; they are generally cheaper than flights of the same distance in Europe, although prices have recently increased and future increases are likely. Flying is a popular means of transport with Iranians and tickets are difficult to buy unless you make a reservation well in advance. It is essential to bear in mind when working out your itinerary that flights are frequently delayed and even cancelled. Reservations can be made in Iran Air offices in all the major cities.

By Train

Trains are a comfortable and relatively quick way of getting around, but the railway system is rather limited; there are no railway lines, for example, to Shiraz or Hamedân. The east–west line goes from Tabriz (and Turkey) to Mashhad, via Zanjân, Tehran and Semnân. A smaller line links Tehran with the Caspian coast and passes through Sâri and Gorgân. The second main line leaves Tehran for the south, splitting at Qom into two separate lines, one running south–east to Yazd and Kermân, and the other south–west to Ahvâz and the port of Abâdân. There are three classes of seats and berths in the overnight trains. Tickets have to be bought at the station except in Isfahan, where there is a ticket office in town at Enqelâb-e Eslâmi Square.

By Coach

The inter-city coach system covers the entire country. The various bus companies have been organized into cooperatives, each one identified by a different number, such as Cooperative Bus Company No 1, also known as Iran Peima 1, No 2, or No 5. The main towns have several coach stations, some of which are shared between companies, while others belong to a single company. Seats on the buses are numbered and it is wise to buy one's ticket ahead of time.

By Bus and Taxi

For getting round within a city, there are both buses and taxis. Unless you can speak and read a minimum of Persian, the bus system can turn out to be extremely complicated as stops are not always well indicated and the number of the bus as well as its destination are written in Persian only. Taxis are either collectively owned or belong to agencies; they can be hired from the hotels for short excursions or ones lasting up to a whole day.

Maps, Books and Newspapers

The best places to find maps of Iran, city maps and books about the country in foreign languages are the bookshops in the hotels Esteghlal and Azâdi Grand in Tehran, and opposite the Abbâssi Hotel in Isfahan. As yet, few hotels have shops in them, so it is best to buy maps, postcards and dictionaries at the beginning of your trip before you leave Tehran.

Foreign language books are also on sale in some bookshops in Tehran (try on khiabân-e Enqelâb, near the University), and in Isfahan (opposite the Abbâssi Hotel).

Two English-language daily newspapers are published in Tehran, the *Tehran Times* and the *Keyhan*, both of which are available in the big hotels and are occasionally sold in the streets in the main cities (outside Tehran they are usually a day or so out of date).

Tourist Offices

The governmental tourist information service is run by the Ministry of Culture and Islamic Guidance and the tourist offices in the main towns are generally to be found in the ministry building (ask for the Edâre Ershâd Eslâmiye). All provincial capitals have tourist offices, which can probably provide you with town maps and a few practical tips. These offices vary considerably in helpfulness from town to town and do not all have English-speaking staff. The offices are closed Thursday afternoons and Fridays and are open on other days from 8 am till 2 pm.

The main offices are the following:
Tehran Department of Tourism and Pilgrimages, 5th floor, 11 khiâbân-e Dameshq, khiâbân-e Vali-e Asr. Tel 892 212, extn 29
Isfahan corner of khiâbân-e Shâhid Madani and khiâbân-e Chahar Bagh, opposite the Abbâssi Hotel. Tel 21555
Mashhad Ministry of Culture and Islamic Guidance, 2nd floor, Eslâmi Road, khiâbân-e Bahâr. Tel 48288
khiâbân-e Kermân Ershâd, khiâbân-e Ferdusi. Tel 25098

Language

The official language of Iran is Persian, or Fârsi, an Indo-European language (more specifically Irano-Aryan) which was once the dialect spoken in the province of Fârs, hence its name. Until the Arab invasion in the eighth century, classical Persian, derived from older forms known as Middle and Old Persian, was written with a variant of the Assyrian alphabet; it is this script which is seen in the Sassanian rock inscriptions. At the time of Arab domination, the Arabic script was adopted and modified slightly to adapt it to a non-Semitic language. The result is an alphabet which includes most of the letters used in Arabic, with the addition of a few new letters. Words borrowed from Arabic are generally written in their original form, although their pronunciation in Persian may differ from that of the Arabic.

While Fârsi is the national language, other Iranian dialects, such as Kurdish and Baluch, are also spoken in some regions. Arabic is spoken in Khuzestân, on the Iraqi border, Turkish Azeri in Azerbaijân and another Turkish dialect, Turkoman, in the northeast. The tribal communities generally speak their own dialects, such as Lur or Bakhtiâri, as well as Fârsi.

For the non-Persian-speaking tourist, a knowledge of English is essential as it is spoken in most hotels and in many shops in the main towns. See page 245 for a short language guide with a note on the pronunciation of Persian words.

Clothing

Iran is an Islamic republic and the *hejâb*, or Islamic dress, must be worn by all women. This does not mean having to wear a *châdor*, but rather covering one's head and neck with a scarf, and wearing long sleeves and a long dark coat (preferably calf-length). Feet and any part of the legs left showing should also be covered (with socks or thick tights), even when wearing sandals. Do not wear lots of jewellery; try to keep to plain rings and discreet makeup.

Hejâb must be worn in all public places (even in restaurants and regardless of the temperature!). In practice, this means that the only time it can be taken off is in the privacy of your hotel room. But do not forget to put your coat and scarf back on when you go to answer the door! Some state hotels are very strict about *hejâb* in the lobby and may ask women to readjust their scarves if a few locks of hair have managed to escape.

The problem of packing for a trip to Iran is simplified for women by the rules concerning clothing: do not bother taking along your best dresses for the evenings as no one will see them! On the other hand, a selection of scarves and a change of coat will come in handy. Scarves as well as long coats in a surprising variety of colours can be bought quite cheaply in Iran. Be careful when buying cloth in the bazaars as most of it is synthetic and very uncomfortable in hot weather. Trousers (jeans are perfectly acceptable) and long skirts or dresses are the most practical way of dressing. Be aware that wearing *hejāb* can be difficult in hot weather, particularly if you are overdressed; loose and light cotton clothing is best of all.

In certain holy places, such as the mausoleums of the descendants of the Imams, women must wear a *chādor*, but these can usually be borrowed at the entrance gate. There is no need to buy one for the purpose. Be careful not to tread on the ends of your *chādor*: walking with a *chādor* on is not always as easy as it looks, especially if it is slightly too long!

Even if these rules concerning clothing seem restrictive, it is very strongly advised that you stick to them (remember that, travelling in a group, you may simply be sharply reprimanded for improper dress, but it could be an entirely different matter later for your Iranian guide). If you are not prepared to obey these rules, then it is probably better not to visit Iran at the moment.

The rules concerning clothing for men are much simpler: shorts should not be worn and arms should be covered, particularly when visiting holy shrines. Note that all these rules are more strictly observed during the months of Ramadan and Moharram.

Given the great temperature swings between day and night, as well as differences in altitude (when travelling by car in the Zagros, for example, it is quite possible to go from the central plateau at a height of 1,000 metres [3,280 feet] above sea-level to a mountain pass at 2,500 metres [8,202 feet] several times in one day!) it is important to have several layers of clothing handy that can be taken off or put on as need be. In winter, warm clothes are essential except along the Persian Gulf.

Photography

Although the Iranians themselves enjoy taking photos of their families, they are not yet used to the sophisticated photographic equipment that foreign tourists like to deploy, and may well regard some of it as highly suspicious, especially zoom lenses. Groups of tourists descending from a bus with their cameras at the ready and shooting off in all directions make policemen particularly nervous. Be careful where you point your camera and avoid taking pictures of policemen and soldiers. It is strongly recommended that you do not take pictures in or around airports, military installations of any kind, barracks, frontiers and any other sensitive area. If in doubt, ask your guide (policemen have been known to forbid pictures being taken in the street, especially in small towns). When taking photos of people, particularly of women, ask their permission beforehand.

Photography is permitted at most historic sites and even in some museums (without flash) but not around certain holy shrines such as Mashhad and Qom. In *imâm-zâdeh* check first with a guardian to make sure that photos are allowed.

Health

There are no compulsory vaccinations for entering Iran but it is a good idea to be vaccinated against tetanus and typhoid. Malaria is present in some areas, such as Sistân and Baluchestân, southern Fârs and Khuzestân, particularly in summer. Check with your doctor about which anti-malarial drugs to take, and make sure you have insect repellent with you.

Take a small medical kit with the usual basic items (such as plasters, aspirin, anti-diaorrhea pills) as well as any particular medicine you might need.

The tap water can be drunk almost everywhere; if in doubt, take water purifying tablets with you. In many of the smaller towns, the water comes directly from the *qanât*, which are fed by melt water and is therefore relatively safe. However, in out-of-the-way places and in the heat of summer it is better to take proper precautions.

Accommodation

Hotels (*mehmânkhâne* or *hotel*) in Iran are classified in categories from one to five stars, and guesthouses (*mosâferkhâne*) in superior, first and second class. The *mosâferkhâne* offer rudimentary services, particularly second class ones, but are very cheap and can often be paid in rial, whereas most hotels now ask foreigners to pay in US dollars. The star system for the hotels bears little relation to the systems in use in the West, and the quality of hotel within any one class can vary quite considerably. In general, a five-star room is a 'deluxe' one with private bathroom. Do not expect the words ex-Hilton or ex-International to indicate the equivalent of those hotels in Europe. Most hotels were built in the 1970s and are now somewhat run down, although generally perfectly acceptable. In many hotels, even in the four-star category, the bedroom toilets may be of the squat variety rather than a Western-style one.

The names of hotels are liable to change when the owner changes. It is worth enquiring about previous names of a hotel if you can, and making sure that you have as exact an address as possible (street names frequently change too).

Theoretically, only married couples may share a hotel room. This rule is strictly applied in the case of Iranians but hotel staff may be more lenient towards foreigners, especially those in a group. However, be aware that the rule exists and do not assume that it will be waived just for you.

For a list of the main hotels, see Practical Information page 240.

Money

The basic monetary unit in Iran is the rial. While written prices are usually given in rial, it is very frequent when giving a price orally to do so in toman (one toman is equal to 10 rial, 100 toman are 1,000 rial). There are banknotes of 100, 200, 500, 1,000, 2,000, 5,000 and 10,000 rial, as well as coins of 10, 20 and 50 rial. In autumn 1992, 1 US$ was worth 1425 rial.

US dollars cash, and traveller's cheques in dollars and in some foreign currencies (yen, Deutschmark, pounds sterling, Swiss francs) are generally accepted, but outside the major cities it is best to have dollars in cash. Credit cards (American Express and Visa) are increasingly accepted in the big hotels in Tehran and Isfahan, but do not rely on them as your only method of payment.

The best place to change money is at the bank: since the beginning of 1991, bank exchange rates have been equivalent to those on the black market. Branches of the major banks can be found at Tehran airport and in most of the big hotels. If you want to change your rial back when you leave the country, make sure you have kept the bank exchange certificates and your customs declaration form. Banks are usually open from 9 am to 4 pm or 4.30 pm from Saturday to Wednesday, and are closed on Thursday afternoons and Friday.

Do not change too much money when you first arrive; US$50 go a long way, particularly if you are travelling with a group. If you are travelling alone, remember that most hotels will ask to be paid cash in dollars. Food and transport within the country is very cheap, and hotels will probably be your biggest expense.

Telecommunications

Hotels are by far the most convenient place from which to telephone abroad and long-distance calls are relatively cheap. From Tehran hotels, the connection is usually quite quick, but it may be necessary to wait an hour or two when calling from smaller towns as all calls abroad have to go through a receptionist.

It is also possible to send telegrams and telexes within the country or abroad from post offices in the larger towns. These services are also available in the bigger hotels.

Time Zone

Tehran time is GMT plus three and a half hours. Iran has now introduced daylight saving time (the clocks change by an hour in March and September) so that for a few weeks there may be an extra hour's difference with Continental Europe.

Opening Times

Friday is the day of prayer in Iran and all shops, businesses and offices close then. Thursday is half-closing day for many shops and offices. On other days, opening hours can vary quite considerably from one region to another. In general, shops close for an hour or two at lunchtime and stay open until 8 pm, whereas government offices are only open from 8 am to 2 pm.

Mosques, Museums and Historical Sites

There is generally no problem for non-Muslims to visit mosques in Iran, except perhaps during Friday prayer. Shoes can be worn inside the mosques but should be taken off where carpets have been laid down, usually in front of the *mehrab*. However, in the *imâmzâdeh* (mausoleums of the descendants of Imams), it is necessary to take one's shoes off before entering the building. Remember to ask permission to take photographs inside the *imâmzâdeh* even if there are no signs expressly forbidding it. In some *imâmzâdeh*, such as Abdol Azim's in Ray, women must wear a *châdor*, which can be hired at the entrance.

At Qom and Mashhad, the most important pilgrimage centres in Iran, entrance to the holy shrine is forbidden to non-Muslims (with the exception of certain areas in Mashhad).

The opening times and days of museums and historical sites is often one of the most frustrating problems for the tourist in Iran. Most museums have fixed opening times, with one closing day a week. Unfortunately, these times can change suddenly and those tourists with itineraries fixed in advance may have to cancel some visits or replace them. The opening times given in this guide are for winter 1993.

At the most important sites, such as Persepolis, Pasargadae, or Susa, tickets are sold at the entrance, but some sites, particularly those away from the major towns, are unfenced and do not even have a guardian. Occasionally, it will be necessary to find the guardian and get him to unlock the gate. Should he be absent, you may even have to come back later or the next day. It is therefore recommended to have as

Plan of the haram-e motahar, *the holy precinct around the shrine of Imam Rezâ, in Mashad*

flexible an itinerary as possible if you are determined to see a particular place, or to telephone in advance to be sure of getting in. Sites well away from large cities are often impossible or extremely difficult to get to by public transport; for these, it is best to hire a car and a driver if you are not travelling with an organized tour.

Calendar

There are three different calendars in use in Iran. The first is the Persian calendar, a solar one, the direct descendant of the Zoroastrian calendars of pre-Islamic Persia, which has years of 365 days divided into 12 months of 30 or 31 days each. Despite its apparent resemblance to the Gregorian calendar, it differs on several important points: the first six months of the year have 31 days, the next five have 30 days and the last month 29 days, or 30 days in leap years. New Year's Day corresponds to the first day of spring, the 21st of March, which is the time of the great festival of Noruz. The years are counted from the first day of spring of the Hegira (622 AD). It is this solar calendar which is the most widely used in Iran today. For a quick conversion, add 621 to the Iranian year for the approximate date in the Christian calendar.

The names of the months are as follows: Farvardin (21 March–20 April); Ordibehesht (21 April–21 May); Khordâd (22 May–21 June); Tir (22 June–22 July); Mordâd

(23 July–22 August); Shâhrivar (23 August–22 September); Mehr (23 September–22 October); Abân (23 October–21 November); Azar (22 November–21 December); Dey (22 December–20 January); Bahman (21 January–19 February); and Esfand (20 February–20 March).

The second calendar is the Islamic lunar calendar used in all Muslim countries, and which serves to fix the religious festivals and ceremonies. With this system, the year is also divided into twelve months, but is only 354 days long. For this reason, the gap between the solar and lunar years is constantly growing (33 lunar years are equal to 32 solar years), and there is now roughly a forty-year difference between the Islamic and Persian calendars although both start with the year of the Hegira. Because the first month of the Islamic year, Moharram, can begin at any time in the Gregorian calendar, it is very difficult to calculate the exact equivalent of an Islamic date, and conversion tables have been worked out for this purpose.

It is worth noting also that there is a small difference between the Islamic calendars in Iran and in other Muslim countries. As the calendar is fixed according to the visibility of the moon, which appears a day later in Iran, there is a one day difference in the dates of the big religious festivals in Iran and in other Muslim countries.

The Gregorian calendar is also used in Iran and appears, for example, on the newspapers alongside the other two calendars; thus the newspaper published on the 5th of October 1992 was also dated 13th Mehr 1371 (Persian solar calendar) and seventh Rabi-ol-sani 1413 (lunar calendar).

Festivals and Holidays

RELIGIOUS HOLIDAYS

These days are determined according to the Islamic lunar calendar. As the equivalents in the Gregorian calendar vary from year to year, only the Muslim dates are given below, in the order in which they appear in the Islamic calendar:

9 Moharram Tâsuâ	Eve of the martyrdom of Imam Hussein
10 Moharram Ashurâ	Anniversary of the martyrdom of Imam Hussein, killed at Kerbala
20 Safar Arba'in	40th day after the death of Imam Hussein
28 Safar	Anniversary of the death of the Prophet and of the martyrdom of Imam Hassan
17 Rabi-ol-avval	Anniversary of the birth of the Prophet and of Imam Ja'far Sadeq
13 Rajab	Anniversary of the birth of Imam Ali

27 Rajab Eid-e mab'as Day when the Prophet began preaching
3 Sha'bân   Anniversary of the birth of Imam Hussein
15 Sha'bân   Anniversary of the birth of the Twelfth Imam
1 Ramazân   Beginning of the month of fasting
21 Ramazân   Anniversary of the martyrdom of Imam Ali
1 Shavvâl Eid-e fetr   Festival to mark the end of the month of fasting
25 Shavvâl   Anniversary of the death of Imam Ja'far Sadeq
11 Zighade   Anniversary of the birth of the Eighth Imam, Imam Rezâ
10 Zihajje Eid-e qorbân Day of sacrifice to the pilgrims at Mecca
18 Zihajje Eid-e qadir Anniversary of the naming of Ali as successor to the Prophet

NATIONAL HOLIDAYS
These holidays are calculated according to the Persian solar calendar and rarely vary
in date in the Gregorian calendar:

1–4 Farvardin (21–24 March) Noruz, the Iranian New Year
12 Farvardin (1st April)   Islamic Republic Day
13 Farvardin (2 April)   Sizdah bedar, the 13th day of the New Year
14 Khordâd (4 June)   Anniversary of the death of Imam Khomeini in 1989
15 Khordâd (5 June)   Anniversary of the popular uprising in 1963, which
                             followed news of the arrest of Imam Khomeini
17 Shahrivar (8 September)   Day of the Martyrs of the Revolution
22 Bahman (11 February)   Victory of the Islamic Revolution (1979)
29 Esfand (20 March)   Oil Nationalization Day (1951)

Shopping

Iranian arts and crafts are extremely varied and, in most cases, have a very long tradition behind them. They include carpets, kilims (*gelim*), printed cloth, brocade, inlaid
wood, miniatures, and copper and brassware, to name just a few. Unfortunately,
these crafts have been declining in quality for a few years and the hotel and airport
shops—when they exist—offer only a limited choice, which is soon repetitive. The
bazaars have a much wider choice, but do not forget to bargain for anything you buy
there, particularly in Isfahan. The bazaar is the best place to buy gold jewellery (in
small quantities if you want to avoid trouble when you leave the country), textiles or
a *châdor*.

Persian carpets are still of very high quality; as well as the traditional motifs there
are now a variety of modern ones, including the portrait of Imam Khomeini, some of

which are of foreign inspiration. Because of the strict rules governing the export of carpets, it is best to buy them at a shop which has an exporting licence and which will take care of sending them to you, in your home country, against a down payment. If a carpet seller assures you that the laws on exporting carpets have just changed, check with your guide or at the hotel before buying. The same pre-cautions are valid for antiques. Be careful with recent antiques, cloisonné fresh out of Chinese workshops and miniatures painted on ivory, bone or even plastic.

Caviar can be bought in Iran at extremely low prices, particularly along the Caspian. Theoretically, its export is forbidden unless it has been bought at the airport shop located after customs, where, although more expensive, it is still considerably cheaper than the prices on the European market.

Part of the Isfahan bazaar

Food and Drink

The basic foodstuff in Iranian cuisine is rice, served either as a *chelo* or a *polo*. *Chelo* is the plain cooked rice which is served with meats or stews (*khoresh*), while *polo* is rice mixed with other ingredients such as fruits (cherries, dried fruit), meat, or vegetables. Meat, particularly chicken and lamb, is frequently served skewered (*kebâb*): the *chelo kebâb* is meat with plain rice, while *luleh* and *kofteh kebâb* are made from minced meat. The stews (*khoresh*) are simmered for a long time and are always served with *chelo*. One of the most famous *khoresh* is *fesenjân*, usually made with duck or chicken, pomegranate juice and walnuts. Among the numerous other forms of khoresh are *khoresh mast* (with yoghurt), *khoresh bademjân* (with eggplant), *khoresh beh* (with quinces) and *khoresh rivas* (with rhubarb). This combination of fruit and meat which gives the dishes a unique sweet and sour taste is characteristic of much Iranian cuisine and produces some extremely interesting and successful dishes.

Vegetables are used in salads, in *khoresh* or in *polo*, but are also very often made into *dolmeh*, when they are stuffed with rice, meat and various seasonings. In addition to the ubiquitous *dolmeh barg* (stuffed vine leaves), there are *dolmeh bademjân* (eggplant), *dolmeh beh* (quince) and *dolmeh sib* (apples).

Iranian cuisine is not very highly spiced but uses large quantities of herbs, such as mint, dill, parsley, coriander and chives. These herbs serve as seasoning for *khoresh* and *polo*, such as for *sabzi polo va mahi* (rice with herbs and fish), but are also frequently eaten raw with bread and goat's cheese (*sabzi khordan*) as a starter. A bowl of yoghurt (*mast*), sometimes flavoured with chopped raw garlic, *torchi* (small pickles), cucumber, spinach with yoghurt and various vegetable salads are also served with the meal.

Soups (*âsh*) also come in a wide variety of flavours and are usually quite filling. Like the *khoresh*, they make use of vegetables, fruit and meat. One of the most common is *âsh-e jo*, a barley soup, but it is worth trying more unusual ones such as *âsh-e ânâr*, a pomegranate soup, *âsh-e torsh*, a dried fruit soup, or *âsh-e mast*, a yoghurt soup.

Apart from rice, the other staple food of Iranian cuisine is bread (*nân*). Vast quantities of bread are eaten every day and around lunchtime it is common to see men leaving bakeries with armfuls of long, flat bread. There are several varieties of bread, of different shapes and sizes, including *nân-e lavâsh*, very thin and often served for breakfast, and *nân-e sangak*, a thicker variety eaten while it is still warm.

Desserts and pastries, which are extremely popular in Iran, are often flavoured with rose water, saffron, almonds or honey. Some towns are famous for their sweets:

Qom is known for its *sohân*, a flat biscuit-like sweet flavoured with saffron, and Yazd for its *pashmak*, a strongly perfumed candy floss. Isfahan is the home of *gaz*, a sort of nougat flavoured with rose water and pistachios based on a substance called *gaz* or *gaz angebin*, usually translated as manna. This manna, exuded by insects living on certain shrubs, particularly on the manna tamarisk, forms a dried layer on the leaves which can easily be collected. It is beaten with eggs and sugar and then flavoured. Ice-creams, particularly rose water (*bastani gol-e sorkh*) and saffron (*bastani zafrane*) ones, are excellent, and are of a slightly thicker consistency than European ones. They can generally be found in the *châikhâneh*, or tea houses.

The most common drink in Iran is tea (*châi*), traditionally served in small glasses and very sweet (the sugar cube is not placed in the glass, but held in the mouth between the teeth so that it dissolves slowly). With meals, one may drink *âbdugh*, yoghurt or buttermilk diluted with water and slightly salty. Although an acquired taste, it is very thirst-quenching. In summer, try the traditional drinks such as *afshoreh*, *sharbat* and *sekanjabin*. *Afshoreh* are fruit or flower syrups (orange blossom, rose or violet) served with ice. *Sharbat* is another form of syrup made from fruit and sugar heated together. *Sekanjabin* are infusions of mint, vinegar and sugar served chilled.

Unfortunately, many foreign visitors will have few opportunities to try the traditional dishes unless they are invited into an Iranian home, or able to go to some of the few restaurants in Tehran and Isfahan that have a menu really representative of the variety and originality of Iranian cuisine. The majority of restaurants, large and small, offer only a limited number of dishes, which recur with remarkable consistency from one place to the next. A soup, a salad, three or four different *kebâb* served with or without rice, and perhaps a *khoresh* or a *polo*, make up the usual restaurant menu. Most people get tired of this rice and grilled meat very quickly, and vegetarians should be warned that they may find themselves restricted to a diet of salad and plain rice. Drinks in restaurants are limited to the ubiquitous Coca-Cola (local brew) and to Islamic beer (usually sparkling, and which varies considerably in taste from one town to another). Bottled mineral water is available in the larger cities. It is impossible to buy alcohol openly in Iran, even in the large tourist hotels.

History

Prehistory

The long prehistoric period in Iran is known to us mostly from excavation work carried out in a few key sites, which has led to the establishment of a chronology of distinct periods, each one characterized by the manufacture of certain types of pottery, tools and other objects in daily use. Among the most important sites are Tappeh Sialk, near Kâshân, which was first occupied in the fourth millennium BC, Tappeh Giyan near Nehâvand and Tappeh Hissar near Dâmghân.

The Birth of Cities in Iran: Susa and Elam

It was in the Susian plain, near Iraq, that urban civilization first developed in Iran as a direct result of the presence nearby of Mesopotamia and the Sumerian civilization of Uruk. In the sixth millennium BC, a first centre had already been established in Susiana at Choga Mish, and around 3900 BC, a religious and administrative town was built nearby at Susa. During the fourth millennium BC, the region remained under the influence of Sumer, but was invaded by a new culture, known today as proto-Elamite, which occupied all the mountainous areas from Fârs to Kermân and even into Sistân. Because of its geographic location, the fate of the Susian plain was closely linked to that of Mesopotamia. With the rise of the archaic dynasties at Babylon, around 2800 BC, Susiana once again came under the influence of Sumer and, around 2300 BC, was annexed by Sargon, founder of the empire of Akkad.

Babylonian sources mention the presence of other peoples in western Iran at this period, notably the Guti, the Lullubi and the Kassites. These peoples, who lived in the mountainous areas separating the Mesopotamian plain from the Iranian plateau, controlled many of the routes that crossed these regions, in particular the Hamedân–Baghdad road which was one of the few natural ways onto the plateau from the West. These tribes took advantage of periods of weakness of Babylonian power to rush down and raid the settlements of the plain, and, around 2200 BC, the Guti even succeeded in invading Babylon, causing the fall of the empire of Akkad.

This fall allowed Elam, which, in the meantime, had become an independent state, to capture Susa, a city which was to be one of the capitals of the kingdom. Until approximately the 15th century BC, Elam continued to be strongly influenced by Mesopotamian culture while gradually developing its own identity. During the 13th and 12th centuries BC, at the height of its glory, Elam defeated Assyria and Babylon,

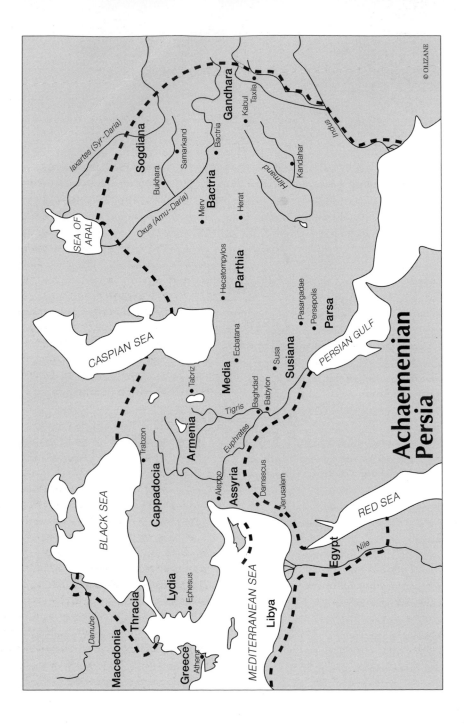

Achaemenian Persia

© OLIZANE

Sogdiana — Iaxartes (Syr-Daria), Samarkand, Bukhara, Oxus (Amu-Daria)

Gandhara — Kabul, Taxila, Indus

Bactria — Merv, Bactria, Herat, Kandahar, Hilmand

SEA OF ARAL

Parthia — Hecatompylos

CASPIAN SEA

Parsa — Pasargadae, Persepolis

Media — Ecbatana, Tabriz

Susiana — Susa, Babylon, Baghdad, Tigris

PERSIAN GULF

Armenia

Cappadocia — Trabzon

Assyria — Aleppo, Damascus, Jerusalem

Euphrates

BLACK SEA

RED SEA

Egypt — Nile

Lydia — Ephesus

Libya

MEDITERRANEAN SEA

Thracia

Macedonia — Danube

Greece — Athens

capturing from the latter fabulous treasures, including the famous Code of Hammurabi, now in the Louvre Museum in Paris.

The Medes

In the second and first millennia BC, successive waves of Indo-European tribes arrived on the Iranian plateau, either from the Caucasus, or through Transoxiana (Central Asia). The Persians, having settled for a while around lake Orumieh, finally moved to the present province of Fârs and the Bakhtiâri mountains, while the Medes occupied the Hamedân plain. The Medes, known for being fierce warriors and skilled horse breeders, were at first organized as independent tribes. Under constant pressure from their powerful neighbours, Urartu and Assyria, and following the arrival of two new war-like groups from the Caucasus, the Scythians and the Cimmerians, the Median tribes gradually developed a more cohesive political structure. The unification of the Medes, which was begun by a tribal chief, Deioces, was completed in 673 BC by his son Phraortes and the Median capital was established at Ecbatana or "Place of Assembly", modern Hamedân. Under the rule of Cyaxares (633–584), the Medes put an end to centuries of war against the Assyrians, capturing Niniva in 612 and thus bringing down the Assyrian empire. For more than half a century after the fall of Niniva, the Medes ruled over a vast empire that stretched from Afghanistan to Turkey.

The First Persian Empire: the Achaemenians

At the beginning of the seventh century BC, the Persian tribes which had settled in Fârs formed a small state, under the leadership of king Achemenes. His son, Teispes (675–640), extended the kingdom which, on his death, was divided between his successors: thus Ariaramnes became king of Parsa and Cyrus I, king of Anshân.

In 558 BC, Cyrus II the Great, a grandson of Cyrus I, was enthroned at Anshân. Within a few years, he succeeded in conquering an immense empire that extended from Pakistan to the Mediterranean coast, first conquering Media, his former suzerain, then Lydia and the Greek colonies of Ionia. In the east, he crossed the Oxus (Amu–Daria) and Iaxartes (Syr–Daria) rivers in Central Asia before following the Indus south. In 539, he conquered Babylon, entering the city as a liberator and sparing the population, a rare enough event in those times. This policy of tolerance and integration of the various peoples that made up his new empire was to characterize the reign of Cyrus. In 529, he died in battle and his elder son Cambyses II succeeded him.

Unlike his father, Cambyses (530–522 BC) ruled as a complete autocrat. After a victorious campaign against Egypt he annexed that country to his father's empire, but during his absence the throne was usurped by the Magus Gaumata and the king died in mysterious circumstances in 522 BC.

The reign of the usurper lasted only a few months and he was executed by Darius I (522–486 BC), a descendant of Ariaramnes, who proclaimed himself the legitimate king. Despite the speed with which he overthrew Gaumata, it was to take the new ruler almost two years to establish his authority throughout the empire because of certain rebellious provincial rulers. He then began the reorganization of his vast empire, creating 23 provinces, or satrapies, and building the administrative and religious cities of Susa and Persepolis. His military campaigns extended the frontiers of the empire previously forged by Cyrus: in the east, around 512 BC, he conquered Gandhara and the Indus Valley, while in the west, he attacked the Scythians, whom he never managed to subdue, and then turned against Greece. In 490 BC, came the humiliating defeat of Marathon, near Athens, which occurred while he was attempting to put down a rebellion in Egypt. Darius died in 486 BC without renewing his attack on Greece.

After the death of Darius, the immense empire established under the first Achaemenian rulers was threatened as Persian authority was no longer able to contain the rebellions of the satrapies. Xerxes (486–465 BC), the son of Darius, put down the revolts in Egypt and Babylonia with great severity and renewed the struggle against Greece. He quickly subdued Thessaly and Macedonia, then captured Attica and Athens, which he burned. Despite these successes, the Persian fleet was destroyed at Salamis in 480 BC. Discouraged, Xerxes returned to Persia, which he never left again. Gradually, the immense empire disintegrated; the Greek cities in Ionia, Egypt, then Pheonicia and Syria broke away, followed by the regions to the west of the Euphrates. Artaxerxes III (358–338) made one last attempt to reunify the empire, brutally taking back Egypt and quelling the revolt of the satraps, but a new power was already emerging in the west—Macedonia.

Alexander the Great

The conquest of Persia by Alexander the Great's armies marks a major turning point in the history of the vast region lying between the Euphrates and the Iaxartes. It is the beginning of a long period of Hellenization which was to have a far-reaching effect on culture and the arts in areas well beyond the actual frontiers of the empire. This conquest, planned by Philip of Macedonia and carried out by his son Alexander (356–323 BC), began with a series of lightning victories—Granica in 334 BC, Issos in 333, and Gaugamela in 331—which left the Persian army in complete disarray. Alexander captured Babylon, Susa and then Persepolis before setting off towards Bactria and Sogdiana in Central Asia, where he founded a number of military colonies. From there, he moved towards the Hindu Kush and India. In 324, having travelled down the Indus as far as its delta, he returned to Babylon where he fell ill and died in 323, at the age of 32.

The Hellenistic Period: the Seleucid Dynasty

After Alexander's death, his former companions in arms, the diadocs, fought among themselves over the partition of the empire. In 301 BC, after the battle of Ipsos, a threefold division emerged, with the Ptolemaic Dynasty ruling Egypt, a Macedonian monarchy in Europe and the Seleucid Dynasty in the East, with its capital at Antiochus. Founded by Seleucos (358–280 BC), a Macedonian general, this empire covered Mesopotamia, Iran, Syria and Bactria.

During the reign of the Seleucids, the empire was to go through a period of intense urban development as a result of a policy of colonization which lead to the establishment of Greek towns or military colonies. While there appears never to have been any forced Hellenization of the native population either by the government or the colonists, certain aspects of Greek culture were nevertheless rapidly adopted. The Greek language, for example, replaced Aramaic as the lingua franca of the empire and continued as the language of trade and commerce long after the fall of the dynasty.

The main difficulty which the Seleucid rulers faced was how to maintain the unity of an empire composed of a mosaic of different cultures and ethnic groups, with separatist tendencies, and governed by independent-minded satraps. A new menace was added to this, that of the Parthians, a nomad people of Iranian origin who had settled in the region between the Caspian and Aral seas. In 250 BC, Bactria proclaimed its independence, followed shortly afterwards by Parthia. Antiochos III (223–187) and his successor Antiochos IV (175–164) attempted to keep the empire together but in 190 BC, the Roman army won a decisive victory against the Persians at the battle of Magnesia. Taking advantage of this weakening of Seleucid power, the Parthians conquered northern Iran and set up their capital at Hecatompylos, near Dâmghân.

The Parthian Empire

Under Mithridates I (171–138 BC), the Parthians continued their conquests and annexed Media, Fârs, Babylonia and Assyria, creating an empire that extended from the Euphrates to Herat in Afghanistan, a restoration of the ancient Achaemenian empire of Cyrus the Great.

In addition to the nomads that were a constant menace on the eastern frontier and the state of Kushan, a Buddhist kingdom in India, the Parthians had also to face another powerful adversary, Rome. For almost three centuries, Rome and Parthia were to battle over Syria, Mesopotamia and Armenia, without ever achieving any lasting results. In 53 BC, during the reign of Orodes II (56–37 BC), a reign which marked the highpoint of Parthian power, the Roman army was severely beaten at Carrhae. But despite this victory and the signing of several treaties, the wars recurred throughout the first and second centuries AD. However, the fall of the Parthian Dynasty was provoked not by an external enemy but by an internal rebellion.

The Sassanians

During the Seleucid and Parthian dynasties, the region of Fârs had maintained some of the ancient imperial traditions, and Greek influence was less strong there than in other areas. When the local Sassanian Dynasty began to expand its territory out of Fârs into neighbouring areas, it was thus able to present itself as the true inheritor of the Achaemenian dynasty and of an authentically Iranian culture. In 224 AD, the Sassanian ruler Ardeshir I (224–241) rebelled against the Parthian overlord Artabanus V; within twenty years, he created a vast empire that stretched as far as the Indus. His son Shâpur I (241–272) continued this expansion, conquering Bactria, forcing Kushan to recognize Sassanian suzerainty and leading several campaigns against Rome. In 260, the Persian army captured the Roman emperor Valerian at the battle of Edessa and more than 70,000 Roman soldiers were exiled in Iran.

During the Sassanian Dynasty, Zoroastrianism was firmly established for the first time as state religion, a development which was accompanied by periodic repressions of foreign, heretic faiths, including Manicheism, Mazdakism and Christianity. Armenia in particular suffered from its conversion to Christianity as the Sassanians suspected it of having close links with Rome.

For nearly four centuries, foreign wars and internal struggles gradually exhausted the Sassanian Empire. The wars against Rome started up once again during the reigns of Bahram II (276–293) and Shâpur II (309–379). In the fifth century, a new enemy appeared in Central Asia, the Hephtalite Huns who defeated the Persians in a series of battles, killing King Peroz in 484. It was not until the reign of Khosroe I (531–579), one of the greatest Sassanian rulers, that the Huns were beaten.

Khosroe's expansionist policy was continued by Khosroe II (590–628), who re-established the old Achaemenian frontiers, regaining Damascus, Jerusalem (614) and

Egypt (618). He also carried out important reforms to restore royal authority by reducing the excessive power of the nobility and thereby strengthened the bureaucracy, which he reorganized into divans, or ministries. But despite these reforms, the Sassanian Empire did not last long after the death of Khosroe. Twelve kings succeeded each other over a period of fourteen years, and the power of the central authorities passed into the hands of the generals. When the Arab army launched its first attacks in 633, Persia was already considerably weakened.

Arab Conquest: the Umayyad and Abbassid Caliphates

After the death of the Prophet in 632, the direction of the Islamic world was handed over to the caliphs (from the Arab word *khalifa*, successor or replacement). The first four caliphs, Abu Bakr, Omar, Osman and Ali, were elected by the Muslim community. But the assassination of Osman and the election of Ali as successor created a political crisis which ended in the replacement of Ali by his rival Mo'awiya. The latter transferred the capital from Medina to Damascus and set up a hereditary caliphate, known as the Umayyad Caliphate (661–750). This move aroused the anger of two groups: the inhabitants of Medina, who favoured an electoral system for the nomination of the caliphs; and the Shi'ites, for whom the leadership of the community should be handed over to the descendants of Ali (see section on Shi'ism, page 90).

In 633, shortly after the Prophet's death, the first caliph Abu Bakr sent an Arab army to conquer Iraq. The last Sassani-

Achaemenian bas-relief from Persepolis of two officials en route for the New Year celebrations; on the left a Persian, on the right a Mede

Ferdusi and the *Shâhnâmeh*

The *Shâhnâmeh*, or *Book of Kings*, is the national Iranian epic. Fifty thousand distichs long, it relates the history of the country from the creation of the world to the Arab conquest in the seventh century. The figures in the *Shâhnâmeh* and their adventures—sometimes glorious, sometimes pathetic—are known to all in the Persian-speaking world, and even further afield, in India and Turkey. The most famous episodes have become the favorite subject-matter of miniature painters: the battles of the hero Rostam against the Central Asian state of Turan; the death of Sohrab, killed by Rostam, his father, unaware of his son's true identity; the revenge of the young prince Siavush; the love of King Khosroe and Chirine; the fight between King Bahram Gur and a fearsome dragon. The main themes of the *Shâhnâmeh* are those of the Sassanian period: the legitimacy of the ruling king; the loyalty of vassals; the inexorability of fate; and the fight between Good and Evil symbolized by the battles between Iran and Turan.

The author of the *Shâhnâmeh*, Ferdusi, was born near Tus, in Khorâssân, between 932 and 942. For twenty-five years he worked on this vast epic. In 1010 he presented the finished work to the ruling Ghaznavid sultan, Mahmud, but, after a disagreement with the king, he was forced to flee the court and to live a life of wandering. He returned to his native village to die in 1020. According to tradition, Sultan Mahmud, realizing too late the poet's genius, sent him as a reward a caravan-load of treasure, but it arrived after Ferdusi's death.

While writing the *Shâhnâmeh*, Ferdusi drew from a very rich and varied literary—and probably oral—corpus. From these sources he produced a work that represents the entire memory of the Iranian people. In the tenth century, heroic and romanesque narratives were still very much alive in Iran, despite the Arab conquest. In addition to the ancient romanticized histories written in Pehlevi (Middle Persian) and the royal chronicles of the Sassanian Dynasty, there existed a *Book of Kings* from the end of the Sassanian period as well as several *Shâhnâmeh* written in prose in the ninth and tenth centuries, including one begun by Abu Mansur in 957. A few years later, at the request of a Samanid emir, the poet Daqiqi began a verse *Shâhnâmeh*. After his sudden death in 975, Ferdusi took over the project, incorporating Daqiqi's verses into his own work.

Unlike Persian lyric poetry, which borrows heavily from Arabic, Ferdusi's verse has retained many archaic Persian words, close to the Pehlevi, which confer a certain nobility to the text and fit perfectly its heroic tone. Although the author uses hyperbole and complex metaphors, his style is nonetheless simple and the rhythm of the verse subtly entrancing.

an ruler, Yazdgard III (632–651), was powerless to prevent its advance; in 637, the Persian army was defeated at al-Qadisiyah and the Sassanian capital, Ctesiphon, fell. In 642, Sassanian power was destroyed once and for all at the battle of Nehâvand, near Hamedân, and Yazgard fled to Merv, where he was assassinated in 651.

The conquest of Persia continued during the rule of the first Umayyad caliphs; in a very short time, Afghanistan (651) and then Transoxiana (674) also fell. But opposition to the caliphate was growing and a series of rebellions and riots broke out, one of which, supported by the Shi'ites, led to the restoration as caliph in 750 of Abul Abbâs, a descendant of the Prophet.

The Abbasid Dynasty (750–945) established its capital at Baghad, near the old Sassanian capital. For a century, the empire experienced a time of unprecedented cultural, artistic and economic development, particularly during the reigns of Hârun al-Rashid (786–809) and al-Mamun (813–833). Persian scholars and artists played an important role in this intellectual activity· from the very beginning of the Abbasid Caliphate, they had been placed in charge of the highest court functions to which they had not had access in Damascus, and a large number of Iranian customs and traditions were rapidly adopted in Baghdad.

From the second half of the ninth century, a period of decline began which was marked by the growing power of the Turkish and Slav mercenaries who had been the caliph's guards. In 908, the head of the guard was named Emir of Emir's by the thirteen-year old caliph, and thus became the de facto ruler of the empire. The governors of the Iranian provinces took advantage of this period of anarchy to break away from Baghdad, forming small local dynasties. In the east, in Khorâssân, these were the Tahirid (821–873), Saffarid (867–963) and Samanid (892–999) dynasties. The Samanids, whose capital was at Bukhara, favoured Persian culture and literature, introducing Persian as the written language of the bureaucracy.

In the west, there was a general movement of people from the mountains near the Caspian Sea towards the plateau, first the Ziyarids (928–1077), then the Buyids (945–1055), a Shi'ite dynasty that took control of Khuzestân, Shiraz, Iraq and finally Kermân. In 945, the Buyid prince Mu'izz al-Daula entered Baghdad and the Abbasid caliph promptly named him Emir of Emirs.

The Turkish Dynasties: the Seljuqs

This period of successive Iranian dynasties came to an end with the appearance on the political scene of the Sunni Turks who had, until then, served as soldiers or military chiefs at the Persian courts. In 976, one of these military leaders took advantage of the weakening of Samanid power to proclaim his independence and to found the

Ghaznavid Dynasty (962–1186) in present-day Afghanistan. His son Mahmud (998–1030) took control of Sistân and Baluchestân to the west and the Punjab to the east.

But the Ghaznavids were unable to prevent the arrival of yet another powerful force, the Seljuqs, a clan of Oghuzz Turks, who settled first in Transoxiana and latterly at Bukhara. Under the leadership of Toghrul Beg, who established himself at Neishâbur in 1038, the Seljuq army overthrew the last Buyid ruler, capturing Isfahan (1051) and Baghdad (1055). The three great Seljuq rulers, Toghrul Beg (1038–1063), Alp-Arslan (1063–1072) and Malik Shâh (1072–1092), managed to create a centralized state with an efficient administration and a powerful army, thanks largely to the help of their vizier Nizâm al-Mulk (1020–1092). This brilliant administrator and author of a treatise on government, written for the use of princes, was also the founder of the nizâmiyeh or madresseh, institutions for higher religious teaching which fixed the Sunni orthodoxy throughout the empire.

At the death of Malik Shâh, the empire broke up and local dynasties were founded by provincial governors, particularly in Azerbaijân, Luristân, Fârs and at Yazd. Khorâssân recognized the suzerainty of the princes of Khwârezm (1153), a Turkish state in Central Asia which quickly occupied the whole of eastern Iran. In 1217, the Khwârezmi armies even reached as far as the Zagros Mountains but were never able to consolidate their conquests as by that time a new menace had appeared in Central Asia: the Mongols.

Mongol Invasions from the 12th to 15th Centuries

The Mongol conquest of the Persian world brought with it terrible destruction and large-scale massacres. In 1219, Gengis Khân's army attacked the state of Khwârezm, capturing Transoxiana, Samarkand (1220) and Khorâssân (1221), while a detachment penetrated as far as Azerbaijân. In 1256, a second expedition led by Hulagu (1217–1265), Genghis Khân's grandson, subdued the whole of Persia. In 1258, Baghdad was captured and the caliph put to death, bringing the Abbasid Caliphate to an end. Hulagu's successors, who took the title of il-khân, established their capital at Tabriz.

The death of Sultan Abu Said in 1335 lead to the division of the Mongol Empire of Persia. Once again, local chiefs took advantage of this to declare themselves independent: a Persian Shi'ite dynasty, the Sardebarians (1337–1381), settled in the northwestern part of Khorâssân while the Mozzafferids (1340–1392) took control of the south from Fârs to Kermân. But these dynasties were to be short-lived as a third invasion, this time of Turko-Mongol nomads lead by Tamerlane, or Lame Timur, swept across the region. The east of Iran fell in 1380, and Azerbaijân, Iraq and Fârs a

few years later. Like his predecessors, Tamerlane left a trail of destruction in his wake; the sack of Isfahan is said to have caused 70,000 deaths.

Tamerlane's immense empire became the object of intense fighting after his death in 1405, but the Timurids who settled in eastern Iran and Afghanistan were paradoxically active protectors of Persian culture, in particular Shâh Rokh (1405–1447): this was to be a period of great flourishing of the arts, especially of the schools of miniature painting at Shiraz and Herat, and of architecture.

The Safavids

At the same time, northwestern Iran, where rival Turkoman groups contended with each other for power, went through a different historical development from the east. From 1275, the Turkoman Dynasty of the Kara-Koyunlu, or Black Sheep (1275–1468) set itself up at Tabriz; it was later replaced by the Ak-Koyunlu, or White Sheep (1434–1514). Meanwhile, a third Turkish dynasty, the Safavids (1502–1737), often considered the founding dynasty of modern Iran, emerged in Azerbaijân under the leadership of Shâh Ismâil (1487–1524), who rapidly conquered a vast territory extending from Herat in the east to Baghdad in the west. This dynasty, whose origins go back to a Sufi order, called Safawiyya from the name of its founder Sheikh Safi al-Din Ishaq (died in 1334), was first of all centred around the town of Ardebil. In the 15th century, its rulers decided to change their religious title of sheikh to the more secular one of sultan.

The height of Safavid glory was the reign of Shâh Abbâs I (1571–1629), who encouraged contacts and trade with Europe and transformed his new capital, Isfahan, into one of the most magnificent cities of Persia. The presence at the Safavid court of foreign travellers and merchants was later to have a great influence on the arts and literature in Europe.

The adoption of Shi'ism as state religion by the Safavids was an important unifying factor throughout the empire, which, while taking advantage of a latent nationalistic feeling, also brought Persia in direct conflict with the staunchly Sunni Ottoman Empire. Two centuries of intermittent wars followed which produced only minor territorial changes.

The last Safavid rulers were much weaker than Shâh Abbâs, and despite the luxury and glory of the court, the dynasty went into decline. Rebellions broke out on the frontiers of the empire and, in 1722, an Afghan army invaded Khorâssân and captured Isfahan, killing all the Safavid princes except for one, Tahmasp, who fled and took refuge on the Caspian coast.

Kajaveh traditionally used by Persian ladies when travelling, late 19th century engraving by Jane Dieulafoy

Nâder Shâh and the Qâjâr Dynasty (1794–1925)

Afghan rule in eastern Iran lasted only a short period of time (1722–1729); the second ruler, Ashraf Shâh, was overthrown by a young chieftain from Khorâssân, Nâder Shâh, who had rallied to the cause of the Safavid prince, Tahmasp. After a brief restoration, the Safavid Dynasty was definitely abolished when Nâder Shâh set himself on the throne in 1736.

Sometimes described as the last great conqueror of Asia, Nâder Shâh (1736–1747) managed in the space of just four short years to conquer Afghanistan and to capture New Delhi (which yielded fabulous treasures), Bukhara and Khiva, creating a kingdom even more extensive than that of Shâh Abbâs. He was, however, a dictatorial and cruel ruler and was assassinated in 1747.

Nâder Shâh's empire broke up after his death; an ephemeral dynasty, founded by Karim Khân Zend (1747–1779) and based at Shiraz, succeeded him but was defeated by a Turkish tribe, the Qâjâr. One of the Qâjâr leaders, the eunuch Aghâ Muhammed Khân, succeeded in bringing the whole country under his authority and was crowned shâh in Tehran in 1796.

The history of Iran in the 19th and early 20th centuries is dominated by the rivalry between Russia and Great Britain, the former hoping to reach the Persian Gulf and the Indian Ocean through Iran, and the latter trying to protect its sea and land routes to India and to slow down Russian expansion. In 1813 and 1828, the shâh was forced to cede Georgia and part of Armenia to Russia, which gradually became the main political power in the north of Iran, a position occupied by Great Britain in the south of the country. Russia and Britain obtained concessions from the Iranian government which gave them control of the country's principal natural resources, due in part to the indifference of Naser od-Din Shâh (1848–1896) and his successor Muzzaffer (1896–1907). This foreign control of the country's economy provoked strong feelings of discontent among religious leaders on the one hand, and among partisans of reform on the other, and eventually led to the establishment of a parliamentary system in 1906 and the promulgation of a Constitution in 1907.

The Pahlavi Dynasty and the Fall of the Monarchy

At the end of World War I, the British attempted to extend their control over southern Iran to the whole country at a time when Soviet troops were pulling out from the north. Incidents broke out, and in February 1921, Sayyed Ziya od-Din and Rezâ Khân, a colonel in the Persian army, organized a coup to make Ziya od-Din prime minister. In October, Rezâ Khân took over the Premiership and in December 1925 proclaimed himself shâh of Iran, thus founding the Pahlavi Dynasty.

Although Rezâ Shâh's reign (1925–1941) brought a certain economic development to the country and saw the repeal of the privileges granted to the foreign powers, it was also marked by a tightening of police control of the people.

During World War II, Iran—the name was officially adopted in 1934—declared itself neutral, but after the Shâh's refusal to expel German nationals, British and Soviet troops entered the country in August 1941. One month later, Rezâ Shâh was forced to abdicate in favour of his son Mohammed Rezâ. However, even at the end of the war, the problem of foreign intervention in Iran was far from resolved. In 1951, Doctor Mossadegh, elected to the post of prime minister, decided to nationalize the oil industry. The increasing popularity of his nationalist movement worried not only the Monarchists but also overseas powers with oil interests in Iran. In 1953, the government was overthrown by a coup d'état. Despite this, the nationalization of oil became the symbol of the resumption of Iranian control over its own economy.

In 1962, the Shâh launched a series of reforms, known as the White Revolution, aimed in particular at the rural population who formed the majority of the country. However, the redistribution of land and the reforms concerning the status of women aroused the anger of the large property owners and of religious circles. Unrest broke out in 1963, and in November 1964, the Ayatollah Khomeini, who had become more and more critical of the government, was exiled to Turkey and then to Najaf, in Iraq. The Savak, the political police, intensified its activities, notably by clamping down on leftists, intellectuals and students.

Economic success relegated the internal political problems that the country faced to a secondary position: the huge revenue from the oil industry from 1973 allowed the Shah to carry out a vast programme of industrial expansion, but this was criticized for concentrating on extravagant and costly projects badly adapted to the immediate needs of the country. Social issues were hardly addressed and the massive rural exodus of the 1970s continued to swell the population in the poorer areas of the big cities where unemployment was chronic.

In 1977, Iran had to face a sudden deterioration of the economic situation: the cost of living shot up dramatically while a slump in oil sales between 1975 and 1977 forced the government to reduce social spending even further to finance building projects and the purchase of armaments. This situation benefitted the opposition and demonstrations were organized in the large towns, openly demanding the return from exile of Ayatollah Khomeini. 1978 was marked by violent riots, most notably in Tabriz, Qom and Tehran. On 7 September, during the month of Ramadan, there were calls for the abolition of the monarchy at a demonstration in Tehran in which over a million people took part. Starting in October, strikes broke out throughout the country, paralysing the administration and industry, and even suspending the export of oil, which was essential to the country's entire economy. In December, the Shâh tried to save the situation by naming Shapur Bakhtiâri prime minister, but on 16 January 1979, he was forced to flee with his family to Egypt. His departure was taken as an abdication by the crowds in the streets and greeted with great rejoicing.

The Founding of the Islamic Republic

The coalition which had united against the monarchy, composed of different social classes each with its own political aims, collapsed as soon as the latter was abolished, leaving two main forces in confrontation: the army, which the Bakhtiâri government was unable to control; and the clergy. The return of Ayatollah Khomeini to Tehran on 1 February 1979 marks the beginning of the last phase in the formation of an Islamic government. On 9 February, clashes broke out between the imperial guard and units of the air force faithful to Khomeini. This was followed by two days of insurrection during which the inhabitants of Tehran took over several strategic buildings in the capital. On 12 February, a provisional Islamic government was named with Mehdi Bazargân as prime minister. The Islamic Republic was proclaimed by Ayatollah Khomeini during the night of 1 April 1979.

But important political differences emerged, even within the religious circles. These were divided between radical elements, partisans of ayatollahs Khomeini and Beheshti, and progressive elements who followed Ayatollah Taleghani and were closer to leftist groups such as the Mujahedin-e Khalq. Autonomist movements broke out in Azerbaijân, Kurdistân and Khorâssân. The hostage-taking at the American embassy in Tehran on 4 November occurred just at the right moment to reinforce popular unity.

The Iran–Iraq War

From July 1980, the skirmishes at the Iranian and Iraqi frontier, which had begun several months before, intensified and in September Iraqi forces entered Khuzestân: this was the beginning of a long war of attrition which was to last eight years. But instead of causing the immediate collapse of the Iranian government, the Iraqi attack served to unite most of the political and religious groups around the regime of Ayatollah Khomeini and Iranian resistance proved much more effective than Iraq had expected.

The political, military and economic goals of the war were considerable. For Iraq,

It Is Time To Pick Roses

If you welter my homeland in blood,
Rose after rose will sprout in this rose-garden.
You may burn my body, or stick it with arrows,
You may sever my head from the body,
But how can you, oh foe, rob me of my love for homeland?
A muslim, I am, and martyrdom is my desire;
My death is but a manifestation of life.
Presume not that this fire will become extinct;
It will rise from my tomb after my death.
No surrender, no compromise, no tribute, no plea;
All your plots I will bring down in ruins.
Rivers of people are now a seething sea;
All my harvest has turned grapes of wrath.
I am liberal-minded; one from the country of the high-minded;
My skirt nourishes the flower of fortitude.
I drink only from the cup of unification;
Even if you sever my head with the sword of oppression.
My lofty star, my leader, has arrived;
It is spring and time for me to pick roses.

Ali Khazaee-Far, translator, Poetry of the Islamic Revolution: A
Collection of Poems with Persian Texts, 1986

This poem represents two typical songs of the Islamic Revolution.

which hoped to take over the leadership of the Arabic world and wanted to take advantage of the lack of organization in the Iranian army, the main aim was to cause the fall of the Shi'ite regime and to increase its own access to the Persian Gulf by taking the Arvand-rud (better known in the West under its Arabic name, Shatt al-Arab) and the province of Khuzestân (ex-Arabistan), where the main Iranian oil fields are located.

The Iraqi advance lasted until September 1981, but despite months of seige, Saddam Hussein's troops were unable to capture Abâdân. The liberation of the town by Iranian forces marks the beginning of the Iranian counter-offensive; within a few months, the Iraqis were pushed back to the border and, in July 1982, Baghdad requested a cease-fire. By then, the Iranian government had set itself new objectives, including the overthrow of the Ba'assist regime in Iraq, the condemnation of Saddam Hussein as a war criminal and the occupation of Najaf and Kerbala, two holy Shi'ite towns located in Iraqi territory. Fighting continued until July 1988, when Iran accepted the United Nations Resolution 598 for a cease-fire which became effective a month later. Negotiations began between the two countries, but the war did not end officially until just before the Gulf War when Iraq accepted, in August 1990, a return to the pre-war frontiers defined by the Algiers Accord signed in 1975.

The consequences of eight years of war were very severe: according to diplomatic sources over a million people were killed; considerable material damage occurred in the entire frontier zone with Iraq, particularly at Abâdân and Khoram Shahr; thousands became refugees; the economy was shattered.

Post-war Reconstruction

The death of Ayatollah Khomeini on 3 June 1989, only a few months before the tenth anniversary of the fall of the monarchy and the victory of the revolution, lead to huge demonstrations of collective mourning throughout the country. Ali Khamenei succeeded as head of state and Guide of the Revolution and, the following month, Ayatollah Hashemi Rafsanjâni, former president of the parliament, was elected president of the republic. The new government concentrated on the economic reconstruction and the rebuilding of the defensive capabilities of the country. This latter objective is well under way to completion, but the former one will take longer to achieve. A high rate of inflation, a certain social discontent and problems related to an inadequate industrial infrastructure are slowing down the expected economic growth. In addition, despite its low profile during the Gulf War and the influence it exerted towards a positive outcome for the Western hostage crisis in Lebanon, the West is still far from ready to accept Iran back into the community of nations. Relations were further

Portrait of Imam Khomeini on the wall of a school

strained by the issue of the death sentence in a *fatwa* to the author Salman Rushdie in 1989 on publication of his controversial book *The Satanic Verses*.

Since the breakup of the Soviet Union, Iran has turned more and more towards the republics of Central Asia. Although only one republic, Tadjikistan, is Persian-speaking, there are nonetheless strong cultural and historical ties between Iran and the entire region. A certain rivalry has developed between Iran and Turkey over this issue, as Turkey has similar ties with the same republics and is unwilling to allow Iran to be the sole beneficiary of the commercial possibilities that are opening up. Various economic and cultural projects between these countries are currently under discussion, perhaps leading in the long term to the formation of a new, 21st-century version, of the Silk Road.

Chronology

IRAN	BC	REST OF THE WORLD
First city built at Susa	c. 3900 BC	
	c. 2700–2300 BC	Old Kingdom in Egypt, pyramids of Giza
	c. 2350 BC	Reign of Sargon, founder of the Akkadian Empire
Akkad annexes Susa	c. 2300 BC	
Susa becomes part of Elam	c. 2200 BC	Fall of Akkad
	2065–1785 BC	Middle Kingdom in Egypt
	c. 1730–1680 BC	Reign of Hammurabi, king of the first Babylonian Empire
	16–12th centuries BC	Kassite Empire of Babylon
Height of the Elamite Empire	13–12th centuries BC	
	1193–1184 BC	Trojan Wars (traditional dates)
Destruction of the Kassite Empire of Babylon by Elam	1160 BC	
Median capital established at Ecbatana	673 BC	
Assyrian sack of Susa (Elam) under Assurbanipal	646 BC	
Medes' capture of Niniva		
Fall of the Assyrian Empire	612 BC	
	605–562 BC	Reign of Nebuchadnezzar II in Babylon
Persian Achaemenian Empire	550–331 BC	
Reign of Cyrus II the Great	558–529 BC	
Reign of Darius I	522–486 BC	
Rebuilding of Susa	521 BC	
	509 BC	Establishment of Roman Republic
Building of Persepolis	500 BC	
Reign of Xerxes I	486–465 BC	
	490 BC	Greek victory over the Persian army at Marathon
	480 BC	Greek victory at Salamis
	431–404 BC	Peloponnesian War between Athens and Sparta
	336–323 BC	Reign of Alexander the Great

Persian defeat at Gaugamelus	331 BC	
Death of Darius III, last Achaemenian ruler		
Seleucid Dynasty	312–44 BC	
	264–146 BC	Punic Wars between Rome and Carthage
Parthian Dynasty	250 BC–224 AD	
Reign of Mithridates I	171–138 BC	
Parthian victory over Rome at Carrhae	53 BC	
	27 BC	Founding of the Roman Empire by Augustus

AD

	117–138	Reign of Hadrian
Mani, founder of Manicheism	216–277	
Sassanian Empire	224–642	
Reign of Shapur I	241–272	
Roman emperor Valerian taken prisoner at Edessa	260	
	330	Constantinople becomes capital of the Holy Roman Empire
	395	Division of the Roman Empire into east and west
	410	Sack of Rome by Alaric
Massacre of the Mazdakites	c. 528	
	622	Mahommed flees to Medina (Hegira)
	632	Death of the Prophet Mahommed
Defeat of the Persian army at Nehavend by the Arabs	642	
Umayyad Caliphate	661–750	
	680	Death of Imam Hussein at Kerbala
	732	Victory of Charles Martel over the Saracens at Poitiers
Abbassid Caliphate	750–1258	
	751–987	Carolingians in France
Reign of Caliph Hârun al-Rashid	766–809	
	768–814	Reign of Charlemagne

Iranian dynasties

Tahirid	821–873	
Saffarid	867–903	
	871–899	Reign of Alfred the Great in England
Samanid	892–999	
	909–1171	Fatimid Caliphate in Egypt
Ziyarid	928–1077	
Buyid	945–1055	
Ghaznavid	962–1186	
Reign of Toghrul Beg, founder of the Seljuqs	1038–1063	
	1066	Battle of Hastings
Occupation of the castle of Alamut by Hassan Sabbâh	1090–1124	
	1096–1099	First Crusade, capture of Antiochus and Jerusalem by the crusaders
	1171–1193	Reign of Saladin in Egypt and Syria
Arrival in Iran of Genghis Khân's Mongol army	1221	
	1260–1295	Travels of Marco Polo
	1304–1377	Ibn Battuta, Arab geographer and traveller
	1337–1453	Hundred Years' War
	1336–1405	Tamerlane, Turko-Mongol conqueror
Timurid Dynasty in Persia	1405–1517	
	1508–1512	Michelangelo paints the ceiling of the Sistine Chapel
	1509–1547	Reign of Henry VIII of England
	1520–1566	Reign of the Ottoman sultan Suleiman the Magnificent
	1539–1588	The architect Sinan works for the Ottoman sultans
	1558–1603	Reign of Queen Elizabeth I of England
Reign of Shah Abbas I, reconstruction of Isfahan begins	1571–1629	
Reign of Nâder Shâh	1736–1747	
Zend Dynasty, capital moved to Shiraz	1747–1779	

	1775–1783	American War of Independence
	1789	Beginning of the French Revolution
Qajar Dynasty moves capital to Tehran	1794–1925	
	1815	Battle of Waterloo, Napoleon exiled to St Helena
	1861–1865	American Civil War
Adoption of a constitution	1907	
	1922–1923	Kemal Atatürk abolishes Otto-man Sultanate, proclaims the Turkish Republic
Reign of Rezâ Shâh Pahlavi	1925–1941	
Reign of Mohammed Rezâ Shâh Pahlavi	1941–1979	
Nationalization of Oil; Mossadegh becomes prime minister	1951	
Fall of Mossadegh government	1953	
	1964–1978	Ayatollah Khomeini exiled in Iraq
	Oct 1971	Celebration at Persepolis of the 2500th anniversary of the Persian Empire
	Oct 1978	Ayatollah Khomeini arrives in France
Return of Ayatollah Khomeini to Tehran	1 Feb 1979	
Proclamation of the Islamic Republic	1 Apr 1979	
Iran–Iraq war	Sept 1980–Jul 1988	
Death of Ayatollah Khomeini; Sayyed Ali Khamenei becomes the Guide of the Revolution	4 June 1989	
Ayatollah Hashemi Rafsanjâni becomes president of the republic	July 1989	

Geography

The Plateau and the Mountains

Iran, which has a surface area of some 1,648,000 kilometres^2 (636 miles$^{2)}$, is an elevated plateau with an average height of over 1,000 metres (3,000 feet) above sea level, set between two depressions, the Caspian Sea to the north and the Persian Gulf to the south. The central desert plateau is surrounded by tall chains of mountains. In the north, the Alborz Range creates a formidable but narrow barrier between the plateau and the fertile coastal plains along the Caspian. The physical differences on either side of the mountains are striking: from the heat and dust of Tehran (1,100 metres, 3,600 feet) the road climbs quickly up to the mountain passes before descending again to the humidity and luxuriant vegetation of the coast situated at an average of 40 metres (130 feet) below sea level! While the annual rainfall in Tehran is only 210 millimetres, it is as high as 1,224 millimetres at Rasht, by the sea. It is in this coastal area that rice, tea and various citrus fruits are grown.

The Alborz Chain includes several peaks over 4,000 metres (13,000 feet) in height, including the Alam Kuh (4,840 metres, 15,875 feet) and Mount Demâvend (5,671 metres, 18,600 feet), an extinct volcano which dominates the skyline of Tehran. The chain stretches east into Khorâssân Province but is lower there than further west and cut by fertile valleys. This region is one of the few areas giving easy access onto the Iranian Plateau and has been used for centuries by nomads and invaders from Central Asia.

To the west of the plateau, the Zagros Chain stretches south from Lake Van in Turkey to the Persian Gulf, and also reaches over 4,000 metres (13,000 feet) in height in places. The mountain ridges, which lie in regular folds running from the northwest to the southeast, are cut by transverse valleys. The remains of what were once vast oak, pistachio, almond and walnut forests are visible on the mountainsides, now occupied mainly by grazing herds of sheep and goats. In the valleys, wheat, cotton, tobacco and barley are grown.

To the southeast of the plateau, the Makrân Chain forms a barrier between the sea of Oman and the central plateau, while along the frontier with Pakistan is yet another chain. Its highest point is Mount Taftân (4,042 metres, 13,260 feet), a still active volcano, near the town of Zâhedân.

The plateau itself has an average height of 1,000 metres (3,300 feet) above sea level. In the centre of it are two areas of desert: the Dasht-e Kevir, the salt desert in the north, and the Dasht-e-Lut, the sand desert in the south. These are among the most arid areas in the world. While the Dasht-e Kevir does have some oases in it, the Dasht-e-Lut cannot support any form of life at all. The zones of human settlement are therefore to be found mostly along the edges of the plateau and in the oases.

To the southwest of the Zagros lie the plains of Khuzestân, a sort of enclave of the Mesopotamian plain through which flow the Arvand-rud (better known as the Shatt el-Arab) and the Kârun. The coastal area of the Persian Gulf, which stretches for some 800 kilometres (497 miles) from the Iraqi frontier to the Straits of Hormuz, is arid with only very little natural vegetation and a few palm groves. The main source of income in the region is oil, first drilled for here in 1908. To the east, near Bandar-e Abbâs, are several offshore islands which belong to Iran, including Qeshm, Kish, Kharg and Hormuz.

Like the neighbouring states around the Caspian Sea (Turkey, Armenia, Azerbaijân and Turkmenistan), Iran is located in an active earthquake zone and tremors are a frequent phenomenon, sometimes occurring very violently. The area around Tabriz, Qazvin and the Caspian has suffered considerably from earthquakes over the centuries, most recently in September 1978 when 25,000 people were killed in the region of Tabas, and in June 1990 when another earthquake hit the towns of Rudbâr and Rasht in Gilân Province, leaving 48,000 people dead. Other regions of the country are also prone to earthquakes, particularly in the south, from Fârs Province east to Baluchestân.

The Water Problem

Iran has only one navigable waterway, the 850 kilometre (528 mile)-long Kârun, which originates in the Zagros Mountains and joins the Arvand-rud at Khoram Shahr before flowing into the Persian Gulf. Most Iranian rivers, however, are not permanent and never reach the sea. The Zayandeh-rud, for example, which flows through the city of Isfahan, ends up in the Ghavkhuni marshes nearby.

Iran's largest lake is Lake Orumieh (4,368 metres^2, 47,016 feet^2) in Azerbaijân. Like most of the other lakes, such as the Salt Lake (daryâcheh-ye Namak) near Qom and Lake Bakhtegân near Shiraz, it has a high salt content. Several fresh water lakes are to be found in the east, in Sistân, including the largest one, the Hâmun-e Sâberi, fed by the Hirmand from Afghanistan. Since the construction of a dam on the river, however, the volume of water in the lakes has considerably decreased.

The problem of obtaining water is a serious one in Iran and has existed since antiquity. South of the Alborz in particular, rain is very rare and tends to fall mainly between November and April. Under these conditions, agriculture is only possible if combined with irrigation. The mountains, however, serve to collect the winter pre-

cipitation in the form of ice and snow and release it slowly during the drier spring and summer months. But a dry winter is only too often a sign of drought for the following summer.

One solution to the problem which is particularly well adapted to the country is the *qanât*, an underground canal which captures the water directly from the water tables in the foothills of the mountains and carries it onto the plains. The *qanât* system was first devised by the Medes and Persians and has remained essentially unchanged ever since. The series of small depressions that can often be seen crossing the desert reveal the presence of a *qanât* below the ground: they are the vertical wells dug at regular intervals to provide fresh air and light for the workers below, to allow the rubble to be cleared and maintenance work carried out. Some *qanât* are tens of kilometres long and may be dug 300 metres (984 feet) below the surface. Many oases are entirely dependant on *qanât* for their survival rather than on well or spring water.

Dams also appeared very early on in Iran. The first bridges with sluice gates were built by the Sassanians in the third century AD to irrigate the plains of Khuzestân. The Khaju Bridge at Isfahan is based on the same principle and serves not only for irrigation purposes, but also to control the volume of water in the river. In the 20th century, several dams and mountain reservoirs have been built, particularly in the Alborz, in order to increase the surface area of arable land available and to satisfy the demand for water from Tehran and the large industrial centres (there are dams, for example on the Sefid-rud near Rudbâr, and in Khuzestân Province, near Dizful).

Descent to the Caspian Sea from the Elborz Mountains

Flora and Fauna

The vegetation in Iran is remarkably varied from one area to another. Iran is situated at the junction of four different phyto-geographic regions (the Irano-Turanian, Euro-Siberian, Saharo-Arabian and Sudanian) and has over 8,000 species of plants, of which about 20 per cent are endemic. These endemic species are now to be found mostly in isolated spots, on the peaks of the Zagros and Alborz, on a few mountains of the central plateau and on the ridges south of Kâshân and Yazd and north of Ker-mân. Although 60 per cent of the land is classified as arid or semi-arid, these areas are not entirely barren and can sustain a sparse vegetation, adapted to the dryness and salinity of the soil (*Acacia, Ziziphus, Heliotropium, Astragalus, Artemisia*).

The natural vegetation of the Zagros is one of oak forests up to 2,200 metres (7,220 feet), and above that of mixed forests of oak and juniper. The slopes of the Alborz which face the plateau were also originally covered in juniper forests but on the north side facing the Caspian Sea the forests are very dense and of great botanical complexity; there are even species there representative of Tertiary flora which have survived the ice age. The forests here are mainly composed of deciduous trees (elm, oak and beech) with box, elder and vine. Along the coast itself are marshes and mangrove swamps.

Iran is also at the junction of different faunal regions (the Palearctic, Oriental and Ethiopian), and its great climatic and geographic diversity has led to the establishment of an extremely rich and varied fauna (jungle cat, brown bear, wild boar, mouflon, ibex, goitred and Dorcas gazelles, crested porcupine). Until the 1940s, tigers, lions, panthers and leopards were hunted in Iran, but today only the panthers and leopards still survive. Iran is one of the most important regions in the whole Middle East for bird migration, particularly in the Ansali marshes, the salt lakes of Orumieh (Azerbaijân) and Bakhtegân (Fârs), the Shadegân marshes (Khuzestân), lakes Parishan and Arjan (Fârs) and the Persian Gulf. Over 500 species of bird have been recorded in Iran, of which 325 breed there. Among the more interesting species are the Iranian bee-eater, the grey-necked bunting, the crowned and black-bellied sandgrouse, the great rock nuthatch, the houbara bustard, the white-throated robin, and the Socotra cormorant.

Unfortunately, centuries of tree felling, grazing herds of sheep and goats, cultivation, as well as modern pollution and urbanization have had a serious impact on the environment. The vast stretches of primary forest have been seriously depleted and a large part of the Zagros, now covered in grasses and bushes, is suitable for grazing but no longer supports trees. In the past fifteen years or so, the Iran–Iraq war, and atmospheric and maritime pollution brought about by the burning of the Koweiti oil fields during the Gulf War, have also had an effect on the Iranian environment, although its extent has not yet been properly evaluated. The Shadegan marshes and the Khor al-Amaya and Khor Musa tidal mudflats, for example, have been contaminated, probably by Iraqi chemical weapons. The draining of marshland and its conversion into arable land has lead to the disappearance of numerous species of birds, frogs and insects. Twenty years ago, more than 12 million birds migrated regularly through the Iranian marshes; today there are just over one million. Although hunting and pollution have contributed to this decline, the main factor behind it is the loss of the birds' natural habitat. This draining of the marshes is sometimes linked to irrigation projects: the Hâmun-e Sâberi Lake in Sistân was practically dry during the winter of 1976 because of the construction of a dam on the Hirmand in Afghanistan.

Natural reserves have existed in Iran since 1927. In 1974, four categories of protected area were established (national parks, wildlife refuges, protected areas and national natural monuments). In addition to these, there are forest parks, protected rivers and coastal areas, as well as Ramsar sites (named after the town in which a convention was signed in 1975) for the protection of wetlands. Today, Iran has over 70 of these reserves of various types, scattered throughout the country and with a total surface area of just over 10 million hectares (25 million acres) in 1991. Among the most accessible and interesting parks and reserves are the Kavir National Park in the desert southeast of Tehran (Dorcas gazelles, ibex, bustards, sandgrouse, desert larks), the Golestan National Park near Gorgân and the Caspian Sea (goitred gazelles, wild boar, Isabelline shrike, grey-necked buntings, wheatears), the Mian Kaleh wildlife refuge, also on the Caspian coast (a wetland park), and the Arjan protected area near Shiraz (waterbirds, sombre tit, masked shrike).

Agriculture, Animal Husbandry and Fishing

Iran remains today a mainly agricultural country although less than half the population still lives in the countryside and only a third of the arable land is systematically irrigated. Wheat accounts for just over 50 per cent of Iran's agricultural production, followed by barley (17 per cent) and fodder crops (6.5 per cent).

In mountainous areas, the valley floors offer relatively sheltered and easily irrigable land for growing wheat, barley and various fruits and nuts (grapes, apricots, peaches, pistachios). On the plateau, sugar beet and potatoes are also grown, while in more arid areas one can find plantations of dates, jujubes and tamarisks.

In the coastal provinces of Gilân and Mâzanderân which have high rainfall, rice can be cultivated (approximately four per cent of the country's agricultural production). Gilân used to be known for its silk, especially at the end of the 19th century, but the province's main crop is now tea, a relatively new plant in the area which was introduced at the beginning of this century. Cotton, tobacco and citrus fruit are also grown along the coast.

Animal husbandry is mainly practised by the nomadic or semi-nomadic tribes over vast areas of now poor pasture-land. At present, there are some 35 million sheep, 19 million goats and five million cows in Iran. A few horses are raised in the north and in the Zagros. The herds winter in the valley bottoms and move slowly to higher pastures in spring. This seasonal migration was traditionally done on foot, although now it has become partly mechanized and many animals are transported by lorry.

Fish has traditionally been a major element of the diet of the people living along the Caspian Sea and Persian Gulf, and because of the demographic increase in the country as a whole, fish is gradually gaining in importance for the inland urban populations too. But the seas and lakes are still badly exploited and the catches are consequently relatively small. Because of irregular fishing, there is some concern over the long-term survival of shrimp beds in the Persian Gulf. There is heavy sea pollution in the Gulf as well as in the Caspian. Since the breakup of the Soviet Union, there has been an increase in industrial waste dumped in the Caspian, a situation which is seriously endangering the reproduction of the sturgeon and thus threatening one of the region's main luxury products, caviar.

Sturgeon are fished in the mouths of the rivers that flow into the sea. Caviar is one of Iran's best-known export products. From 1888 to 1927, the exploitation rights to caviar on the north coast of Iran were held by a Russian firm, Lianosov, and almost the entire production was exported to Russia. In 1928, the Iranian government granted the monopoly to a mixed Iranian and Soviet firm, and the fisheries were modernized. In 1953, the caviar industry in Iran was nationalized. Present production (government figures for 1988) is estimated at about 300 tons a year, of which two-thirds are exported. The sturgeon, which generally weigh between 40 and 300 kilos according to the species (but which can weigh up to 600 kilos [1,323 pounds]!) are also an important source of meat (about 1,500 tons a year).

Industry

Iran's main industry is of course oil, followed by mining, textiles (wool and cotton) and food. Apart from oil, the Iranian soil contains large amounts of coal and many minerals (iron, copper, lead, zinc, manganese, chromium) which are mined mostly for domestic use.

Oil was first discovered in Iran in 1908 at Masjed-e Suleiman, near Dezful, in Khuzestân Province. The following year, the Anglo-Persian Oil Company bought the concession and in 1913 was granted the right to prospect for, exploit, refine and export all Iranian oil. This British control lead to a political crisis in 1951 when the Iranian Prime Minister Mossadegh decided to nationalize the oil industry. After 1954 and the signing of a series of agreements, the control of the industry passed into the hands of an international consortium which paid part of the proceeds over to the Iranian National Oil Society. Production, which was of 31 million tons in 1950, quickly increased to 80 million tons in 1964 and reached 300 million tons at the end of the 1970s.

During the Pahlavi Dynasty, Iran's industrial sector, financed mostly by revenues from the oil industry, developed very fast. Under Rezâ Shâh, emphasis was placed on light industry (sugar refineries, textile mills, canning factories) but in the 1960s this trend was reversed in favour of heavy industry, particularly petrochemicals, steel-works and coal mining. This industrial expansion increased after 1973 when petro-dollars started pouring in, while other sectors of the economy, particularly agriculture and light industry, were neglected. The revolution and the war with Iraq inter-rupted most of the large-scale industrial projects that were underway. Oil refineries, especially those in the Persian Gulf, became prime targets for Iraqi attacks. The Abâdân refinery, the largest in the world at the time, and the refinery at Bakhtaran, were completely destroyed. Faced during the war with a critical economic situation, the government did everything it could to ensure a constant flow of petrol to foreign countries. Today, oil-based products are still Iran's main source of revenue and ac-count for 94 per cent of its exports.

The economy now has a chance to recover from the war years, largely due to the adoption of Five-Year Plans aimed at encouraging economic growth, but several sectors still need urgent development, especially the road and rail networks, as well as port facilities. The 4,500 kilometres (2,796 miles) of railway lines in Iran, for example, are completely inadequate for the country's needs and do not even extend as far as certain provincial capitals such as Shiraz or Hamedân. A very large propor-tion of goods transported around the country is done so by lorry and as a result the roads are overused and overcrowded. The construction of sections of motorway between Tehran and Qom, Tehran and Qazvin, and around Isfahan, as well as the widening of some of the other major roads has helped to ease the traffic somewhat, although a long-term solution to the problem has still to be found.

Population

Since the beginning of this century, the population of Iran has increased at a very rapid rate. In 1875, it was estimated at six million people; in 1956, the first official census recorded over 18 million. At the time of the last census (1976) this figure had grown to 49.4 million people. The present population is estimated at 55 million and is expected to reach 60 million by the year 2000.

One of the main features of the population distribution in Iran during the second half of the 20th century has been the rural exodus towards the large urban centres, particularly Tehran, Mashhad, Tabriz and Shiraz. This movement, at its strongest during the 1960s and '70s, has now slowed down somewhat although it is still noticeable. A few figures are revealing: at the end of the World War II, 75 per cent of the work force was engaged in agriculture, whereas in 1976 this had decreased to 34 per cent. In 1986, over 54 per cent of the total population lived in urban areas, and Tehran on its own accounted for 16 per cent of it.

Ethnic Groups in Iran

The numerous migrations of peoples who have passed through Iran, sometimes settling there, have created an ethnically diverse population. The biggest influence has come from Central Asia, first the Indo-European tribes that arrived on the plateau in the second and first millennia BC, and then the Turkish and Mongol tribes in the 12th to fourth centuries. Movement of peoples from the West (Jewish and Greek colonists, then Arabs from the seventh century onward) have only played a minor role on the national scale.

Traditionally, there has always existed a close link in Iran between the ruling dynasty and the domination of one particular tribe or ethnic group (Seljuq, Zend, Qâjâr). In the 20th century, some governments have attempted to carry out national integration of this heterogenous population, in the hope that tribal and cultural distinctions would disappear with the economic and political development of the country. Under Rezâ Shâh in particular, the Persianization of the population was carried out by vigorous methods, including a policy of enforced settlement of the nomadic tribes. Today, cultural pluralism is officially admitted but the changes that have occurred since the beginning of the century are in most cases irreversible. The traditional way of life of the nomad groups has been drastically altered by their settlement in villages and by the agricultural reforms of 1962, which were accompanied by land redistribution. Traditional pastures are shrinking under pressure from agriculturalists and large-scale nomadism was reduced by the sealing of the political frontiers with the former USSR.

The main ethnic minorities live in the mountain regions along the edge of the central plateau (several provinces, such as Baluchestân and Kurdistân, take their names from the dominant group living in them). There are no precise or recent official figures concerning ethnic minorities; however, Iranian minorities (groups speaking Iranian languages other than Fârsi) are estimated at about 30 per cent of the total population of the country and Turkish-speaking groups at 25 per cent. About 1.5 million Arabic-speakers live in Khuzestân.

The main Iranian minorities are the Kurds, the Lurs, the Bakhtiâri, the Baluch and a few groups along the Caspian Sea such as the Gilâni, Mâzandarâni and Tâleshi. The **Kurds** are descendants of the Indo-European tribes that arrived in Iran in the first millennium BC, and they regard themselves as the descendants of the Medes. Today, the Kurds are to be found mainly in Iraq, Iran, Turkey and Syria. Almost nine per cent of the population of Iran is Kurdish, about 5.5 million, living mostly in Azerbaijân, Bâkhtarân, Ilâm and Kurdistân provinces. The Kurds speak Kordi and are Sunnite.

The **Lurs** live mainly in Bâkhtarân and Lurestân, south of Kurdistân. They speak Luri, a language related to Pehlevi (Old Persian) and are currently estimated to number 2.5 million. Like the Kurds, the Lurs were once a sedentary nation that made only short pastoral migrations. Their way of life was radically changed with the arrival of the Turks and Mongols whose armies devastated the countryside, forcing many of the sedentary villagers to take up a nomadic lifestyle.

The **Bakhtiâri** live in the Zagros Mountains to the west of Isfahan, around Shahr-e Kord, moving in winter to the kinder plains around Dezful, Susa and Râmhormoz. They are divided into two main groups, the Haft-Lang and the Chahâr-Lang, subdivided in turn into several tribes and sub-tribes, or *taifeh*. Most Bakhtiâri speak Fârsi or a Luri dialect, although part of the population, concentrated in the towns and villages in the south, speaks Arabic. The total number of Bakhtiâri is currently estimated today at about 900,000.

The **Baluch** live in the far southeast of Iran, in the Makrân Mountains of Baluchestân, but they originated much further north, in Khorâssân, which they were compelled to leave in the 12th and 13th centuries by the invading Turkish armies. In Baluchestân they mingled with the local population, which included several very ancient tribes. Among these are the **Brahui**, who speak a Dravidian language, and who have almost completely disappeared except in a few isolated pockets. In this extremely arid and inhospitable area, the Baluch adopted a nomadic way of life, spending summer in the inland mountains and descending to the coast in winter. Agricultural reforms and forced settlement have driven them to find work in urban centres such as Zâhedân. The Baluch population is estimated at 1.2 million.

The origins of the Turkish-speaking minorities in Iran date back to the invasions and migrations that occurred between the tenth and fourth centuries BC. These peoples are divided into several groups which live for the most part in the north and southeast of the country. The **Azeris** are by far the most important ethno-linguistic

64

Congratulations for a Girl?

I was born on New Year's Day in Iran, Norooz, the twenty-first of March, the first day of spring. In Iran Norooz is a major celebration. People prepare months in advance. They spring-clean, buy new clothes, decorate and prepare delicacies. Having survived the harsh winter they celebrate, every-thing is cleaned and freshened, people wear their new clothes. If adults can't afford them somehow they manage for the children. They have to. Everyone tries to wear something new. People start visiting to wish each other Happy New Year, the senior members of the family first, grandparents, great uncles and aunts, senior members, who give presents to the young ones. Children receive coins from aunts and uncles, and coloured eggs and sweets from friends. Young married women receive a trayful of goodies from their parents and brothers—sweets, cakes, coloured eggs, a scarf, bits of jewellery maybe, and a piece of material for a dress, usually, or a chador, and this is called pi, a share, signifying that the women still play parts in their lives, that they have not been forgotten. Women who live far away receive their presents a few days before.

I was born early in the morning at about five o'clock. The news of my birth was taken to my father who stayed in a nearby house as was the custom in the village. 'Congratulations, it's a girl,' the messenger shouted.

'Congratulations for a girl?' my father asked. The woman expected this response. She wasn't dismayed. The news had to be taken. She'd done her duty. 'It would have been better if a child had brought the news,' she thought, but it was too late. Had it been a boy it would have been totally different. The women would have arrived breathless with running. 'You have a boy.' 'Wonderful,' he would laugh. 'Here.' And he would place a coin in her hand. He would go out and treat everyone in the neighborhood to fruit and sweets. Everyone in the village would know that he had a boy. He would hold his head high, proud. In some cases, fathers of daughters would not return home for a while, or not speak to their wives for a time. What does a wife expect, giving birth to a girl? It wasn't too bad in my case, since luckily my father already *had a son . . . . Ali, the eldest, the first male, was always given special treatment. He was given the best of the soup, the best of everything. He was the family's hope, because he was male, the first son, the eldest. The first son was always regarded as the family's future security. He would carry the family burden, look after his parents in their old age. He was the life line of the generations. Daughters left home when married but sons stayed, even after they had married. The eldest son always stayed with the parents, and eventually took over the running of the household. There was great prestige in giving birth to a male child first. It was even more wonderful if the second and third were also male, just in case something happened to the first son. The parents would register the birth of a son late, thus their age was given as a few years younger on the birth certificate and the parents could benefit from having their son stay with them longer before he had to leave to do national service. On the other hand daughters were registered as a few years older than they actually were so they could be married off early. The legal age for marriage was fifteen so, a girl would often, in fact, be married at twelve. National service for boys was at eighteen but they often went at twenty-one or twenty-two.*

Gohar Kordi, An Iranian Odyssey, 1991

Gohar Kordi was born in a small Kurdish village in Iran. At the age of four, she became blind. She writes of her growing up in a working-class family in the country, the family's move to Teheran and her personal struggle to obtain an education and become the first blind woman student at the university.

minority in Iran, with a population of over six million living in the two provinces of Azerbaijân and Zanjân. The settlement of this part of Iran by the Oghuzz Turks, to which the Azeris belong, dates back to the 11th century but, unlike the Turks who settled in Anatolia and who remained Sunni, the Azeris converted mostly to Shi'ism.

The **Turkoman** who live in Khorâssân in northeast Iran also arrived very early on, in the 11th century. Traditionally they are nomads and extremely proud of their warrior past: until recently, they were greatly feared around Gorgân and Dâmghân for the ferocity with which they swept down to pillage caravans and villages. The Turkoman were traditionally divided into two groups whose life-style was governed by their geographic environment. The Sarwa, nomad herders, lived in the steppes of Khorâssân and the present Republic of Turkmenistan, moving each year with their herds across vast distances in regions unsuitable for agriculture. The Somir, on the other hand, were semi-nomadic agriculturalists who lived between the Gorgân and the forests of the Alborz, in Mâzanderân Province, where they grew mainly wheat. While the Somir would strive to better their social status and become nomadic herders, it was not uncommon for financially ruined Sarwa families to settle down and become farmers, or even to make for the Caspian coast and work as fishermen. The closure of the frontier with Soviet Russia in 1928 suddenly cut off the traditional migration routes and profoundly modified the way of life of the Sarwa. Today, the Turkoman are mostly sedentary and have become agriculturalists and fishermen. Unlike the other Turkic groups, they are Sunni.

The **Shâhsevan**, who live in the northeast of Iran, in the province of East Azerbaijân, differ from other groups in that their formation was the result of a political decision and not a spontaneous movement on the part of the nomads themselves. In the 17th century, Shâh Abbâs I created a militia from tribes of diverse origins, most of them Turkish-speaking, that would serve to put down the rebellions of other nomadic groups. After the fall of the Safavid Dynasty, the Shâhsevan became a tribal confederation. Like the Turkoman, their traditional territory has been divided in half by the closure of the frontier with the former-USSR.

The dominant ethno-linguistic group in Fârs Province are the **Qashqâi**, Shi'ite Turkish-speakers organized into a confederation composed of five main tribes and a few smaller ones. Traditionally, the Qashqâi wintered on pastures in the foothills of the Zagros to the south and west of Shiraz, near the Persian Gulf, and moved north to the mountains in the spring. The Qashqâi confederation was sufficiantly powerful in the 19th and early 20th centuries to play an important role regionally, and at times even nationally, as the provincial authorities frequently relied on the tribal leaders to maintain law and order in rural areas. In the 1960s, Mohammed Rezâ Shâh attempted to reduce their power by disarming them and nationalizing their pastures. Since then, many Qashqâi have been forced to settle or to become semi-nomads. In the 1950s they

Kurdistan village

were estimated at about 400,000 but are thought to be considerably fewer in number now.

Fârs Province also includes a rival confederation, the **Khamse**, formed in the middle of the ninth century by a rich merchant family from Shiraz who wanted to protect their caravans on the way to the Persian Gulf. The Khamse are a confederation of five tribes (Khamse means five in Arabic), of Persian, Arabic and Turkish origin.

The **Afshâr** arrived on the Iranian Plateau in two waves, first of all in the 11th century under the Seljuqs, and then in the 13th century with the Mongols. They served the Safavid rulers and were given posts all over the empire. As a result, the Afshâr were split into several groups. Today, the main groups are to be found in Azerbaijân, between Lake Orumieh and Qazvin and Hamedân, and in an area between Kermân and Bandar-e Abbâs, in the south of Iran. Traditionally, the Afshâr are pastoral nomads but many have now settled down and become farmers.

In addition to these various ethnic groups, there are also a number of religious minorities living in Iran. Zoroastrians, Jews and Christians are recognized as minorities by Article 13 of the constitution, which guarantees them freedom of religion. The Ba'hai are not recognized as a religious minority. The **Zoroastrians** still practice the ancient pre-Islamic religion, whose origins go back to the beliefs of the Indo-European immigrants of the first millennium BC and which became the state religion under the Sassanians (see page 86). After the Arab conquest and the arrival of Islam, the Zoroastrians were recognized, along with the Christians and Jews, as People of the Book, or *ahl al-dhimma*. The Arab policy of religious tolerance towards non-Muslims living in the conquered territories provides them with a legal status within the Muslim community. This status was determined by a pact, or *dhimma*, said to exist between the two communities. According to this pact, non-Muslims accepted a subordinate position with certain social restrictions and the payment of tribute, in return for which they were guaranteed physical protection against their enemies, freedom of worship and a great autonomy in the running of their community. Despite conversions and emigration, there are currently about 30,000 Zoroastrians still living in Iran, mainly around Isfahan, Yazd and Kermân.

The history of **Christianity** in Iran is closely linked to that of the Armenian community there. In the first century AD, Christianity spread from Antiochus to Armenia and Upper Mesopotamia where several communities established themselves, including Nestorians, Baptists and Monophysites. Armenia converted to Christianity during the reign of its king Tiridates III (294–324). After the Arab conquest, Christians were recognized as *ahl al-dhimma*, and the Nestorian Church even went through a period of great expansion in Central Asia where it remained active until the Mongol conquests. An important Christian community settled in Isfahan in 1603 when Shâh Abbâs forcibly moved families of Armenian merchants there from Jolfâ in Azerbaijân. Today, Christians form the largest religious minority in Iran with a population estimated at around 200,000, most of whom are Armenian and live in Tehran.

The presence of a **Jewish** community in Iran dates back to the period of the first Achaemenian conquests and the capture of Babylon by Cyrus the Great in 539 BC. Cyrus freed the Jews who had been deported to Babylon by Nebuchadnezzar and gave them permission to return to Jerusalem and rebuild their temple. At that time, Jerusalem was placed under Persian administration, as it was again under the Seleucid Dynasty, between 197 and 129 BC. During the Islamic period, the Jews were also considered *ahl al-dhimma* and were thus able to continue living and working on Persian soil. The exact number of Jews now living in Iran is unclear but is thought to be around 60,000.

Islamic Art and Architecture

In any discussion of Islamic art it must always be remembered that the artistic tradition of the Muslim faith developed not only over a long period of time beginning with the Hegira in 622 AD, but also over a very wide geographical area extending from Spain and Morocco to Central Asia, India and Indonesia. Given these conditions, it would have been surprising for a single, homogenous artistic tradition to emerge. Indeed, the very richness and variety of Islamic art is due in part to the appearance of regional trends within the Islamic world, particularly once the Umayyad Caliphate began to weaken in the tenth and 11th centuries, thus allowing the formation of local political powers. The ethnic diversity of the Muslim world—which includes Arabs, Iranians, Turks, Indians, Berbers and more—the variety of pre-Islamic traditions that existed in the newly-conquered territories, and the continued presence of non-Muslim communities in those areas, all contributed to the creation of an art with strongly marked regional characteristics. This diversity was to be emphasized by the almost complete lack of any imposed directive or code concerning the work of the artist.

And yet, despite this tendency towards specific regional characteristics, other forces were at work which tended towards the development of a universal and unified art. The main force was of course Islam itself, the basis of the whole civilization. Along with faith came an entire way of life, as well as certain attitudes and a vision of the world which were common to all regions concerned. Unlike Christianity, Islam never developed an exclusively sacred art. The proper functioning of the mosque required only a few elements (*mehrab*, *mimbar*, prayer carpet) and none of the ritual or liturgical paraphernalia present in temples of other faiths. The decorative motifs used in the mosques were by no means limited to a strictly religious context but could equally well serve as secular ornaments, on a wide range of media. Calligraphy, for example, the natural vehicle for the divine message transmitted by the Prophet, plays an important role in mosques but is also largely used on ceramics, textiles and in handicrafts in general. The almost complete absence of sculpture, with a few rare exceptions, is another universal characteristic of Islamic art influenced partly by the rejection of human representation as it appears in the *Hadith* (*Traditions*). It should be noted, however, that despite this disapproval, humans and animals have frequently been depicted on ceramics and are the favourite subject-matter of miniature painting, one of the most creative art forms in Persia, Turkey and Moghol India.

A second unifying factor in Islamic art has been the great mobility of people within the Muslim world, either as individuals or in groups. There have been numerous cases, particularly in Iran, of rulers who were foreign to the region or the country

they governed. It is no coincidence that these mixed courts were often the ones in which the arts flourished the most, a direct result of the interaction between the local, traditional styles and those brought by the newcomer. Artists, architects and poets travelled over great distances in their search for benevolent patrons. Other migrations were not undertaken voluntarily: large numbers of refugees and conscripts have, at various times, been compelled to start a new life in new lands. But it was particularly trade along the maritime and overland caravan routes that was behind the widest artistic exchanges. As a result, artists came into contact with new decorative motifs and new techniques which were quickly absorbed into the local artistic repertoire.

Islamic Architecture in Iran

MOSQUES

The centre of Islamic religious life is the mosque, or *masjed* in Arabic, literally the 'place of prostration'. The first mosque, which served as a prototype, was the house of the Prophet himself in Medina. It was composed of a central courtyard with a portico of palm trunks along one wall supporting a roof of palm fronds. This wall, or *qebla* wall, indicated the direction of Mecca and of the Ka'ba. According to some sources, the Prophet delivered his addresses from a pulpit, known as *mimbar*, resembling a tall chair with three steps. These basic elements, the assembly area, the portico, the *qebla* wall and the *mimbar*, were all to be adopted in later mosques, along with a new feature, the *mehrab*, a niche set in the centre of the *qebla* wall which developed during the first century after the Hegira.

The Umayyad caliphs of Damascus (661–750) decided at an early stage to build monuments to the Islamic faith capable of rivalling the imposing Christian basilicas which existed in their newly conquered lands. In some towns, churches were converted into mosques, and the original orientation towards Jerusalem to the east was replaced by an orientation towards Mecca, to the south. In other places, however, entirely new monuments were built. These first mosques, including those of Basra and Kufa in Iraq, have almost completely disappeared but they appear to have been simple in shape, with a square, central area and a deep portico along the *qebla* wall. The caliphs' first major construction, and the oldest Muslim building still standing today, is the Dome of the Rock in Jerusalem (built between 687 and 692), a holy place of Islam associated with the Prophet's miraculous night-time journey to Heaven.

The development of Umayyad mosques lead to the recreation of the hypostyle mosque (a building with a roof held up by columns) by extending the use of the portico to the other three sides of the central courtyard. Two new elements also ap-

Friday Mosque, Isfahan

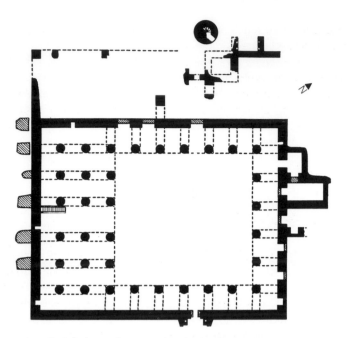

Plan of a hypostyle mosque (Tarik Khâneh Dâmghân)

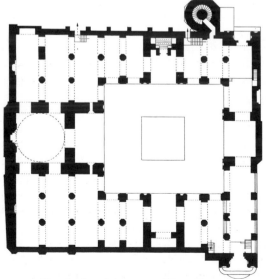

Plan of a four-eivân mosque (Zavâreh)

peared at this period: the *maqsura*, an enclosure reserved for the prince in the *qebla* wall of the larger mosques, and the minaret.

The development of the mosque under the Abbasid caliphs (750–950) is still unclear. In Iran, there was a period of adaptation and experimentation of Islamic forms which lasted until the beginning of the 11th century, and which was influenced to some extent by the older native architectural forms. Square domed buildings with plans reminiscent of the Sassanian fire temples (*chahâr tâq*) seem to have been added to certain mosques, probably to serve as *maqsura*. When found on their own, usually in villages, these buildings are termed kiosk mosques. Lacking a courtyard, they were inadequate for large congregations. Among the oldest mosques in Iran are those of Susa and Dâmghân (eighth century), Fahraj (ninth century) and Nâin (tenth century), all of them hypostyle, and occasionally domed, mosques.

From around 1086 on, during the Seljuq Dynasty (1038–1157), a remarkable series of mosques were built along the edge of the central desert, particularly in Isfahan, Ardestân, Zavâreh and Qazvin. The main novelty was the integration of a domed pavilion with the central courtyard (*sahn*) surrounded by arcades. In the centre of each side of the court was an *eivân* (or *iwan*, a barrel-vaulted room open on one side); the *eivân* in the *qebla* wall gave directly onto the *mehrab*, itself set at the back of a domed room. This combination of domed chamber and *eivân* had already appeared in Iran in the earlier Sassanian palaces. The oldest Islamic example of this is in Zavâreh (1136), although the most remarkable example is undoubtedly the Friday Mosque in Isfahan, which was built in several phases.

Once the plan of a courtyard with four *eivân* had been established, it changed very little through the centuries, and most later developments concern decoration, and the relative proportions of decorated and plain surfaces. The culmination of nearly six hundred years' development of the four-*eivân* mosque is, as Alexander Pope observed, the superb Imam Mosque (ex-Shâh's Mosque) in Isfahan, built in the reign of Shâh Abbâs (built 1611–1638).

MAUSOLEUMS

The mausoleum, or *imâmzâdeh*, is another major type of Islamic construction in Iran. Although the veneration of the saints is expressly denounced in the Koran (Surat IX, 31), a number of commemorative monuments were built over important burial places, particularly those of Shi'ite saints, around the ninth and tenth centuries. In Iran and Central Asia, further constructions commemorated local rulers, Biblical figures, Companions of the Prophet, scholars and even popular heroes.

The first Iranian mausoleums, which date back to the tenth century, are represented today by two types, the canopy tomb and the tower tomb. Canopy tombs are square buildings with openings on all four sides. The best examples can be seen in outer Iran, in particular the tombs of Ismâil the Samanid at Bukhara (914–943) and of Arab-Ata at Tim, near Samarkand (977). Of the tower mausoleums, the most spectacular is without doubt the Gonbad-e Kâvus built in 1006 near Gorgân, in northeast Iran. This conical tower, star-shaped on the outside but circular inside, is 51 metres tall and shows great purity of line and a masterly use of brick.

These two forms of mausoleum were to undergo great diversification from the 11th century onward. The tower-shaped tomb adopted a circular plan, seen in Dâmghân (1027 and 1056), and at the Gonbad-e Ali at Abarkuh (1056), all of which are much shorter than the Gonbad-e Kâvus. The canopy tomb can be square, hexagonal, or octagonal, such as those at Demâvend and Kharaqân. Unlike the tower tombs, of which only the upper sections are decorated, the entire surface of the canopy tombs' outer wall is decorated with geometric brick motifs.

A third very important style at this period, which appears mostly in the northwest, in Azerbaijân, seems to incorporate elements from both the above styles. A good example is the Gonbad-e Qabud at Marâgheh, a domed tower with corner columns, entirely decorated outside. This type of mausoleum, which appears in a variety of shapes (square, circular or polygonal) continued to be built for several centuries.

The tomb of Sultan Uljaitu Khodâbendeh at Soltânieh, near Zanjân, built in 1304, is another form of mausoleum reminiscent of the earlier monuments in eastern Persia such as the tomb of Sanjan at Merv (c. 1152) or the Gonbad-e Hâruniye at Tus, in Khorâssân (early 14th century). These mosque-mausoleums are characterized by their great height, the elevation of the dome itself and the presence of a gallery around the base of the dome.

In addition to these isolated tombs, which are generally built for sultans or local rulers, there are other infinitely larger and more complex mausoleums in Iran which commemorate the Shi'ite Imams or their descendants and which have become important pilgrimage destinations. Two of the main mausoleums of the Shi'ite faith, those of Ali and Hussein, are actually located outside the borders of modern Iran, at Kerbala and Najaf, in Iraq. Among the most popular in Iran itself are the tombs of Fatima, at Qom, of her brother the Imam Rezâ, at Mashhad, and, a more recent addition, that of the Ayatollah Khomeini near Tehran. In these holy cities, the tombs are part of vast complexes which include a large four-*eivân* mosque and sometimes one or more *madresseh*. While the sites of these tombs are generally quite old, the buildings themselves are often more recent. At Qom, for instance, the sanctuary of Shâh Ismâil (1503–1524) is located among Qâjâr and Pahlavi buildings, while at Mashhad the main mosque was built onto a tenth-century sanctuary between 1405 and 1417.

THE MADRESSEH

The *madresseh* is a place of higher religious education. At first privately run and of

Classes in the madresseh are often held in the open air (Madresseh of the Shah's Mother, Isfahan)

modest size, the first real *madresseh* were founded in the 11th century, when they became political institutions under state control and served to fix the Sunni orthodoxy—the first Shi'ite *madresseh* was founded around 1050 at Najaf, in Iraq, by the Shi'ite scholar Tusi. Among the most famous *madresseh* of the period were those founded by the great Seljuq vizier Nizâm al-Mulk (and therefore called *nizâmiyeh*), most notably those in Baghdad, Neishâbur and Isfahan. Almost nothing remains today of the early Iranian *madresseh*, probably built during the Ghaznavid Dynasty (962–1186), and very little of the Seljuq buildings. According to some scholars, these *madresseh* probably consisted of four-*eivân* courtyards similar to those of mosques, a plan which was adopted again later for *madresseh*, particularly under the Safavids. The *eivân* of the *madresseh* served as classrooms; the students lived in the small rooms behind the double arcades surrounding the courtyard.

THE DOME

With the importance that the dome and the vault rapidly gained in Islamic architecture, it soon became necessary to devise a solution to the problem of the transition zone between the square chamber and the dome above it, namely from a square plan to a circular one. The basic solution depended on the squinch, an arch set at an angle across each corner of the building. In the 11th and 12th centuries, the corner squinches were generally variants on the following scheme: centred; set over the corner; a small barrel-vaulted squinch flanked on either side by a quarter dome with the whole composition enclosed within a larger broken arch. Between each of these corner squinches, centred above each side of the square chamber, is a similar lobed arch. In this way, an octagon is created over the base of the chamber. Above these squinches a row of smaller arches, set over the angles of the octagon, thus form a sixteen-sided polygon. This so-called *muqarna* system appeared in a simple form at the end of the tenth century at Tim, in Central Asia, and then at Yazd, in the Davazde Imâm Mosque, built in 1037. It reappears frequently afterwards, particularly at Ardestân and at Isfahan in the Friday Mosque.

The small triangular squinch was to have multiple applications, even covering, in superimposed rows, the entire interior surface of *eivân* domes. Each row is shifted sideways in relation to the ones below, and each squinch becomes gradually narrower towards the apex of the arch. Under the Safavids, each row was shifted slightly forwards so that it jutted out over the one below it, forming a network of cells, or hanging stalactites.

Another important building technique was the use of a double-shelled dome to lighten and strengthen the structure. In Iran, the oldest examples of this technique appear in the Kharaqân tombs, in Zanjân Province, built at the beginning of the 11th century. This technique enabled the inside and outside of the dome to be designed in different shapes. Good examples are the spectacular Timurid and Safavid domes, such as those of the Gur Emir Mosque at Samarkand (1434) and of the Sheikh Lotfollâh and Imam mosques in Isfahan (1598 and 1611).

Decoration

BRICK AND STUCCO

Colour did not play a major decorative role in the earliest mosques. Instead, much emphasis was placed on using the building materials themselves, most commonly brick, to create a decorative effect. In its simplest form, this technique consisted of placing the bricks alternately on their short or long sides to create zigzag motifs. At Marâgheh and Kharaqân, a more sophisticated use of bricks of different sizes, some with a solely decorative function, gives extremely successful and more complex results.

A second very widespread, decorative method was carved stucco, or *gach*. This was either applied to entire walls, or restricted to a particular architectural feature, such as the *mehrab*, a gate, or niches (Nâin, Ardestân, Dâmghân). Stucco had the advantage of being a relatively cheap and abundant material, easy to work and long-lasting. Examples of decorative stucco have been found that date back to the Parthian and Sassanian dynasties, but the most complex and the most beautiful stucco work was executed in the Islamic period, between the 11th and the 14th centuries. The *mehrab* of Sultan Uljaitu in the Friday Mosque in Isfahan is one of the best preserved pieces; its decoration is of extraordinary intricacy, resembling in places the finest of lacework.

TILEWORK

During the Seljuq period (1038–1157), the use of coloured tiles on buildings gradually became more common, although at the outset they served mainly to accentuate certain elements of the interlaced geometric designs created in brick. It has been suggested that the early development of colour was an attempt to make the Koranic inscriptions on the exterior of mosques more legible. The usually turquoise tiles appeared sparingly in the 11th century on funerary towers at Dâmghân and Kharaqân. Within a century, this use had increased dramatically: on the Gonbad-e Kabud in Marâgheh (Azerbaijân, 1196) the entire upper section of the tower, that is to say the niches, the band of interlaced inscription, the stalactite cornice and the pyramidal roof, is decorated with glazed tiles.

The mausoleum of Sultan Uljaitu Khodâbendeh at Soltânieh, near Zanjân, built in the first decade of the 14th century, marks a turning point in architectural tilework: the exterior of the dome, as well as the stalactite cornice, was entirely covered in turquoise tiles, while the entire interior surface of the walls of the great hall and of the dome were originally decorated with tiles and stucco. Up to the Safavid period, this type of ornamentation increased until it covered the entire visible surface area, inside as well as out. The range of colours also increased, first by the addition of white and two different blues, a turquoise and an ultramarine, followed by ochre, olive green and brown (the last colours were used in the Blue Mosque at Tabrîz, built in 1465, which is often considered the greatest example of glazed tilework decoration in Iran).

During the reign of the Safavid ruler Shâh Abbâs I (1571–1629), decorative tilework underwent a major technical change. In the midst of an ambitious building programme, and finding the traditional methods too time-consuming and laborious, Shâh Abbâs approved the adoption of a new technique, that of polychrome painting, or *haft rangi*, or 'seven colours'.

The earlier method involved the creation of a cut faïence mosaic, requiring great patience, skill and precision to carry out. First a full-scale drawing of the final design was made on paper, which was placed over a layer of plaster. The lines of the design were pricked out with a needle and covered with a coloured powder to transfer it to the plaster beneath. The different elements of the mosaic were then carved out of the plaster. The pieces of paper from the original stencil were stuck onto a glazed sheet of

(Left) *Glazed tile mosaic design: the edges of each piece of the mosaic are clearly visible, modern period, tomb of Kemâl al-Mulk, Neishâbur;*

(right) *haft rangi polychrome tile, the complete overglaze design is painted before firing instead of being made up of separate pieces, Safavid Dynasty, Qadamgâh*

the desired colour. Once these tile sections were cut out and filed down, they were placed, glazed side down, into the corresponding holes in the plaster mould. When all the pieces were in place, a layer of mortar was poured over the whole as a fixative. The panel was then set against the wall in its final position, leaving a small gap between it and the wall into which more mortar was poured to hold it firmly in place.

With the new *haft rangi* technique, the motif was no longer created by mosaic but painted directly onto the tile. There was therefore no longer any need to cut out the elements of the design and assemble them, but just to place the tiles side by side on the wall (dome exteriors were covered with glazed bricks, never with these painted tiles, which were too fragile). Unfortunately, this method is shorter-lived than the older one and the tiles, fixed to the wall with plaster, easily become detached.

After Shâh Abbâs' reign, the palette of colours changed once again and reds, yellows and even oranges were added to the earlier blue harmony. At the beginning of the 18th century, the reds disappeared and a golden yellow appeared which was

often used together with blues. A very fine example of this is the west *eivān* of the Friday Mosque in Isfahan, redecorated during the reign of Shāh Sultan Hussein (1694–1722). But glazed ceramics gradually declined in quality, continuing a process which had already begun after the reign of Shāh Abbās.

Zend and Qājār tilework shows a completely new departure from that of the Safavid period. For the first time, representations of people and animals form the main subject matter: there are hunting scenes, illustrations of the battles of Rostam, the hero of the national epic, the *Shāhnāmeh*, soldiers, officials, scenes of contemporary life and even copies of European illustrations and photographs. The figures are usually shown against a white background, sometimes set within a floral medallion. Large panels of still life fruit and flowers, with rather dominant yellows and pinks, were another favorite motif. Shiraz, followed by Qazvin and Tehran, became the centres of this new style which was used in the decoration not only of mosques and *madresseh* but also of administrative buildings and royal palaces.

ISLAMIC CALLIGRAPHY

Calligraphy occupies a privileged place in Islamic culture. From the moment when it became destined to reproduce and transmit the Word of God contained in the Koran, it acquired a sacred function. But very rapidly it was also employed for decorative ends in secular as well as religious contexts. Metal bowls and vases, for example, are often decorated with a combination of floral scrolls and inscriptions which quote the verses of a well-known poet, express wishes of happiness and prosperity or list the titles of a ruler.

The Arabic system of writing, derived from the Syriac and the Nabatean, is characterized by a contrast between vertical lines and the horizontal base line formed by the links between the letters. The aesthetic potential of this system was exploited very early on and a large range of different scripts has evolved over the centuries. New styles are created by altering the various components of each letter, either by extending or shortening the base line, by varying the slope of the vertical strokes, or by changing the curve of the loops which descend below the horizontal line. But calligraphers are not entirely free to play around as they wish with these elements and are restrained by very strict stylistic rules.

Among the numerous calligraphic styles which have developed, some are more common than others. A first very important category covers the so-called Kufic scripts, which are very angular and are used mainly in religious contexts, such as for reproductions of the Koran and for inscriptions in mosques. Among the different variants are floral Kufic (al-kufi al-mukhamal), in which the inscription is set against a background of leaf and flower arabesques, and square Kufic (al-kufi al-handâsi or ma'qeli), which avoids all curved lines.

The non-Kufic scripts are sometimes called cursive. Naskh, which has a very regular and balanced appearance, has been widely used as an everyday writing style and for reproducing books. Thulth, on the other hand, has rounded letters, and may be written in lines so close to one another that elements of the letters intersect. This is a difficult style to master and requires a great deal of practice. From the 11th century, Persian calligraphers developed a new cursive style known as Ta'liq, which made use of elements from other styles including Naskh. Later, a variant of this style called Nasta'liq was created which rapidly became one of the most popular ones in Iran. This style is characterised by the extension of the horizontal lines and by a perfect balance between these and the vertical or rounded elements. The elegance and lightness of the words on the page make it an ideal complement to a painting or book illustration.

The Ma'qeli Kufic style, composed only of straight lines. The blue tiles repeat the name of God to infinity. (Imāmzādeh Mahruq, Neishābur)

A modern example of Shikastah Ta'liq, a style designed for rapid writing which was mostly used in the Persian administration but was gradually replaced by Nasta'liq. (Mausoleum of Omar Khayyām, Neishābur)

Thulth is frequently used in the decoration of mosques; the best examples are those of the Safavid calligrapher Ali Reza Abbassi, which can be seen in Isfahan and Mashhad. (Imāmzādeh Mahruq, Neishābur)

Handicrafts

PERSIAN CARPETS

Carpet weaving is by far the most widespread handicraft in Iran; it is also the best-known one abroad. The origins of the carpet date back to antiquity: texts and carvings tell us that the ancient Sumerians and Egyptians owned carpets, as did the Achaemenians in Persia. The oldest known knotted carpet was found at Pasyryk in the Altai (Siberia) and is thought to have been made in Persia around the fifth century BC. Despite the existence of this ancient example, little is known about the subsequent history of the carpet in Iran until the 16th century. Traditionally, carpets were made by the nomadic tribes, whose herds of sheep and goats provided them with high-quality, durable wool. The sale of this wool, either untreated or in the form of textiles and carpets, was for a long time one of the major sources of income for the nomad communities.

In the Safavid period, an entirely new development revolutionized the production of Persian carpets: until this period, the manufacture of carpets was carried out on a relatively small scale by geographically dispersed groups, but as royal manufacturers and independent workshops opened up in the large urban centres it grew into a national industry. Carpets began to figure among Persian export products to Europe, India and even the Ottoman Empire. Under the influence of contemporary miniature painting and Chinese and Arabic designs, new motifs were created. Gradually, hunting scenes, animals, flowers and figures were added to the older, purely abstract or stylized designs.

In addition to the carpets produced in the urban workshops, there existed an important production of tribal carpets, often less well known abroad. Qashqâi, Turkomans—in particular the Yomut and Tekke tribes—Afshâr, Shâhsevan and Bakhtiâr each had their own motifs and styles. Certain designs, transmitted from generation to generation, are very old; they are reproduced from memory without the use of a model or a design cartoon. Carpet weaving was one of the most important tasks for nomadic women and was taught to girls at a very young age. The carpet held such economic importance for the group that a woman's ability to weave was a major criterion in the choice of a wife.

Tribal carpets are frequently made on small, horizontal looms which are easy to dismantle and to transport. The size of the loom determines that of the finished product, and many tribal carpets are therefore traditionally narrower than those made in urban workshops where there is room for the larger vertical looms.

Persian carpet makers use two types of knot, the Turkish knot and the Persian knot (both these knots are used over a wide geographical area and these terms do not necessarily imply a connection with linguistic or ethnic borders). The Turkish knot, also called the symmetrical knot, is tied with a hook and produces a rigid carpet; the back, however, appears less uniform and coarser than a carpet made with the Persian knot. The latter, also known as the asymmetrical knot, is hand-tied and produces more flexible, softer carpets with a flat and uniform back. The tighter and closer together the knots, the clearer and more focused the designs; most Persian carpets have between 120 and 180 knots per square inch, but the finer ones may have between 600 and 800.

TEXTILE PRINTING

The technique of cloth printing using carved blocks (*qalam kâr*), known in India for centuries, was already well established in Persia in the Sassanian period when it was used for the decoration of woollen, silk and linen cloth. Later it was used for cotton, and today Isfahan is still famous for its printed textiles. The cloth used for this technique is usually a light beige calico decorated with four colours, black, red, blue, and yellow, applied in that order. A wooden block, carved with the motif in reverse, corresponds to each colour. The black colour serves to fix the outline of the design. A fifth colour, green, is sometimes added as well.

WOODWORKING AND INLAY

There is a very long-standing tradition of woodworking in Iran. The mountains, and particularly the forests of Mâzanderân, once provided an abundant supply of a great variety of different trees. Although few examples of antique woodwork exist today, many of the handicrafts still produced attest to their long heritage, particularly carved beggars' bowls, latticework panels used as doors and windows, and textile printing blocks.

One of the traditional handicrafts that the visitor to Iran cannot fail to come across is marquetry (*khâtam*), a delicate decorative technique that requires great precision and a steady hand. The oldest examples of wood inlay date back to the Safavid period (1487–1722); *khâtam* was then so highly esteemed at court that certain royal princes were taught it in the same way that they were taught music or painting. In the 18th and 19th centuries, marquetry went through a period of decline but was revived by Rezâ Shâh (1925–1941) who founded several specialized schools for handicrafts in Tehran, Isfahan and Shiraz.

As harmonious colour combination is vital to the overall effect of *khâtam*, the craftsman selects a variety of different types of wood (jujube, orange, ebony, teak, rosewood), metals (brass or even gold and silver) and bone or ivory. Very fine strips of wood or bone are filed into triangular lengths two to six millimetres wide. These pieces are assembled and glued together in strict sequence to form a cylinder, which provides the basic decorative unit; a six-pointed star set within a hexagon. The cylin-

der is cut into sections, which are then stuck close together between two fine strips of wood. Once this has dried, it is cut in half lengthways revealing a design formed by a repeat of the basic unit. These are applied to the surface of the object to be decorated. Rezâ Shâh had entire pieces of furniture from the Marble Palace in Tehran covered in this way (now on show in the Museum of Decorative Arts), although *khâtam* is more commonly used in the decoration of picture frames, boxes, musical instruments and lecterns.

METALWORK

The use of metal in Iranian decorative art dates back to well before the Islamic period; some of the most beautiful examples of metalware are gilded silver cups and dishes, decorated with royal hunting scenes, of the Sassanian Dynasty. From the seventh century, many everyday objects used by the middle classes were made of metal, such as serving dishes and trays, candlesticks and incense-burners. Over the centuries, the shapes and decorative motifs of these objects have been copied by craftsmen in the bazaars for a much wider clientele, and today every bazaar still has an alley for coppersmiths, tinsmiths and engravers. The techniques used vary from simple hammering of copper or tin sheets to nielloed, embossed or engraved designs.

The manufacture of jewellery was traditionally an important occupation of the silver or goldsmith. Although the heavy pieces of jewellery inlaid with semi-precious stones of the Turkoman and Qashqai tribes are rarely on sale, the buying and selling of gold and gold jewellery still flourishes in the bazaar.

The Ardabil carpet, 1539, possibly the world's most famous carpet. It is one of a pair said to have been formerly at Ardabil, the ancestral shrine of the Safavid dynasty that ruled Iran during the 16th and 17th century. Enormous in size, it bears the name of Maqsud of Kashan, probably the weaver. The design follows a pattern that is found also on book-bindings, illuminations and other decorative arts of the period. Courtesy of the Board of Trustees of the Victoria & Albert Museum.

Religion

Pre-Islamic Religions

In the second and first millennia BC, the native population of Iran adopted the cults of the Indo-European tribes who had recently arrived on the plateau. These cults, known generically by the term Mazdaism, were to develop along separate lines in different regions but most of them recognized a god called Ahura Mazda (or Ormazd). Very little information is available about this ancient past, which predates the Achaemenian period, and our present knowledge of these cults is based largely on the study and comparison of ancient Iranian and Indian texts. Because of their common Aryan heritage, the Iranian cults show a close relationship with the ancient Indian religion as it appears in the *Vedas*, particularly in the names and functions of the gods, and the division of society into three classes: priest, warrior and pastoralist-agriculturalist.

The Aryan religion was a polytheistic one which recognized a principal god, Ahura Mazda (Varuna in India), who was surrounded by a group of divinities known as the Amesa Spenta. The worship of these gods centred around two essential elements, fire and *haoma*. Fire, by nature sacred and purifying, remained the central element of Zoroastrianism, and is so today. *Haoma* is the equivalent of the Indian *soma*, an inebriating drink, honoured as an equal of the gods, which was used during sacrificial rites. The bloody sacrifice of animals, usually of bulls, was one of the main rites associated with the worship of the gods.

ZOROASTRIANISM

Zoroastrianism is the religion which developed from the reforms of the old cults carried out by Zarathustra (or Zoroaster in its Hellenized form). Numerous legends exist about Zarathustra's life and it is often difficult to distinguish the fact from the fiction. The present consensus gives Zarathustra's place of birth as somewhere in eastern Iran; he is thought to have been born between 1000 and 600 BC and would therefore have lived slightly before the great Achaemenian kings. The main events of his life are known in part thanks to the hymns, or *gâthâ*, which are attributed to him and which form part of the *Avesta*, the holy book of the Zoroastrians.

Zarathustra appears originally to have been a priest who was expelled from his country for his strong heterodox views. He succeeded in converting Vishtaspa, the ruler of a Bactrian tribe, who became his protector and helped him spread his new doctrine. This was often done through the use of force. This doctrine inevitably aroused strong reactions when placed in oppositon to the traditional beliefs, and

Zarathustra is said to have been mercilessly killed while at prayer in a temple.

Of the old Indo-Iranian pantheon, Zarathustra retained only Ahura Mazda, a beneficent god from whom all things originate. Subordinate to Ahura Mazda were the two twin spirits, Spenta Mainyu (the Holy Spirit) and Ahura Mainyu (the Spirit of Evil), better known as Ahriman, personifications of the battle between Good and Evil, and Light and Darkness. This dualism is fundamental to Zoroastrianism: man is blessed with free will, and the choice of the road he takes in life is thus entirely his own. The supreme virtue of Ahura Mazda is Goodness, and one whose deeds, thoughts and words have been good during his lifetime, and who will thus have lived in accordance with God, will be rewarded after death by a place in His kingdom.

One of Zarathustra's greatest reforms was to introduce the idea of monotheism into Mazdaism. The supreme god Ahura Mazda does not take part in the cosmic battle between Ahriman and Spenta Mainyu; the dualism represented by these two spirits is only temporary and will end with the final victory of Good over Evil. At the appointed time for the Last Judgement, a great trial by fire and molten metal, presided over by Ahura Mazda, will punish the evil and reward the good with spiritual resurrection.

Zarathustra appears as a strong opponent of some of the practices of the Aryan religion, in particular of bloody sacrifices and the use of *haoma*. For Zarathustra, the suffering and death of a bull were incompatible with the doctrine of goodness and wisdom associated with the God to whom the animal is sacrificed. As for *haoma*, its intoxicating effects lead men astray.

The spread of Zarathustra's doctrine did not entirely supersede traditional Mazdaism and a certain syncretism occurred under the Achaemenians, most notably by the incorporation into Zoroastrianism of some of the practices of the Magi. The Magi had for centuries formed a priestly cast with hereditary politico-religious functions in the Median Empire. After the conquest of Media by the Achaemenians, they became the priesthood of the new dynasty. Fundamentally conservative, they did not always adopt the radical ideas of Zarathustra, and animal sacrifice was therefore maintained and the worship of *haoma* reintroduced.

Under the influence of the Magi, several of the old Indo-Iranian gods were reinstated into the pantheon, particularly Anâhita, associated originally with water and rivers, and Mithra, associated with the sun. A rock inscription dated to the reign of the Achaemenian king Artaxerxes II (404–359 BC) invokes for the first time, and together, Mithra, Anâhita and Ahura Mazda, signalling a change from the practice of earlier reigns when only Ahura Mazda was called upon. Mithra was also the god of war, and presided over the bull sacrifices and the *haoma* rituals. His cult, known as Mithraism, spread throughout the Greek and the Roman worlds, and was particularly popular in the army.

88

Under the Sassanians, who were themselves descendants of a high priest of
Anâhita, Zoroastrianism became a state religion, a theocracy organized around the
Magi. At the beginning of the Sassanian period, there still existed a variety of Mazda-
ian doctrines, but an orthodoxy gradually developed under the influence of a priest
named Kartir who lived during the reigns of Shâpur I (241–272 AD), Bahram I (273–
276) and Bahram II (276–293). Kartir's actions are known to us through a series of
inscriptions, a form of apologia, in which the priest describes the main events of his
career. Kartir was not alone in having built fire temples throughout the empire or in
destroying pagan places of worship, but he was much more aggressive than his predecessors. He reorganized the priesthood and openly attacked heretic doctrines, particularly the Manichean, Christian and Jewish faiths. The compilation at this period of a
canon, the *Avesta*, from texts of various origins, contributed to fix the orthodoxy of
this state Zoroastrianism, also known as Neo-Mazdaism.

ZERVANISM
By the time of the Parthian Dynasty, another branch of Mazdaism had developed
which was particularly popular in Media: Zervanism. Its name was derived from that
of its supreme god, Zervân, who represents unlimited time. Once again, a cosmic
battle between Good and Evil is represented, but unlike Zoroastrianism, it is Ormazd
(Ahura Mazda) himself who battles with Ahriman and not Spenta Mainyu. According
to Zervanism, the history of the world will last a span of 9,000 years (some texts say
12,000), divided into cycles of 3,000 years. The first two periods, those of the reigns
of Ormazd and Ahriman, represent an alternation of the reigns of Good and Evil, a
concept which is completely absent from Zoroastrianism. In the final period, Light
and Darkness battle with each other, creating a mingling of Good and Evil, until the
final victory of Light. In this battle, Mithra plays the role of arbiter and mediator.

MANICHEISM
In the third century AD, during the Sassanian Dynasty, a prophet by the name of
Mani preached a new, syncretic doctrine in Iran, influenced by Zoroastrianism,
Christianity and Buddhism. Born around 216 AD, Mani was brought up in a Gnostic
Baptist sect in Babylonia. At the age of 24, a few years after having received his first
revelation from God, he left the community and set off on a long journey through
Iran as far as the Indus Valley. On his return, King Shâpur I invited him to court to
expound his doctrine, and gave him permission to preach throughout the empire. But
Manicheism suffered badly from the religious persecutions of the period directed by
the high priest Kartir. In 277, during the reign of Bahram I, Mani was imprisoned and
died in captivity.
    The belief in the two opposite principles of Light and Darkness appears once

Those who wish can listen to readings from the Koran before entering an imâmzâdeh

more in connection with Manicheism. Here again, events unfold over three periods; in the first one, the two principles are separate, each in its own kingdom, until Darkness invades the world of Light. Then begins the middle period, that of the mingling of the principles. Primordial Man, an emanation of God, is defeated by the demons who take away his armour (Light). The particles of Light thus captured are mixed with Darkness and Matter (*hule*). While some particles are recovered by the Living Spirit to create the Moon, the Sun and the Stars, the more defiled ones remain captive. At this point, the Archonts, demons bound by the Living Spirit and who beget the plants and the animals in which the particles of Light are incorporated, intervene. The human species was created by Concupiscence in the hope that as he multiplied, Man would scatter the particles and prevent their return to their own kingdom. To frustrate this plan, the Saviour communicates to the First Man, Adam, the Gnosis, or total knowledge about his origin and his vocation: although his body was engendered by demons, his soul is capable of freeing itself and returning to the Light. In the last period, when all the particles have returned, Light and Darkness will once again be separated and the demons and the damned enclosed for eternity in the world of Obscurity.

The death of Mani and subsequent religious persecution led to an exodus of Manicheans to the ends of the Sassanian Empire. Many fled to Egypt, and even to Chinese Turkestan, where their faith survived at least until the 11th century. But in Muslim as well as in Christian territory, the Manicheans were considered heretics; in Iran, they represented a religious and political threat to the new Arab government which feared that they would form a rallying point for the strongly nationalistic opponents to the new regime. The persecutions continued and, at the beginning of the tenth century, the Manichean Church left its native region for Central Asia.

MAZDAKISM

At the end of the fifth century, there appeared in Iran a movement called Mazdakism, named after its founder, Mazdak, whose religious teachings incorporated the dualism and Gnosis of Manicheism. But

Mazdakism is better known as an economic and social movement than for its religious doctrines. At a period of serious social unrest, the message of Mazdak, who defended the lower classes and preached the sharing in common of lands and women, captured the attention of the very poor. For Mazdak, all men were born equal, and the evil in the world stemmed from hate and social differences. Like Manicheans, Mazdakites were persecuted and the movement lost its religious character and became more revolutionary. As a result of excesses committed by adherents, such as the capture and sacking of castles and kidnapping, the ruler Kavadh I (488–531) was faced with the prospect of serious social upheaval. In 528 he ordered the massacre of the Mazdakites. The sect went underground and was still in existence during the Islamic period.

Shi'ism

The two main branches of Islam are the Sunni, which includes the majority of Muslims, and the Shi'ite, which accounts for slightly over ten per cent of the Muslim community, living mostly in Iran, Iraq, Lebanon, the Arab Peninsula, Afghanistan, Pakistan and India. The split between Sunni and Shi'ite dates back to the period of the first caliphs elected after the death of the Prophet in 634 (see History section page 31). Ali, a cousin and son-in-law of the Prophet and a popular candidate, was dismissed and had to wait until 656 before his election. The reign of Ali is considered by the Shi'ites as a Golden Age, although it did not last long. A first rebellion lead by Aisha, the Prophet's widow, intent on avenging the assassination of the third caliph Osman, was successfully defeated at the Battle of the Camel, near Bassorah, but was followed by a second revolt lead by the governor of Syria, Mo'awiya, a cousin of Osman. His army and Ali's met at Seffin, in Iraq (658). As the outcome of the battle seemed uncertain, the two sides agreed to an arbitration which turned in favour Mo'awiya. Having lost the caliphate, Ali also had to face a further rebellion, that of the Khajirites who refused to accept a human arbitration for such an essential question as the succession to the head of the Muslim community, believing that this decision should be left to God alone. Ali defeated the Khajirites but was assassinated by one of them at Kufa in 661.

According to Shi'ite tradition, a movement rapidly formed aimed at restoring Ali's line to the caliphate. It soon became a full-scale opposition movement to the Umayyad Dynasty founded by Mo'awiya, which it considered as having usurped power. The word Shi'ism is derived from the name of this movement, the shi'at 'Ali or 'party of Ali'. In 680, after the death of his brother Hassan, Ali's second son, Hussein, took over the leadership of a rebellion against caliph Yazid. On the way to Kufa, they were forced to strike camp at Kerbala, a oasis in the desert. On the tenth day of the month of Moharram, the caliph's army attacked them and massacred Hussein and his followers. Hussein joined the growing list of Shi'ite martyrs, headed by Ali. Hussein later became the principal symbol of Shi'ite resistance and of the Shi'ite struggle for justice.

Sunnis and Shi'ites share certain religious obligations (prayer, charity, fasting, pilgrimage and the *jehâd*, or holy war) as well as certain fundamental beliefs: belief in the *tawhid*, or the oneness of God ('There is no God but God'), in the *nobowwah*, or belief in the mission of the prophets whose duty it is to transmit the will of God and of whom Mahommed was the last in a series; and in the *ma'ad*, the belief in a Judgement Day. In addition to these principles, the Shi'ites believe in the *'adl*, the concept of divine justice, and the *emâma*, the principle according to which Ali and his descendants represent the only legitimate authority on Earth until Judgement Day. Only these descendants, the Imams, are empowered to interpret the Koran as they alone retain the secret knowledge revealed to Ali by the Prophet and transmitted from one Imam to the next. The majority of Shi'ites, or Twelver Shi'ites, recognize twelve Imams; the last one, Mohammed al-Muntazar, disappeared around 873, leaving the visible world. His triumphant return will herald the end of tyranny and restoration of justice and peace on Earth. This messianic Imam, known as the Mahdi or 'well directed', remains even in his absence as the sole legitimate head of the community, and the temporal governments that succeed one another can only act in his name, preferably in consultation with the *mujtahid*, theologians who, after long years of study, are considered authorities in matters of judicial and religious interpretation.

As legitimate successor to the Prophet, Ali is considered to be the First Imam. In principle, the Imam designated his heir during his lifetime and transmitted to him the secrets revealed by the Prophet; in practice, the role of Imam has always passed from father to son, with one exception, that of Hussein, the Third Imam, who succeeded his brother Hassan. For the Twelver Shi'ites, the succession of Imams continued until the Twelfth, but several branches of Shi'ism do not recognize this. The first to detach themselves were the Zaidis who supported as heir to the Fourth Imam a half-brother of Mohammed al-Baqer, who became the Fifth Imam. The Zaidis ruled in Yemen until 1962. A second, more important, division occurred at the succession to the Sixth Imam, Ja'far al-Sâdeq, who died in 756. He had designated as heir his son Ismâil, but the latter died before his father. After Imam Ja'far's death, Musa, a son of Ja'far and a slave, was chosen to succeed him, but part of the community still considered Ismâil the legitimate heir and refused this choice. They became the Ismâilites who recognize only seven Imams, the last of whom, Ismâil, also disappeared in the same manner as the Twelfth Imam (see special topic on the Assassins, page 142).

For centuries, in the absence of a Shi'ite government, the survival of Shi'ism remained precarious. Dispersed Shi'ite communities had settled in centres such as

Qom, or Najaf in Iraq where the *madresseh* taught in accordance with imamist beliefs. But persecutions lead the Shi'ites to adopt the practice of *taqiya*, or mental dissimulation, which allowed them to lie about their faith in order to ensure their own survival and that of their beliefs. Under the Safavid Dynasty, in the 16th century, Shi'ism underwent a renaissance, although Shi'ite knowledge had declined to such an extent that Shâh Ismâil had to invite mullahs from Lebanon to revive the theology. From then on, Shi'ism remained the religion of the majority of Iranians although it has faced further difficulties in modern times, particularly under the Pahlavi Dynasty, which tried to reduce the power of the clergy. This rivalry between political and religious power theoretically came to an end in 1979 with the establishment of the *velâyat-e faqih* system according to which political power lies in the hands of the religious authorities, and more specifically of the *faqih*, or *mujtahid*, specialists trained in jurisprudence.

MOHARRAM AND ASHURA

The lunar month of Moharram with which the Islamic year begins has a particular significance in the Shi'ite religious calendar: it is a month of mourning, the time to commemorate the martyrdom of Imam Hussein, killed at Kerbala. The two days known as Tâsuâ (the day preceding the martyrdom) and Ashurâ (the day of the martyrdom itself), the ninth and tenth of Moharram, are marked throughout Iran by great celebrations accompanied by processions of the faithful, beating themselves on the chest or whipping themselves, laments, music and banners. In the villages there are representations of *taziye*, the popular religious theatre. The plays put on enact various episodes of the life and death of Hussein and are performed on open air stages among a weeping public, carried along by the intense, almost tangible emotion which increases inexorably until the final, inevitable drama, repeated year after year. In other processions, costumed figures represent the various protagonists: Hussein himself and Caliph Yazid; Abbâs, Hussein's brother, whose hands were cut off by one of the caliph's soldiers while fetching water from a well to quench his companions' thirst; Shemr, who advanced at the head of the soldiers and attacked Hussein; Zeynab, the Imam's sister; and Ali, his son, the sole survivors of the massacre.

Wind tower of the Borujerdi house in Kâshân

Approach to Teheran

The city itself was not visible, though we knew we could not be more than twenty miles distant, once we had come round the elbow of the hills at Karkej, and saw Demavend before us, the smooth white mountain, the beacon, soaring into the sky. Teheran must lie there, somewhere, in the dip. To the right glimmered a golden dome, far away; the mosque of Shah Abdul Azim, said someone, and little heaps of stones appeared like mole-heaps by the road, for in Persia, where you first catch sight of your place of pilgrimage, you must raise a heap of stones to the fufilment of your vow. I felt inclined to add my heap to the others, for it seemed to me incredible that I should at last be within walking distance of Teheran. But where was that city? A patch of green trees away to the left, a faint haze of blue smoke; otherwise nothing, only the open country, the mountains, the desert, and little streams in flood pouring at intervals across the road. It all seemed as forlorn and uninhabited as the loneliest stretches of Kurdistan. Yet there stood a gate, suddenly, barring the way; a gate of coloured tiles, a wide ditch, and a mud rampart, and a sentry stopping us, notebook in hand. Persian towns do surely spring upon one unawares, rising in their compact, walled circle out of the desert. But this, no doubt about it, was Teheran. . . .

. . . This country through which I have been hurled for four days has become stationary at last; instead of rushing past me, it has slowed down and finally stopped; the hills stand still, they allow me to observe them; I no longer catch but a passing glimpse of them in a certain light, but may watch their changes during any hour of the day; I may walk over them and see their stones lying quiet, may become acquainted wth the small life of *their insects and lichens; I am no longer a traveller, but an inhabitant. I have my own house, dogs, and servants; my luggage has at last been unpacked. The ice-box is in the kitchen, the gramophone on the table, and my books are on the shelves. It is spring; long avenues of judas trees have come into flower along the roads, the valleys are full of peach-blossom, the snow is beginning to melt on the Elburz. The air, at this altitude of nearly four thousand feet, is as pure as the note of a violin. There is everywhere a sense of oneness and of being at a great height; that sense of grime and over-population, never wholly absent in European countries, is wholly absent here; it is like being lifted up and set above the world on a great, wide roof—the plateau of Iran.*

Vita *Sackville-West*, Passenger to Teheran, 1926

Vita Sackville-West, 1892–1962, was a British writer and gardener. Passenger to Teheran is dedicated to her husband Sir Harold Nicolson, a diplomat, politician and writer, with whom she travelled to Persia.

The City and Province of Tehran

The tourist who arrives for the first time in Tehran hoping to catch a glimpse of the splendor of ancient Persia will quickly be disappointed: Tehran has been a capital for only two centuries and has undergone constant recontruction during that time. As a result, the only traces of the long and tumultuous history of the country are hidden behind the walls of the museums. The modern city is a huge, polluted agglomeration, hot and dusty in summer and beset with seemingly insurmountable traffic problems. It has brought together nearly 20 per cent of the entire population of Iran and has expanded chaotically and too fast. Nevertheless it is well worth spending a couple of days in Tehran, if only to see some of the priceless treasures that are on show in its museums.

In addition to being the political, economic and intellectual centre of Iran, Tehran is also a provincial capital. The province of Tehran extends from the southern slopes of the Alborz Mountains into the Dasht-e Kevir desert and includes several mountain resorts popular with the Tehranis, who are eager to escape the heat and pollution of downtown Tehran. Karâj, 42 kilometres west of Tehran, has become popular for its watersports since the building of a dam nearby. To the east of Tehran, looms the unmistakable shapes of Mount Demâvend (5,671 metres, 18,600 feet), an extinct volcano which provides good skiing, mountain climbing and walking. The road which skirts round the eastern flank of the volcano, following the upper Harâz Valley, from Ab-Ali through the villages of Polur and Reyneh and on to Amol and the coast, offers particularly good views of the mountain. It is from these villages that climbers usually set out for the summit.

History

Although present-day Tehran is a modern city, the region surrounding it has a long history. Remains of Neolithic settlements have been discovered at the small town of Shahr-e Ray, about ten kilometres south of Tehran. During the Achaemenian Dynasty, Ray—then called Ragâ, or Rhages by the Greeks—was an important settlement. It was rebuilt by the Seleucids and remained the main city of Media under the Parthians and the Sassanians.

Partly destroyed after the Arab invasion, Ray was again rebuilt by the Abbasid caliphs and was the birthplace of Hârun al-Rashid (766–809). Very early on, an important Shi'ite community settled there, as well as in the nearby towns of Qom and Kâshân. In the tenth and 11th centuries, Ray was governed in turn by the Samanids,

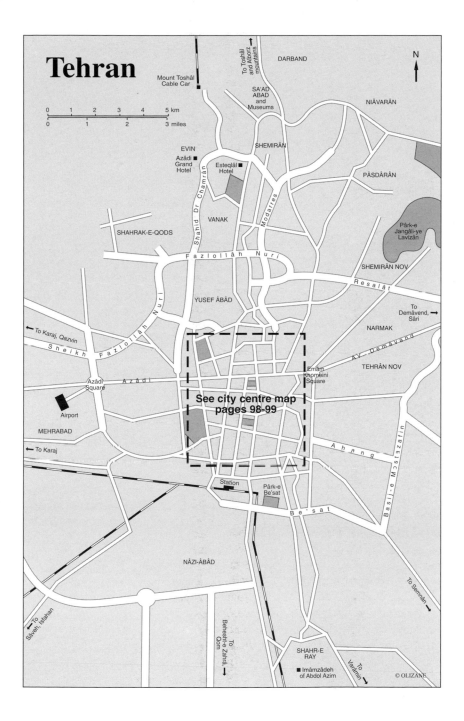

Tehran

Mount Toshäl
Cable Car

0 1 2 3 4 5 km
0 1 2 3 miles

To Toshäl and Alborz mountains

DARBAND

N

SA'AD ABAD and Museums

NIÂVARÂN

EVIN

Azâdi Grand Hotel ■

SHEMIRÂN

Esteqlâl Hotel ■

PÂSDÂRÂN

Shahid Dr Chamran

VANAK

Modarres

Pârk-e Jangâli-ye Lavizân

SHAHRAK-E-QODS

F a z l o l l â h   N u r i

SHEMIRÂN NOV

R e s a l â t

YUSEF ÂBÂD

To Demâvend, Sâri →

F a z l o l l â h   N u r i

S h e i k h

To Karaj, Qazvin ←

NARMAK

A V .   D e m â v a n d

Azâdi Square

A z â d i

TEHRÂN NOV

Emâm Khomeini Square

Airport

See city centre map pages 98-99

MEHRABAD

To Karaj ←

A h a n g

B a s i j - e   M o s t a z a f i n

Station

Pârk-e Be'sat

B e ' s a t

NÂZI-ÂBÂD

To Semnân →

To Sâveh, Isfahan ←

To Behesht-e Zahrâ, Qom ↓

SHAHR-E RAY

To Varâmin →

■ Imâmzâdeh of Abdol Azim

© OLIZANE

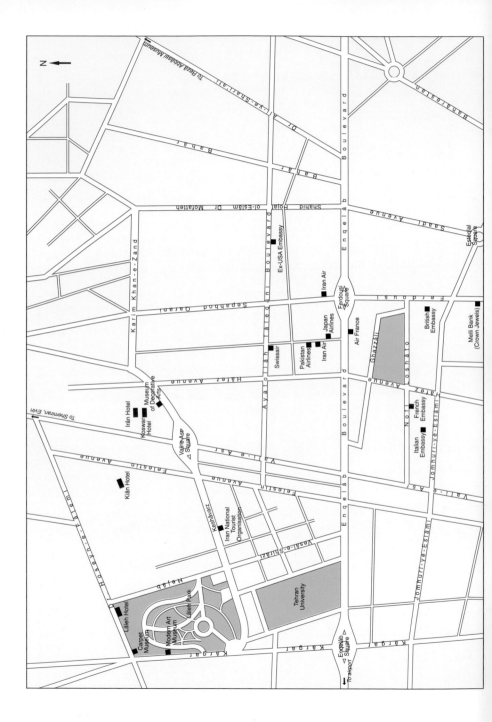

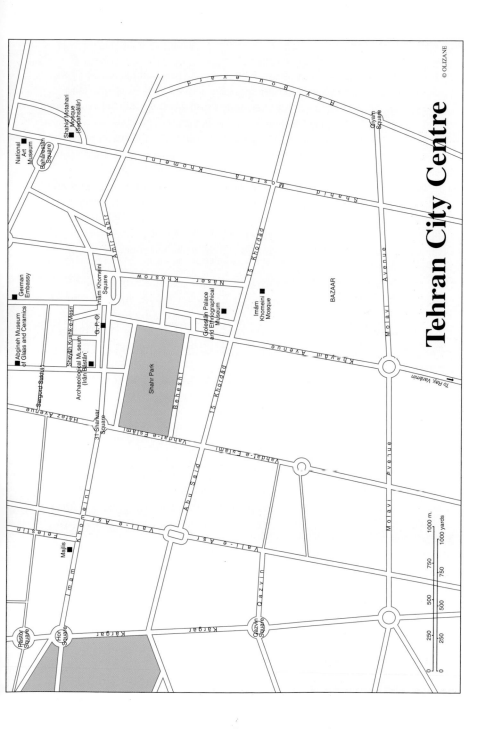

Tehran City Centre

National Art Museum

Shahid Motahari Mosque (Sepahsalar)

Baharestan Square

German Embassy

Abgineh Museum of Glass and Ceramics

Sarguit Sutta

Haféz Avenue

Shaykh Kardk-e-Masn

G.P.O.

Archaeological Museum (Irán Bástán)

31-Shahivar Square

Imám Khomeini Square

Naser Khosrow

Amir Kabir

Shahr Park

Beheshti

Vahdat-e-Eslam

15 Khordad

Golestán Palace and Ethnographical Museum

Imám Khomeini Mosque

Khayam Avenue

BAZAAR

Mostafa Khomeini

Shahid

15 Khordad

Molavi Avenue

Qolyah Square

Boulevard

Majlis

Abu Said

Vali-e-Asr

Imám Khomeini

Feresti

Kargar

Qazvin

Vali-e-Asr

Molavi Avenue

Kargar

Pastur Square

Hort Square

Qazvin Square

To Ray, Varámin

0   250   500   750   1000 m.
0   250   500   750   1000 yards

© OLIZANE

Ziyarids, Buyids and Ghaznavids, before falling into the hands of the Seljuq Turks (1038–1157). During the Mongol invasion (1120), Ray was sacked and never recovered its former importance. A new town developed gradually in its place, Tehran.

The date of the founding of Tehran is unclear but probably occurred sometime in the 11th century. Descriptions from foreign travellers in the 15th century mention the existence of a well-established town, but it was not until the reign of the Safavid ruler Shâh Tahmâsp I (1524–1576) that it was protected by a fortified wall. Shâh Tahmâsp rebuilt the bazaar and added a citadel, or *arg*, in the centre. Tehran became a capital only in 1789, under Qâjâr rule, replacing Shiraz in that function, and in 1796, Aghâ Mohammed Khân was enthroned there. His successor, Fath Ali Shâh (1797–1833), continued the transformation of the town and had the Shâh's Mosque built, while Naser od-Din (1848–1896) enlarged the walls and commissioned the Sepahsâlâr Mosque.

During the 19th century, the centre of the city remained focused around the palace and the bazaar, in other words around the *arg*, the old Safavid centre. But during the reign of Rezâ Shâh (1925–1941), who preferred to live in his palaces to the west of town or in those at Sa'ad Abâd, ten kilometres to the north, the urban plan of Tehran underwent drastic changes. Large avenues were cut to link these different areas together, avenues which still feature among the main roads of the modern town. This was the beginning of the development of the vertical north–south axis which is so characteristic of Tehran. The old walls of Naser od-Din, as well as the monumental tiled gates, were destroyed to make room for large boulevards. An attempt was being made at creating a modern city on a Western model, with large avenues lined with trees and based on a grid plan.

During the 1950s and '60s, Tehran went through intense urban development. At the beginning of the Pahlavi reign (1925), the town had only 210,000 inhabitants, but its population doubled in the next twenty years, reaching 2.7 million in 1966. The railway station, built in the south of the town, prevented much planned urban development in that direction, and it was there that the poor and the peasants who had just arrived from the country lived in hastily erected, overcrowded shanty towns. To the north, between Tehran and the higher ground around Shemirân, in the areas known as Takht-e Jamshid and Abbâs Abâd, residential and business quarters were built for the middle classes and government employees. As empty land between Shemirân and the downtown area gradually filled up, the zones to the east and west of the old vertical axis were also developed. Towards the end of the 1970s, the population had grown to 4.5 million. To satisfy the increased demand for housing, more and more new blocks of flats were built in the empty areas which still remained between the older districts.

Tehran today is the product of these decades of uncontrolled urban growth, carried out without any overall, long-term plan. The city now extends over a radius of 30 kilometres (19 miles) from the centre. The most coveted residential areas, where the air is less polluted and a bit cooler in summer, are located in the north, about ten kilometres from the centre of town, and even further from the poor quarters. Tehran faces a number of serious problems, including overcrowding (the present population is estimated at ten million), severe air pollution and massive traffic jams, which have caused the local authorities to close the city centre to private cars on weekday mornings.

One peculiarity of Tehran remains to be mentioned: the *jub* or open-air canals, lined with plane trees, which run along the main streets. The *jub* network originally served to distribute the drinking water brought into town from the mountains by the *qanâts*. While the water is certainly fresh when it starts its journey through the city in the northern suburbs around Shemirân, it is much less so by the time it reaches the poorer areas at the foot of the hills! After spring storms, the *jub* can become veritable torrents; be careful when getting in and out of cars or crossing the road!

City Tour of Tehran

Tehran's most famous monument is probably the **Azâdi Tower**, a triumphal arch in white stone, standing 45 metres (148 feet) high, and composed of a large central block set on four splayed feet. Designed by a young Iranian architect, the tower was finished in 1971 for the celebrations of the 2,500th anniversary of the monarchy. Once called Shâhyâde, or 'souvenir of the Shâh', it has been rebaptized Azâdi or Freedom. The tower is located to the west of Tehran, at the junction of the roads from the airport and Qazvin, and acts as a grandiose gateway to the capital. A lift (when it is working) takes the visitor up to the top of the tower from where (smog permitting) there is a panoramic view of the sprawl of modern Tehran.

Beneath the tower, is a cultural centre with a library, a museum and art galleries, which put on exhibitions of contemporary artists. Open every day from 3 pm to 5 pm (tel 945029, 948895).

The City Centre
■ THE ARG AND THE BAZAAR
The area round the *arg* (or citadel), the old royal quarter, forms, with the bazaar, the primitive heart of Tehran as it was designed by Shâh Tahmâsp in the 16th century. Nothing is left of the Safavid *arg*, located between the present Nâsser Khosro and Khayyâm avenues and the 15th Khordâd Avenue (ex-Buzardjomehri), but its site is marked by the **Golestân Palace** and gardens, which date back to the Qâjâr Dynasty.

The Azadi Tower, built in 1971, is one of the best known monuments in Tehran

This palace, the Rose Palace, was once the residence of the Qâjâr kings before being used, under the Pahlavi, for specific ceremonies, such as the coronation of the last Shâh in 1967. The first floor was at one time made into a museum; the famous Peacock Throne which was on show there can now be seen with the royal jewels in the vaults of the Melli Bank (see page 105). The gardens and the main buildings of the palace are currently being restored and all visits are temporarily suspended.

Only one of the garden pavilions, which houses the **Ethnographical Museum** (muzeh-ye Mardom Shenâsi, entrance on 15th Khordâd Avenue), is open to the public. This museum contains an interesting collection of everyday objects from all regions of the country from the Qâjâr period onward, including wax models, a variety of household implements, weapons and jewellery. On the first floor are some models of shops, as well as a display of the accessories used during the religious processions of Ashurâ, during the month of Moharram, including a large *nakhl* or ceremonial catafalque. Open from 8 am to 3 pm, closed Thursdays and Fridays. Tel 313335–8.

The **bazaar** and the **Imam Khomeini Mosque** (ex-Shâh's Mosque) are situated just to the south of the Golestân. The mosque, which was begun early in the 19th century and finished in 1830, is now one of the oldest buildings in Tehran. Its main entrance is on 15th Khordâd Avenue but other doors lead directly into the bazaar: to the east they join the tinsmith's alley, and to the west the Great Bazaar (bâzâr-e Bozorg) and the gold and silversmiths' quarter. Although this mosque is not architecturally as interesting as some of the mosques in other cities, its proximity to the bazaar makes it one of the liveliest places in Tehran.

The bazaar has always played a very important role in the economy and social life of Iran. In the broadest sense of the term, the bazaar is an organized system, grouped into guilds. It tends to be rather conservative, and controls almost three-quarters of the country's internal trade, whether it be agricultural, craft, or even industrial products. The bazaar acts as an interface between the town and the country, and has close links with the clergy. It is no coincidence that the Friday Mosques are so often located next to or in the bazaar. The bazaar is an economic power which should not be underestimated, as has been demonstrated on several occasions. When it feels its interests threatened, by the state, for example, or by a foreign monopoly (such as during the events that led up to the nationalization of oil in 1951), the bazaar can close itself down completely, a move which can have dire economic consequences.

In an Iranian bazaar, the shops are usually grouped by profession; thus one alley may be occupied by carpet sellers, another by goldsmiths and yet another by coppersmiths. In Tehran, the bazaar is particularly lively with the constant coming and going of men loading and unloading an amazing variety of goods. The best way of visiting the bazaar is to go in by the 15th Khordâd Avenue entrance and to follow one of the two main alleys, the bâzâr-e Bozorg or the bâzâr-e Kaffâshhâ from which one can easily branch out into the maze of small side streets leading to the Friday and Imam Khomeini mosques.

■ THE ADMINISTRATIVE AND BANKING QUARTERS
The ministries and other government offices, main branches of the large banks, the central post office and some of the foreign embassies (British, French, Italian and German) are located in an area to the north of the Golestân Palace and of Imam Khomeini Avenue, around Ferdusi and Jomhuri-ye Eslâmi avenues.

The **Archaeological Museum** (muzeh-ye Irân Bâstân), which houses one of the most important collections of objects from both the pre-Islamic and Islamic periods, is located on Shâhid Yarjani Street, parallel to Khomeini Avenue. (Two equally important collections are to be found in the Rezâ Abbâssi and Abgineh museums, see below). The museum was built in a style termed neo-Sassanian by the French architect André Godard, director of the Iranian Archeaological Service for nearly thirty years until 1960.

Begin your visit of the museum with the room to the right of the entrance in order to keep to the chronological order of the exhibits. The ground floor presents the pre-Islamic history of Iran, from the neolithic period to the Sassanian Dynasty; it includes some very fine Neolithic pottery found at Tappeh-ye Sialk (fifth to first millennia BC); vases from Marlik, Susa, Choga Zanbil and Turang Tappeh; a copy of the famous Code of Hammurabi, dating from the second millennium BC, which was brought back from Babylon to Susa by an Elamite king (the original is in the Louvre Museum in Paris); Elamite vases made of tar from Susa (second millennium BC); Achaemenian bas-reliefs from Persepolis; a stone statue of the Achaemenian ruler Darius I, which was made in Egypt and brought back by his son Xerxes (end of the sixth century BC), found in Susa in 1972 ; a remarkable little lapis lazuli head of an Achaemenian prince; a bronze statue of a Parthian prince found at Shami (first or second century AD); a bas-relief of the Parthian king Artabanus V (beginning of the third century AD); and Sassanian mosaics from Bishapur, in Fârs (third century).

The first floor is devoted to Islamic art and includes some magnificent *mehrab* decorations (carved stucco from Dâmghân, Ray and Isfahan from the tenth and 11th centuries, a marble *mehrab* from Abarkuh, glazed tiles from Qom and Isfahan), carved wooden doors, a very fine *mimbar* from Fârs (14th century), as well as textiles, miniatures and illuminated manuscripts. Near the stairs is a model of the Tarik Khâneh Mosque in Dâmghân.

The museum is closed on Tuesdays, open other days from 9 am to 4 pm and Fridays and holidays from 9 am to 11 am (tel 672616).

After leaving the Archeaological Museum, turn right along Si-e Tir Street towards Jomhuri-ye Eslâmi Avenue to get to the **Abgineh Museum of Glass and Ceramics** (at the corner of Jomhuri Avenue and Si-e Tir Street). Despite its small size, this museum is without doubt one of the best in Iran. If you have only a short amount of time in Tehran, this is one place you should not miss. The building itself dates from the Qâjâr period; in the 1950s, it housed the Egyptian Embassy and was later bought by the Bank of Commerce before being turned into a museum in 1976 (it opened in 1980). The Abgineh Museum is interesting not just for the objects in it, which are of exceptional quality, but also for the general presentation of the pieces. The layout of the interior was designed by Italian museologists in a very modern style. In many rooms, each object is presented individually in a column-shaped case. It is a remarkable experiment, although for some visitors the modern presentation will clash with the turn of the century ceilings and floors, and with the fine spiral staircase in the hall.

The museum collections include some very fine glass, ceramic and crystal objects from the Achaemenian period to the 19th century, finds from excavations all over the country. In particular, there is a superb Achaemenian glass bowl on the ground floor and some very fine Kâshân ceramics on the first floor. Books, slides and post cards are on sale at the shop by the entrance. Open from 9 am to 4 pm every day except Fridays (tel 678154, 675614).

Still in the same area, on Ferdusi Avenue, stands the large building of the main offices of the Melli Bank. In its vaults are the **Iranian Crown Jewels** (muzeh-ye Javâherât), a vast collection of jewellery and precious and semi-precious stones of incalculable value, the result of centuries of war booty, inheritances and gifts. The most famous of these jewels is undoubtedly the Dariâ-e Nur (Sea of Light), a 182-carat diamond brought back from New Delhi by Nâder Shâh in the 18th century (its sister-stone, the Koh-e Nur, Mountain of Light, was acquired by the British and is now in the Tower of London).

The Peacock Throne (once on show in the Golestân Palace), was also brought back from New Delhi by Nâder Shâh. According to some sources, this is not the real Indian throne but a copy made by Fath Ali Shâh (1797–1833) for a mistress. Among the myriad other treasures on show here are the Pahlavi Crown, made in 1924 by a jeweller from Bukhara and set with 3,380 diamonds, five emeralds, two sapphires, and 368 pearls on a red background; a gold belt with a 175 carat emerald; a globe weighing 40 kilos (88 pounds) and set with 51,000 precious stones; and cases full of stones, aigrettes, tiaras and brooches. If you have never seen what a handful of uncut diamonds looks like, this is the place to go!

Open for visits two days a week only, Tuesdays and Sundays, from 2 pm to 4.30 pm (tel 282031). Needless to say, photography is not permitted inside the vault. Children under 15 are not allowed in either.

To the east of Imam Khomeini Avenue, near Vali-e Asr Avenue and Felestin Street, is the Majlis (Parliament) building, which used to house the Senate, and the **Marble Palace** (Takht-e Marmar), the residence of the last Shâh, now closed to the public.

Bahârestân Square, to the east of Imam Khomeini Avenue, was once the site of a Qâjâr Palace but is now overlooked on the north side by the Ministry of Islamic Guidance and the **National Museum of Art** (muzeh-ye Honarhâ-ye Melli, entrance on Kemâl al-Mulk Street) which houses a very complete collection of Iranian art and handicrafts: marquetry (khâtam), miniatures, brocades, ceramics and mosaics. Open

The Pearls of Persia

The crown jewels are deposited nowadays in a vault of the Central Bank, which has been converted into a special museum. I arrived at the building and, in my quest for an official of whom to ask permission to see the jewels, was sent from one office to the next in a seemingly never-ending round. . . .

'What can I do for you?' asked the ruffled banker defensively.

'I would like to see the crown jewels.'

He broke into a smile. 'I'm afraid the museum is no longer open to the public. A visit is now only the privilege of visiting heads of state, foreign dignitaries and so forth.'

I presented several of my heavily stamped and letterheaded pieces of paper. He skimmed through them. 'What a pity you weren't here this morning,' he said. 'There was a delegation here you could have gone round with. Now I will have to consult the Ministry of Foreign Affairs. Perhaps you will phone me in due course.'

I phoned him every morning. It didn't take long. A couple of days later he gave me half an hour's notice to come over and join some Dutch dipolomats who were going to look round the museum. I was searched and frisked both at the bank's entrance and at the bunker-like entrance to the museum itself. From there, we were escorted to the cavernous vault, where we were treated to a lecture about the Shah's corruption before our visit.

In the dimly-lit chamber the jewels shone like sprinkled stars: emeralds, rubies diamonds from Khorassan and Turkestan; pearls from the Persian Gulf, gifts and war booty, and straight purchases. There were trays of stones piled up like boiled sweets. There was the Darya-i-Nour, the Ocean of Light—the largest diamond in the world, at 182 carats. But such was the richness around that it was just another item on our guide's list. There was a globe five feet high entirely decorated with gems: the seas encrusted with emeralds and the countries with rubies—all, that is, *except England, Iran and France, which were covered in diamonds. And there was the legendary Peacock Throne. We were told that this treasure, the property not of the Crown but of the People, had been hocked as collateral for foreign loans. We were also told that the Shah had postponed his departure from Iran in order to take three crowns with him: his own, weighing two kilos; his wife's, weighing five kilos and studded with over 3,300 jewels. He failed to escape with them and our guide also gleefully pointed to over a million dollars' worth of jewellery commissioned by the Empress Farah from Van Cleef and Arpels. I wondered why this museum was kept so exclusive. The Revolution would hardly find better propaganda material.*

Nick Danziger, Danziger's Travels: Beyond Forbidden Frontiers, 1987

In 1982, Nick Danziger was awarded a Winston Churchill Memorial Trust Fellowship to follow ancient trade routes, and in 1984 he set off to travel from Iran to the heart of China. Out of the experience came Danziger's Travels.

from 9 am to 3 pm, closed Thursdays and Fridays (tel 316329). To the east of the square is the **Shâhid Motahari Mosque** (ex-Sepahsâlâr Mosque). Originally a *madresseh*, it was built between 1878 and 1890 and is one of the most successful examples of late Qâjâr architecture. Today, the building once again serves as a *madresseh* and is therefore closed to the public, but one may still see the tilework decoration of the exterior walls with its floral motifs and figures so characteristic of Qâjâr art.

■ NORTH OF ENQELÂB AVENUE

At its westernmost end, Enqelâb-e Eslâmi Avenue (Avenue of the Revolution, ex-Shâh Rezâ) crosses the university quarter. Here it is lined with bookshops, some of which sell books in foreign languages. When the University of Tehran was first built in 1930 on this avenue, it marked the northern limit of the city.

Directly behind the university, on the other side of Keshâvarz Boulevard, is the large Laleh Park (Tulip Park) which includes within its grounds the Museum of Modern Art and the Carpet Museum. The **Museum of Modern Art** (muzeh-ye Honarhâ-ye Mo'âser, entrance on Kârgar Avenue, tel 655411, 653200), easily recognizable by the sculptures standing in the park, holds temporary exhibitions of contemporary Iranian and foreign artists. Open from 9 am to 12 pm and from 1 pm to 6 pm every day. The **Carpet Museum** (muzeh-ye Farsh, at the corner of Kârgar and Dr Fâtemi avenues) houses a fine collection of carpets and kilim from all regions of Iran dating mostly from the 19th and 20th centuries, with a few older pieces. Open from 9 am to 5 pm, closed Mondays (tel 653027, 657707).

To the east of Keshâvarz Boulevard is Vali-ye Asr Square and the **Museum of Decorative Arts** (muzeh-ye Honarhâ-ye Tazini, 337 Karim Khân-e Zand Boulevard) which houses a collection of craft products from the 19th and 20th centuries (textiles, brocades, lacquerware, miniatures, carved woodwork) including inlaid furniture originally made for the Marble Palace in Tehran. Open from 9 am to 5 pm, closed Mondays (tel 894381).

In the quarter known as Abbâs Abâd, between the centre of town and Shemirân, is the **Rezâ Abbâsi Museum** (927 Dr Shari'ati Avenue, near the Resâlat Highway) which houses an astonishing collection of cultural objects dating back to Neolithic times. If you only have a single day in Tehran, this is the museum to visit, not the Archeaological Museum, due to the exceptional quality and variety of the objects on show. Begin your visit on the third floor and work your way down if you want to keep to the chronological order of the exhibits. On the top floor are Neolithic pottery, Luristan bronzes from the ninth and tenth centuries BC, some superb Median and Achaemenian gold vases and jewellery, Parthian statuettes and Sassanian gold zytons—drinking cups often in the form of an animal's head. Unfortunately, most of the labels are written in Persian only. The second floor is devoted to Islamic arts (bronzes, ceramics, tiles) with some particularly fine *minai* from Kâshân and plates from Neishâbur. The first floor has a very good exhibition of miniatures and illuminated manuscripts, including illustrations from the *Shâhnâmeh*. Open from 9 am to 12 pm and 1pm to 4 pm, closed Mondays (tel 863001–3).

SHEMIRÂN AND THE NORTH OF TEHRAN

The northern suburbs of Tehran, set on the mountain slopes some 800 metres (2,625 feet) above the centre of town—which at times is hardly visible under its brown haze—have always been a much coveted residential area, the symbol of a social as well as a physical climb. Throughout its history, Tehran's urban development has been centred around the gradual progression of the town from south to north, from the plain to the higher slopes. Once a village completely separate from Tehran, Shemirân is now a suburb, linked to the downtown area by the avenues built under Rezâ Shâh and by two new highways. It has a calm and rather select feel to it, far removed from the bustle of the town centre. It is here that one finds the gardens of some of the foreign embassies, private parks, the International Trade Fair compound, the Pârk-e Mellat (Park of the Nation), which has become a popular meeting place for young people, and the large international hotels built in the 1970s, such as the Esteqlâl Hotel (ex-Hilton) and the Azâdi Grand Hotel (ex-Hyatt).

At the north end of Shemirân is the old Pahlavi royal residence, **Sa'ad Abâd**, (majmue-ye Farhangi-ye Sa'ad Abâd, entrance to the north of Tajrish Square, on Alborz Kuh Street) now turned into museums. Open to the public every day from 8 am to 4 pm, closed on national mourning days such as Ashura. The 18 palaces and residences of Sa'ad Abâd, all dating from the 1930s, are scattered in a vast park of some 120 hectares (297 acres), landscaped in a Western style.

The **White Palace**, or Palace of the Nation, is the Shâh's old Summer Palace where he lived for three months of the year. Built by Rezâ Shâh in a style which was to become characteristic of his reign, it resembles more an administrative building than a palace. Fortunately, the tall columns of the front porch restore a certain regal air to it. However, the treasure-filled interior, belies the austerity of the exterior. The Persian carpets are of rare quality and surprising size: woven specially for the palaces and to the exact measurements of each room, some have a surface area of over 100 metres^2 (1,076 feet^2). The palace is tastefully decorated, without deliberate ostentation, so that the furniture and carpets can be fully appreciated. The last Shâh developed a taste for French culture and entrusted the interior decoration of the palace to a French designer. The curtains and much of the furniture is therefore French (including some very fine examples of 16th century furniture); the china comes from France and Germany, while the glass and crystalware are from Bohemia. Outside the

palace, at the foot of the steps, stands an enormous pair of bronze boots, the only remains of a statue of Rezâ Shâh destroyed during the revolution.

The second palace open to the public is that of the **Shâh's mother**, known today as the Palace of Admonition and Reversion. The furnishings are similar to those in the Shâh's Palace, but the interior design of the building is entirely different: all three floors give directly onto a central well which forms the main hall. Here again, carpets, furniture, and china have been carefully selected.

A third palace has been turned into a **Military Museum**. Outside the building, in the park, stand various large modern war machines, including fighter planes. Inside, on the ground floor, is an exhibition of life-size model soldiers wearing uniforms from each dynasty since Achaemenian times, as well as several rooms of armour and weaponry from different periods, including some fine Safavid armour. The 20th century is well represented by a variety of guns and pistols, ranging from the Winchester to the Uzi.

Other buildings in the park open to the public are the Rajeat and Ibrat Palace, the Museum of Fine Arts (water colours, furniture), the Natural History Museum and the Ethnological Research Museum.

The park and museums of Sa'ad Abâd are open from 8 am to 5 pm every day, (tel 282031-9). Cameras, handbags and shopping bags are not allowed inside the park and have to be left at the entrance.

The area known as **Niâvarân**, where the old summer residence of Fath Ali Shâh was located, is to the east of Sa'ad Abâd on the edge of the city. Open to the public from 8 am to 4 pm, closed Thursdays and Fridays.

For those who wish to get away from the noise and heat of town, a short trip into the mountains around Tehran is recommended. From the northern suburbs it is very easy to get into the Alborz. The simplest way is to take the cable car to **Mount Toshâl** (telekâbin-e Toshâl, tel 272733, leaves from Velenjak, north of Evin). The trip to the top takes about half an hour, with several stops on the way. Several paths lead from the top station, including one to the summit of Toshal (3,933 metres, 12,900 feet). Remember that whatever the temperature down in Tehran, it is always much chillier at 3,000 metres, even in mid-summer! Other walks are also possible from Darband, behind Sa'ad Abâd, where numerous little tea houses line the streams that flow down the mountainside.

EXCURSIONS FROM TEHRAN

For those who have a bit more time in Tehran, there are several interesting visits that can be made in the southern suburbs. The closest is to **Shahr-e Ray**, which was an important centre under the Achaemenians and remained so until the Mongol invasion in 1220. Only a single monument remains in Ray of this period, the funerary tower of Tughril Beg, built in 1139 (visits by prior arrangement only). Today, Ray is an industrial suburb with a lively bazaar in the centre of town. Next to it is the *imâm-zâdeh* of **Abdol Azim**, a great-grandson of the Second Imam, Imam Hussein. The sanctuary, with its golden dome, is a very popular pilgrimage site. A second tomb in the same complex is that of Hamze, brother of Imam Rezâ. Women must wear a *châdor* inside the compound (these can be hired at the entrance). The mausoleum of Rezâ Shâh, the first Pahlavi ruler, used to stand beside the *imâmzâdeh*, but has been pulled down and replaced by a new building.

Near the edge of town, on a rock overlooking the spring of Cheshmeh Ali, are several **carvings** dating from the reign of the Qâjâr ruler Naser od-Din Shâh. They represent, in one case, the ruler sitting among his courtiers and, in another case, the king holding a falcon. It was here that the carpets of Tehran used to be washed, as the water of the stream was renowned for its purity. Today, the stream still runs but its banks have been cemented over and the site has lost much of its former charm.

On the right hand side of the road from Ray to Varâmin are the ruins of a **Sassanian fire temple**, built on the top of a hill known as Tappeh Mil. Part of the surrounding walls and two of the arches of the temple are still standing, as well as a long tunnel which ran under the temple. The site has not yet been systematically excavated although there is talk of doing so in the near future.

About forty kilometres south of Tehran is the small town of **Varâmin**. After the destruction of Ray by the Mongols, Varâmin became the regional centre until the 16th century when Tehran superseded it. The **Friday Mosque** (masjed-e Jomeh) was built between 1322 and 1326, during the reign of the Il-Khân sultan Abu Said, son of Sultan Uljaitu Khodâbendeh whose mausoleum can be seen at Soltânieh. The mosque has been partially destroyed, and the west side has disappeared, but the original plan of a four-*eivân* courtyard can still be made out. The decoration is part brick, part glazed tiles. The complex brick motifs on the porch and on the dome of the *mehrab* are particularly fine.

In the centre of town stands a Mongol funerary tower (finished in 1289) known as the tower of Ala od-Din. The only decoration of this circular brick tower is a Kufic inscription around the base of the dome (open mornings only, closed Thursdays).

Leaving Tehran by the main road southeast towards Qom, one cannot fail to notice an imposing golden dome flanked by tall minarets near the cemetery of Behesht-e Zahrâ in the middle of the desert: this is the **tomb of Imam Khomeini** (*haram-e motahar*). The mausoleum complex is not yet completed but there are plans not only to extend the new metro out here, but also to build a town around it. At night, the whole compound is lit up by powerful projectors and can be seen for miles around. The interior is a vast hall measuring 100 metres long, with a carpeted marble floor; in the middle stands the tomb itself surrounded by grills. The size of the building easily absorbs the crowds that come here to pray, mostly people from the poorer areas of Tehran or from the countryside. The atmosphere here is very different, however, from that of the *haram* at Qom or Mashhad: the children are free to run around and slide on the marble and families on a day's outing sit down to picnic quietly in a corner.

The holy town of **Qom** is only 154 kilometres (96 miles) south of Tehran, on the road to Kâshân and Isfahan. Qom is not part of the Province of Tehran but of Markazi, the central province, with its capital at Arak. The early history of Qom is hazy but from the seventh century onwards, it became an important Shi'ite centre, along with Ray and Kâshân. After the death in 816 of Fatima, the sister of Imam Rezâ (the Eighth Imam is buried in Mashhad), it became a pilgrimage site. The sacred precinct with its golden dome is located in the centre of town near the river. The entrance to the shrine is to be found in a small square, dominated by minarets and the main gateway. Non-Muslims are not permitted to go further than this gate and signs in both Persian and English remind one that photography is forbidden. The Safavid Friday Mosque (masjed-e Jomeh) nearby is also forbidden to non-Muslims. As a holy town and a theological centre, Qom has a high population of mullahs, and almost all

Vali Asr Square, Tehran

the women in the streets wear a *châdor* rather than a simple scarf around their heads. It is very strongly recommended that foreign visitors act in as discreet and respectful a manner as possible. Even if the main monuments are out of bounds, a stroll in the streets of Qom can be very interesting. In particular, try the local speciality, called *sohân*, a flat, sweet biscuit made of saffron and pistachios. One remarkable feature about Qom is the number of sweet shops, which appear to have almost overtaken the shops selling religious souvenirs.

The Philosophy of Life

OF THE CUSTOMS OF KINGS

They have related that at a hunting seat they were roasting some game for Nushirowan, and as there was no salt they were despatching a servant to the village to fetch some. Nushirowan called to him, saying, 'Take it at its fair price, and not by force, lest a bad precedent be established and the village desolated.' They asked, 'What damage can ensue from this trifle?' He answered, 'Originally, the basis of oppression in this world was small, and every newcomer added to it, till it reached to its present extent:—Let the monarch eat but one apple from a peasant's orchard, and his guards, or slaves, will pull up the tree by its root. From the plunder of five eggs, that the king shall sanction, his troops will stick a thousand fowls on their spits.'

ON THE PRECIOUSNESS OF CONTENTMENT

Two dervishes of Khorasan were fellow-companions on a journey. One was so spare and moderate that he would break his fast only every other night, and the other so robust and intemperate that he ate three meals a day. It happened that they were taken up at the gate of a city on suspicion of being spies, and both together put into a place, the entrance of which was built up with mud. After a fortnight it was discovered that they were innoncent, when, on breaking open the door, they found the strong man dead, and the weak one alive and well. They were astonished at this circumstance. A wise man said, 'The contrary of this had been strange, for this one was a voracious eater, and not having strength to support a want of food, perished; and that other was abstemious, and being patient, according to his habitual practice, survived it.—When a person is habitually temperate, and a hardship shall cross him, he will get over it with ease; but if he has pampered his body and lived in luxury, and shall get into straitened circumstances, he must perish.'

ON THE BENEFIT OF BEING SILENT

Some of the courtiers of Sultan Mahmud asked Husan Maimandi, saying: 'What did the king whisper to you today on a certain state affair!' He said: 'You are also acquainted with it.' They replied: 'You are the prime minister; what the king tells you, he does not think proper to communicate to such as we are.' He replied: 'He communicates with me in the confidence that I will not divulge to anybody; then why do you ask me!' A man of sense blabs not, whatever he may come to know; he should not make his own head the forfeit of the king's secret.

OF THE DUTIES OF SOCIETY

Riches are intended for the comfort of life, and not life for the purpose of hoarding riches. I asked a wise man, saying: 'Who is the fortunate man, and who is the unfortunate?' He said: 'That man was fortunate who spent and gave away, and that man unfortunate who died and left behind:—Pray not for that good-for-nothing man who did nothing, for he passed his life in hoarding riches, and did not spend them.'

Sa'adi, The Gulistan, c. 1280, translated by James Ross, 1900

Sa'adi began life as a student of the Koran, which he later exchanged for Sufism. He travelled widely, visiting India, Arabia, Syria and working as a slave in Africa in the trenches of Tripoli. The Gulistan is the product of his thoughts and experiences during these years, written on his return to Shirâz aged over 70.

116

The Caspian Coast

The two coastal provinces of Gilân and Mâzanderân in the north of the country present an astonishing contrast to the vast desert lands slightly further south. The Alborz Mountains which separate the plateau from the coast, and which rise to over 3,658 metres (12,000 feet), act as a barrier preventing the moisture from the Caspian from entering inland. Although Tehran is only 115 kilometres (71 miles) away from the sea, it receives on average six times less rainfall than the coastal towns. As a result, while the southern flanks of the Alborz are almost entirely bare of vegetation, its northern slopes are covered in thick forests and rice paddies. The hot, humid climate of the coast generates thick mists which cling to the hills almost all year round.

The Iranian coast of the Caspian stretches for 630 kilometres (391 miles) from Astârâ in the west, on the border with the Republic of Azerbaijân, to the Bandar-e Torkman region in the east, near the Republic of Turkmenistan. Over such a distance, the vegetation and crops, as well as the ethnic groups, are naturally far from homogenous. The western province, Gilân, is mountainous and its population is concentrated in the plain of the Sefid delta, around the provincial capital of Rasht. Gilân has remained relatively isolated through the centuries and its inhabitants have developed their own customs and their own dialect, known as Gilaki. Mâzanderân is much larger and geographically more varied than Gilân. A large part of the province is taken up by the Alborz Range, leaving only a narrow coastal strip in the west. Around Bâbol and Sâri, however, this widens to become a plain which eventually joins the vast Turkoman Steppes in the region of Gonbad-e Kâvus. Unlike Gilân, this eastern region has been more open to influences from Central Asia. It is the land of the Turkoman, a now mainly sedentary nation, but one which is proud of its nomadic past and which has kept its old traditions alive, particularly the breeding of horses and the manufacture of carpets.

Gilân Province

One of the more interesting trips to be done in Iran from the geographical point of view is to cross the Alborz Range by car, from the plateau to the coast. In addition to often spectacular scenery, the most striking feature of the drive is the speed with which the transition from a desert climate to an almost sub-tropical one occurs. From Tehran, the road to Gilân passes through Qazvin and Rudbâr from where it follows the course of the Sefid to Rasht. From Rudbâr, the vegetation, which until then is sparse, suddenly becomes much denser. As one progresses towards the coast, the olive groves give way to terraced rice paddies and then to tea plantations.

The close proximity of Russia has had a strong influence on the history of Gilân, and Rasht, the provincial capital, has been occupied on several occasions by the Russian army, the last time at the end of World War II. In the 17th century, the town was destroyed by a Cossack leader. At the beginning of the 19th century, when fishing rights off the south coast of the Caspian were granted to Russia, an important Russian trade centre was set up at Bandar-e Anzali, the main port north of Rasht.

Rasht has become an important industrial centre, particularly for the processing of agricultural products. Until the 20th century, the town was known for its silk, but this activity has almost completely disappeared. Today, thanks to the road link with Tehran, Rasht has become one of the favourite weekend resorts of the Tehranis. However, it has few attractions for the sightseer other than the museum which contains a collection of local archaeological finds.

The small town of **Lâhijân**, set at the foot of the mountains and famous for its tea, is much more interesting. It has succeeded in preserving some of the old wooden houses with their open-work galleries and sloping tiled roofs. The Chahâr Olyâ Mosque (Mosque of the Four Guardians), more correctly a mausoleum, is built in the same style as the local houses. Just outside town stands a small but attractive mauso-

leum, built in 1419 for Sheikh Zâhed. Its unusual pyramid-shaped roof, decorated with turquoise and yellow tiles, is visible from the road.

Mâzanderân Province

In its western part, Mâzanderân Province is geographically quite similar to Gilân, but the climate becomes gradually drier further east—although still receiving two or three times the rainfall of Tehran—and the crops consequently change, with orchards of fruit trees replacing the tea plantations. In western Mâzanderân are two popular resorts: Ramsar, with a luxury hotel built in the Shâh's time, and Châlus, where the Hotel Enqelab, probably the best hotel in the country at present, is located. A mountain road leads directly from Châlus to Tehran (202 kilometres, 125 miles).

The small town of **Amol**, set slightly inland west of Sâri, the ninth century capital of the Arab province of Tabarestân, a province which corresponded more or less to present-day Mâzanderân. Amol declined after the Mongol conquests and has little to show today of its past. Its main monument is the *mashhad-e* Mir Bozorg, built in the reign of Shâh Abbâs I (1587–1629) and which is currently being restored. This sanctuary is covered by a red brick dome, once decorated with blue tiles.

A few kilometres from Amol is the town of **Bâbol**, once an important river port linked to Babolsar, the main trading outlet on the coast. In Bâbol is a 15th-century funerary tower built for Soltân Mohammad Tâher in a style similar to that of the towers in Sâri.

Sâri, the capital of Mâzanderân Province, is also connected by road to Tehran but is much less developed than Rasht, with fewer tourists. Sâri has a long history and is said to have been the capital of Sassanian Tabarestan before the Arab conquest. Important finds in the area of Sassanian gold and silver artefacts support this theory. The main sites in Sâri are two 15th-century funerary towers in the town centre, near the bazaar. The first, the *imâmzâdeh* Yahyâ, is a somewhat austere circular building with a conical roof, a shape characteristic of the region. The second, the *borj-e* Soltân Zein al-Abedin, is a square construction still bearing a few traces of the original blue decorative tilework. Outside town, to the east, stands another tower, built around 1491, known as the *imâmzâdeh* Abbâs, which commemorates a nephew of Imam Hussein.

Halfway between Sâri and Bandar-e Torkman, in the small town of **Behshahr**, are the remains of a Safavid palace built by Shâh Abbâs in 1612, which formed part of a palatial complex set in large landscaped gardens. The whole complex was severely damaged by the Turkish invasions and only this one building, known as the Safiâbâd Palace, located on the crest of a hill, still remains. It is smaller and much simpler than the contemporary palaces in Isfahan. Unfortunately, the building can no longer be visited, as a military base has been set up on the hill.

From the Bay of Gorgân and Bandar-e Torkman lies a vast fertile plain, caught between the mountains in the south and the Turkoman desert (*Torkaman-e sahrâ*) to the north. Further east, begin the steppes which stretch into Central Asia, the land of the Turkomans. The town of **Gorgân**, once known as Astarâbâd, occupies a key position in this border region between the settled fertile coastal plains and the steppes. Set at the foot of the Alborz Range, Gorgân became an important caravan post and the main market town for the nomadic Turkomans, a meeting point of two completely opposed ways of life. But because of its proximity to the steppes, it was also raided on numerous occasions by the nomads, particularly in the 19th century. Today, Gorgân is a busy provincial town with a lively and colourful bazaar.

In the centre of Gorgân, in the bazaar, is the Friday Mosque (*masjed-e* Jomeh), which has been rebuilt several times and is currently being restored. Its short and stocky minaret, decorated with brick designs, is topped by a wooden roof. Inside, are an interesting tiled *mehrab* and a 15th-century *mimbar*. Near this mosque is the *imâmzâdeh* Nur, a 14th -or 15th-century funerary tower.

Unlike Gorgân, **Gonbad-e Kâvus**, set further inland, is essentially a Turkoman town: in the streets the black *châdor* gives way to the traditional long colourful shawls (which are now imported from Turkmenistan) and Turkoman is spoken as readily as Persian in the shops. Gonbad-e Kâvus, the 'tower of Kâvus', owes its name to its most famous building, a 51-metre (167-foot)-tall mausoleum which is perhaps the most impressive of all the funerary towers in Iran. Built in 1006–07 by Ghabus, a local prince of the Ziyarid Dynasty, it dominates the entire plain from its artificial platform. Circular inside, it is shaped like a ten-pointed star outside and has a conical roof about 12 metres (39 foot) high. The tower, built entirely of brick, is almost completely plain except for two bands of calligraphy around the foot and the top. The artistic origins of this building are unclear although it has been suggested that it is related to some form of Mazdean commemorative monument. Nevertheless, the uncompromising severity of its lines, its size and its remarkable state of preservation cannot fail to impress the visitor.

About 30 kilometres (18.5 miles) north of Gonbad-e Kâvus, on the way to the frontier of Turkomanistan, are the remains of an ancient wall known as the **Sadd-e Eskandar**, or Alexander's Wall. According to popular belief, this wall was built by Alexander the Great although it is more likely that it is of late Sassanian date and was designed to protect the Gorgân Plain from nomad raids. The remains stretch over some 70 kilometres (43 miles), from Gonbad-e Kâvus to the sea, but they have suffered such severe erosion that in many places there is little more than the odd mound left to see. Because of the proximity of the border, it is necessary to get a permit to visit the wall.

The Caspian Coast, near Bandar-e Torkman

From Gorgân, the main road continues east into the province of Khorâssân, passing first through tobacco and cotton fields and then through the mountains and the **Golestân National Park**. This park, opened in 1957, covers some 92,000 hectares (227,337 acres) and is one of the most interesting in the country from the point of view of wildlife and plants. It is unusual in that it stretches over two very different climatic zones and therefore includes both, thick deciduous forests—beautiful in their autumn colours—and semi-arid steppes. There is still an abundant animal life here and it is relatively easy to see wild boar, deer, gazelles and ibex; it is also a paradise for birds of prey. The Caspian tiger that used to live here, however, has not been seen since the 1960s.

The Northeast: the Provinces of Semnân and Khorâssân

Semnân Province

Despite the size of the province, the population of Semnân is very heavily concentrated in the north, along the Tehran–Mashhad road. To the south of this road lies the Dasht-e Kevir, the salt desert, where the extremely hot and arid climate prevents much permanent human settlement. The capital of the province, **Semnân** (200 kilometres (124 miles) from Tehran), was once an important stop along the trade route between eastern and western Persia which enabled caravans to skirt round the desert in relative safety. Due to its favourable location, Semnân has always made a quick recovery from the numerous invasions and raids that have swept through it. Today, Semnân has the appearance of a rather small provincial town. Its most interesting monument is the **Friday Mosque**, built in 1425, which still contains an attractive carved stucco *mehrab*. Next to the mosque is an 11th- or 12th-century Seljuq minaret. The **Imam Khomeini Mosque** nearby is a much more recent. Built by Fath Ali Shâh in the early 19th century, it is one of the more successful examples of Qâjâr architecture. Its tiled entrance *pishtaq* and *mehrab* with stalactites are particularly fine.

About a hundred kilometres (62 miles) from Semnân, on the road to Mashhad, is the small town of **Dâmghân**, famous for its early examples of Islamic architecture, dating from the Abbassid and Seljuq periods. Dâmghân was first settled in the prehistoric period and important excavations have been carried out a few kilometres out of town at Tappeh-ye Hissar (fourth millennium BC). Dâmghân is very probably the site of the Hellenistic town of Hecatompylos, the 'City of a Hundred Gates', first a Seleucid centre and then the capital of the Arsacid Parthians under Tiridates I (around 200 BC). Hecatompylos was located on one of the main trade routes linking Central Asia to the Mediterranean ports, and which passed through Merv and Ecbatana (Hamedân), a location which ensured the prosperity of the town. Like Semnân, Dâmghân was also repeatedly destroyed during the Turkish and Mongol invasions, and has suffered from a number of devastating earthquakes. Despite this, several interesting ancient buildings still remain in the centre of town.

The first of these is the **Tarik Khâneh Mosque**, one of only a handful of early Abbassid buildings in Iran. It was built between 750 and 789 and thus predates the mosque at Nâ'in, which has a similar plan to that of the Tarik Khâneh but was built at the same time as the first Friday Mosque at Isfahan. The Tarik Khâneh is a hypostyle mosque: its central courtyard is surrounded by single arcades on three sides, and by a portico of three rows of six columns along the *qebla* wall (a model of the mosque can be seen in the Archaeological Museum in Tehran). The columns are massive structures made of baked brick. The arcades are of particular interest to the specialist as their shape is reminiscent of Sassanian architecture. In fact, the building techniques used in this mosque and those seen in a Sassanian building excavated nearby at Tappeh-ye Hissar have many common factors. The Tarik Khâneh is therefore considered to be representative of the transition period between pre-Islamic and Islamic architecture in Iran. The mosque has been renovated several times, most notably during the Seljuq Dynasty (11th century), but it has kept its original simple form and has remained undecorated. Near the mosque stands a minaret, built in the middle of the 11th century and entirely decorated in geometric and calligraphic brick motifs. In 1991 and 1992, the mosque was closed to the public while restoration work was being carried out, but is now open to the public every day.

The Seljuq period is also represented in Dâmghân by two funerary towers. The first, the **Pir-e Alamdâr**, was built in 1026, while the second, the **Chehel Dokhtar** (Forty Daughters), was built in 1054. Both are circular brick towers of similar shape. Only the upper part of each tower is decorated with geometric motifs and calligraphic inscriptions in brick.

In the small town of **Bastâm**, near Shâhrud, where a secondary road from Gorgân and the Caspian coast joins the main road to Mashhad, stands the mausoleum complex of Sheikh Bâyezid Bastâmi, a well-known ninth century mystic. The present buildings, covered in blue glazed tiles, were restored during the reigns of the Mongol Il-khân sultans Ghâzân (1296–1303) and Uljaitu (1303–1316). The mausoleum, recognizable by its conical turquoise roof, is built next to a mosque which contains a fine *mehrab* from Ghâzân's reign. The minaret, which predates the restorations, is a good example of Seljuq art (1120). The complex also includes a second funerary tower, the *imâmzâdeh* Muhammad, similar in shape to the first one.

Khorâssân Province

Khorâssân is the largest Iranian province and has a surface area of some 300,000 kilometres^2 (115,830 miles^2), but its population totals only just over five million, of which half live in the Mashhad and Neishâbur area. Khorâssân used to be the easternmost province of Persia—its name means 'land of the rising sun'—and included Afghanistan and Bactria as far the Amu-Daria river. It was through this province that the numerous invasions from the Central Asian steppes reached the Iranian plateau. Not surprisingly, Khorâssân's history has been dogged by frequent changes of ruler.

With the weakening of Abbasid power in Baghdad, several local dynasties established themselves in Khorâssân (the Tahirids, Saffarids and Samanids) before the Seljuq Turks succeeded in uniting the region and settled in Neishâbur. In the 11th century, Khorâssân became the centre of intellectual life in Iran, but after the breakup of the Seljuq Empire, it was overrun by Khwarezm, a Central Asian Turkish state. In 1221, Khwarezm was defeated by Genghis Khân and was to remain under Mongol control until 1337 when another local dynasty, the Sardebarians, proclaimed their independence in the northwest of the province. This dynasty lasted only a short period of time and, in 1380, Tamerlane conquered the entire region. Khorâssân benefitted greatly from Timurid rule, particularly during the reign of Shâh Rokh (1405–1447), a keen patron of the arts, whose wife Gohar Shâd commissioned the superb mosque in Mashhad that bears her name. Timurid rule in Khorâssân was replaced by that of the Safavids at the beginning of the 16th century. After its incorporation into the large Safavid Empire, the history of the province follows closely that of Iran as a whole.

The main road which crosses Khorâssân from east to west and links Tehran with Mashhad passes through the towns of **Sabzevâr** and Neishâbur. Near the former, a solitary minaret, built around 1112, stands out in the plain. It marks the location of the ancient city of Khosrogerd, destroyed by the Mongols in 1220. Sabzevâr, very close to Khosrogerd, was rebuilt after the invasion and briefly became the capital of the local Shi'ite Sardebarian Dynasty (1337–1381).

Today, **Neishâbur** (Nishapur) is a small provincial town containing only a few historical monuments, but it was once one of the most glorious centres of all Persia. Founded in the third century AD under the Sassanians, it was the seat of the Arab governors of the region at the beginning of the Islamic period. Built at the foot of the Binalud Hills on the caravan route between Central Asia and the Iranian Plateau, it quickly became a flourishing trading town and, in the 11th century under the Seljuqs, one of the intellectual centres of Sunni Islam. It was renowned in particular for its Sufi masters and its *nizâmiyeh*, one of a series of *madresseh* founded by the great vizier Nizâm al-Mulk. One of the most famous of the teachers of the *nizâmiyeh* was the theologian al-Ghazâli (1058–1111), known for his attempt to integrate Sufism into orthodox Islam.

However, this glorious period in Neishâbur's history was short-lived and the city fell rapidly into decline in the 12th century after a series of disasters befell it: invasions by Turkish tribes, internal wars, earthquakes and finally the catastrophic arrival of Mongol troops in 1221 and the massacre of the city's entire population. Neishâbur was later rebuilt but it never regained its former position and was supplanted by Mashhad.

The great majority of Neishâbur's ancient buildings have been destroyed. Only a handful of mausoleums remain in the outskirts of the modern town, near which

Caravansaries on one of the old trade routes crossing Iran afford overnight protection from bandits to pilgrims and merchants

more recent commemorative monuments have been erected. The most famous of these is undoubtedly **Omar Khayyâm's tomb**, built in 1934 in the gardens of the *imâmzâdeh* Mahruq, a few kilometres southeast of town. In the West, Omar Khayyâm (1048–c.1125) is best known as a poet, due to Edward Fitzgerald's translations of his works published in the 19th century, but in Iran, Khayyâm is remembered foremost as an astronomer and mathematician. Born in Neishâbur, he served at the court of Sultan Malek Shâh (1072–1092) and worked, along with other mathematicians, at the revision of the calender and the construction of an observatory. His celebrity as a mathematician is due to his treatise on algebra in which he demonstrated how to solve cubic equations by both algebraic and geometric methods. Khayyâm was a contemporary of the great vizier Nizâm al-Mulk, but the legend that these two men were students with Hassan Sabbâh, the founder of the Assassins (see page 142) seems to have no historical basis. Nizâm al-Mulk (died 1092) was some thirty years older than Khayyâm and no record suggests that Khayyâm and Hassan Sabbâh ever met.

Khayyâm's poetry is highly controversial, and although several hundred *rubâ'iyat* have traditionally been attributed to him, it is very difficult to determine exactly which were indeed written by him. The first mention of Khayyâm as a poet dates from half a century after his death and there is little reason to believe that he ever collected his poems into a *divan* (poetry anthology) during his lifetime. The Mongol destruction of the great Islamic centres of learning in Khorâssân, and in particular of the libraries, has undeniably contributed to the loss of a large part of pre-13th-century Persian literature, and perhaps also of poems written by Khayyâm.

It is the subject matter of the works attributed to Khayyâm which attracted strong criticism from orthodox thinkers, especially from the numerous opponents of 'Greek thought', first and foremost the famous philosopher al-Ghazâli. Khayyâm, a disciple of Avicenna, was considered too materialistic and incapable of following Sufic spiritual paths, to the extent that the poet Farid od-Din Attâr (see below) tells of a vision he had in which a shamed and confused Khayyâm is refused entry to heaven because he lacks the spiritual qualities needed to appear before God. Two themes running through Khayyâm's work are pessimism and scepticism, in particular a profound doubt in resurrection and life after death, a fundamental belief of orthodox Islam. Khayyâm's mausoleum is a modern structure said to resemble the shape of an inverted wine cup. Wine, which gives Man temporary respite from his doubts, and the cup, a fragile and ephemeral creation of Man's, are two further themes which appear constantly in Khayyâm's poems. The inside walls of the mausoleum are decorated with a mosaic work of floral designs, while couplets by Khayyâm are reproduced on the outside.

Near Khayyâm's tomb, in the same garden, is the *imâmzâdeh* **Mohammad Mahruq**, a 17th century Safavid building commemorating one of the Prophet's descendant who died as a martyr.

In a small park nearby stands the **tomb of Farid od-Din Attâr**, one of the greatest Iranian Sufi poets, who was born in Neishâbur a decade or so after Omar Khayyâm's death, and who died around 1220, possibly during the Mongol invasion. Attâr is known principally for his *masnavi*, long, imaginative mystical poems written in a simple style, such as *The Book of God (Ilahi-nâmeh)* and the *Conference of the Birds (Mantiq al-Tair)*. This last work describes in allegorical form the journey of the birds in search of the Simurgh, a mythical beast which represents God. Attâr is also the author of an important work of prose, the *Memorials of the Saints (Tadhkirat al-Auliya)*, a collection of biographies of sufi sheikhs.

The mausoleum itself is an octagonal building with a domed roof and a tall drum. Next to it is a second mausoleum, decorated with floral mosaics, built in memory of a modern painter, **Kemâl al-Mulk** (died in 1938). The architect, who also designed Omar Khayyâm's tomb, has reinterpreted the traditional *eivân* in a very creative manner by placing four *eivân* back to back with arches connecting above the tomb.

About 30 kilometres (19 miles) from Neishâbur, on the road to Mashhad, is the small town of **Qadamgâh** (the Place of the Footstep), where one can visit a sanctuary set in a charming garden, built around a stone bearing the footprints of Imam Rezâ. (Since attempts by some over-enthusiastic pilgrims to take the stone away, it has been set into a wall inside the building.) The sanctuary, built during the Safavid period in the 17th century and later restored, is decorated with *haft rangi* mosaic of high quality, particularly the relief calligraphy inside, and with paintings on the walls and ceiling. Beside the mausoleum is an old caravansarai built by Shâh Abbâs and still very well preserved. The large, elevated arched niches around the central courtyard served as rooms for travellers while their animals filled the yard. Behind the arcades, a covered corridor with similar arches were used as winter quarters.

Nearer Mashhad, at **Sangbast**, stands the mausoleum of Arslân Jâzeb, built in the 11th century. This is a domed building with geometric and calligraphic brick designs inside; note in particular the simplicity of the squinch arches here which allow for a smooth transition from a square plan to a circular one.

MASHHAD

Mashhad is Iran's holiest city, visited each year by more than 14 million pilgrims. Its history is closely linked to that of its main shrine, the tomb of the Eighth Imam of the Shi'ite tradition, Imam Rezâ. Before his death in 809, the Caliph Hârun al-Rashid divided the Abbasid Empire into two, giving half to each of his two sons. In 816, Caliph Ma'mun, ruler of the eastern region, wanted to make the Eighth Imam his heir and invited him to travel to the capital, Merv (near present-day Mary, in the Republic of Turkmenistan). The Imam was at first wary but eventually accepted the invitation and made his way to Khorâssân. While resting in the village of Sanâbâd, he died suddenly after eating some grapes (or pomegranates, depending on the version of the story). Caliph Ma'mun had the Imam buried in Sanâbâd beside the tomb of his own father, Hârun al-Rashid. Word spread that the Imam had been poisoned by the caliph, and his tomb, known as *mashhad* or 'place of martyrdom', soon became a Shi'ite pilgrimage site. In 944, the tomb was destroyed by Saboktagin, founder of the Ghaznavid Dynasty and a devout Sunni, but was rebuilt by his son Mahmud in 1009. In the 13th century, both town and mausoleum were damaged during raids of nomad Oghuzz Turks but Mashhad soon recovered and continued to prosper, finally becoming the capital of Khorâssân in the 15th century. Shâh Rokh (1405–1447), the son of Tamerlane, enlarged the mausoleum, and his wife Gohar Shâd commissioned the building of a mosque next to it (built between 1405–1417).

During the Shi'ite Safavid Dynasty, Mashhad became one of the most important Shi'ite pilgrimage centres as the holy cities of Mecca, Kerbala and Najaf were in enemy territory under Ottoman Sunnite domination. In the 17th and 18th centuries, Mashhad was attacked several times by Uzbek and Afghan troops, although the shrine was never damaged. In 1736, Nâder Shâh established his capital at Mashhad and, although a Sunni himself, he made generous donations to the town and to the mausoleum.

Under Rezâ Shâh, Mashhad was modernized and several wide avenues were built in the old quarter as well as a circular boulevard around the holy precinct. In the past twenty years, the population of the town has grown considerably, from half a million to over two million inhabitants, including a large community of Afghan refugees—some of whom are slowly returning to Afghanistan, although many will undoubtedly remain now that they have made themselves a living in Iran. Mashhad is currently the second biggest industrial centre in the country, and this economic importance is reflected in the bustling activity that is so characteristic of its streets; it is an atmosphere very different from the quieter, more provincial religious centre of Qom.

The goal of the thousands of pilgrims who arrive each day, and indeed the main attraction in Mashhad, is the tomb of Imam Rezâ, in the centre of town, not far from the station, at the junction of Tabarsi and Ayatollâh Shirazi avenues. The holy precinct, the *haram-e motahar*, is set inside a vast circular boulevard. The various constructions on the outside of this boulevard are soon to be pulled down and will be replaced by public buildings such as hospitals, and hostels for the pilgrims.

THE HOLY PRECINCT (*HARAM-E MOTAHAR*)

The tomb of Imam Rezâ and the buildings that are connected to it (including mosques, *madresseh*, libraries, museums and administrative offices) form the only complex of its kind in Iran. A visit to the compound, especially at night when it is lit by projectors, is an unforgettable experience. However, non-Muslim tourists, particularly in groups, are allowed only limited access to the area and are not permitted to enter many of the buildings and inner courtyards. During religious festivals and important pilgrimages, visits for non-Muslims may be curtailed or temporarily suspended. Photography is discouraged inside the precinct and women must wear a *châdor*.

Entering the precinct from the west, along Avenue Ayatollah Shirazi, one arrives at the **sahn-e Atiq**, the 'old court', paved in black stone. In the centre of it stands the Golden Fountain (saqqâkhâne-ye Zarin) built in the reign of Nâder Shâh. In the north and south façades of the court are two large *eivân*; the north one, built by Shâh Abbâs in the 17th century, supports an older minaret, dating from the reign of Shâh Tahmâsp (16th century). The south *eivân*, or *eivân* Talâ-ye Ali Shir Navâ'i, named after the Timurid vizier and Uzbek poet who built it in the 15th century, was restored under Nâder Shâh when it was given its present golden, mirrored frontage.

To the southeast of the courtyard are three **madresseh**, the *madresseh* Parizâd, Do Dar and Bâlâsar; next to the latter stands a mosque of the same name. The Navâ'i *eivân* leads to the Tohidkhâneh, the 'Place of the Unification', and then to the holiest site of all, the **tomb of Imam Rezâ**, which can be seen from the courtyard through a grille (entry to the shrine is strictly forbidden to non-Muslims). The oldest parts of the tomb are said to date back to the 12th century, but there have been numerous restorations and renovations and the present building is an amalgam of different styles: the tombstone itself dates from the reign of Shâh Abbâs while the solid gold chandelier was a gift from Shâh Rokh (1418). The shrine is covered by a large golden dome, rebuilt under Shâh Tahmâsp in 1675.

To the south of the mausoleum is **Gohâr Shâd's Mosque**, by far the most beautiful building in the entire precinct. It was built between 1405 and 1418 by the Shirazi architect Qavâm od-Din for Gohâr Shâd, the wife of Shâh Rokh (1405–1447). This is the best preserved of all the buildings that Gohâr Shâd commissioned, most of which were in the Timurid capital, Herat. It has a classic plan, with a square courtyard surrounded by four *eivân* and arcades entirely decorated with blue tiles. The south *eivân*, flanked by two minarets, has a turquoise dome with yellow inscriptions. Ac-

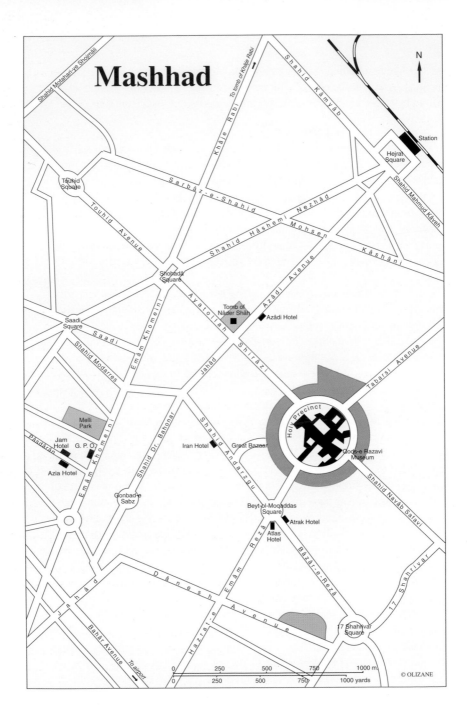

Mashhad

N

Station

Hejrat Square

Shahid Motahari-ye Shojmali

To tomb of Khaje Rabi

Shahid Kâmyâb

Khâje Rabi

Sarbâz-e-Shahid

Touhid Square

Touhid Avenue

Shahid Hâshemi Nezhâd

Mohsen

Shahid Mahmud Kâveh

Kâshâni

Azâdi Avenue

Shohadâ Square

Saadi Square

Saadi

Shahid Modarres

Ayatollah

Jahâd

Shirâzi

Tomb of Nâder Shâh

Azâdi Hotel

Emâm Khomeini

Tabarsi Avenue

Holy Precinct

Melli Park

Jam Hotel

G.P.O.

Pasdarân

Iran Hotel

Great Bazaar

Qods-e Razavi Museum

Shahid Dr. Bahonar

Shahid Andarzgu

Emâm Khomeini

Azia Hotel

Gonbad-e Sabz

Beyt-ol-Moqaddas Square

Atrak Hotel

Shahid Navâb Safavi

Rezâ

Atlas Hotel

Bâzâr-e-Rezâ

17 Shahrivar

Dânesh

Emâm

Avenue

Jahâd

Hazrat-e

Bahâr Avenue

To airport

17 Shahrivar Square

| 0 | 250 | 500 | 750 | 1000 m |
| 0 | 250 | 500 | 750 | 1000 yards |

© OLIZANE

cording to Shi'ite tradition, the *mimbar* next to the *mehrab* is the one on which the Mahdi will sit when he returns for the Judgement. The decoration of the mosque is characterized by the extraordinarily high quality of the workmanship. The finesse of the motifs, the elegance of the calligraphy, the alternate use of matt and glazed bricks and particularly the harmony of the whole, reflect the genius of the architect. But the most successful feature is perhaps the decoration of the interior of the south *eivân* and the *mehrab*, where complex but extraordinarily fine floral designs set on a light ground form a striking contrast to the blue exterior.

To the east of the mausoleum a street leads to the **sahn-e Jadid** or New Courtyard, built by Fath Ali Shâh around 1818 with a very attractive *eivân* in the west façade (*eivân* Talâ-ye Fath Ali Shâh).

The **Qods-e Razavi Museum** (the entrance is on the circular boulevard near Avenue Shâhid Navab Safavi) contains objects of various origins, most of which were gifts made to the shrine, including some magnificent carpets, ceramics, Safavid weapons, Koran lecterns and the old gilt doors of the shrine.

There are several other interesting buildings to visit in Mashhad outside the holy precinct, some of which are located just out of the town centre. To the southeast of the circular boulevard is the **Great Bazaar**, the bazar-e Bozorg; on the first floor are the shops of the turquoise dealers. The area around Mashhad and Neishâbur is known for the quality of its turquoise and turquoise mining has been a major industry here for centuries. In the bazaar, you can watch the stones being cut and polished. If you are buying, be careful to distinguish between synthetic and real turquoise, and remember that, despite what you will be told, turquoise is not cheaper in Mashhad than on the European market. The entrance *pishtaq* and minaret of the old **Mosque of the 72 Martyrs** (previously the Shâh's Mosque), built in the 14th or 15th century, is also to be found in the bazaar. Today it houses the offices of the Pasdaran organization and is therefore closed to the public.

A bit further west, on Avenue Shâhid Dr Bahonar, in the middle of a square, stands the **Gonbad-e Sabz**, or Green Dome, a Safavid mausoleum (partially rebuilt later) which contains the body of a Sufi sheikh, Mohammad Hakim Mo'men.

Further north along the same avenue (now Avenue Azâdi), at the junction with Avenue Ayatollah Shirâzi, is a small park and the **tomb of Nâder Shâh** (1736–1747), a modern 20th-century building with a small adjoining museum of weapons and other 18th-century objects. The tomb is easily spotted by its large statue of the ruler on horseback.

On the other side of the holy precinct, on Boulevard Mosallâ, is a *mosallâ*, an open-air gathering place consisting only of a *mehrab* chamber and an *eivân*, without a courtyard and side walls. The *mosallâ* is dated to 1677 and is still decorated with the original tilework on the outer wall. It is currently under repair and is closed to the public.

■ EXCURSIONS FROM MASHHAD

A few kilometres north of Mashhad is the **mausoleum of Khâje Rabi**, one of the first Shi'ite saints, a disciple of Imam Ali, whose tomb was built between 1617 and 1622 by Shâh Abbâs. Its shape is similar to that of the Hasht Behesht Palace in Isfahan, built about fifty years later: here the four deep *eivân* lead to a central domed room decorated with tiles and paintings which still retain their rich colours. The tile designs are close to those at Qadamgâh (see above). The very fine inscriptions are the work of Ali Rezâ Abbâssi, one of the most famous Persian calligraphers of the Safavid period. The park around the mausoleum has now become a cemetery for the martyrs of the Iran–Iraq war.

The small town of **Tus**, about 30 kilometres (19 miles) north of Mashhad, was once the capital of the region before it was superseded by Mashhad. The Turkish and Mongol invasions, as well as its proximity to the great city of Mashhad, contributed to its decline and today Tus is mostly known for being the native town of Ferdusi, the author of the Iranian national epic, the *Shâhnâmeh*, and of Nizâm al-Mulk, the great Seljuq vizier. **Ferdusi's tomb** is a modern construction built in the second half of this century and composed of various architectural elements borrowed from the Achaemenian period. The overall shape of the tomb is reminiscent of Cyrus the Great's mausoleum at Pasargadae; to this the architect has added capitals from Persepolis and the winged symbol of Ahura Mazda. In a room dug underneath the tomb a series of modern bas-reliefs illustrate a few episodes of the *Shâhnâmeh*.

Just south of Tus stands another tomb, **boqe-ye Hâruniye**, which is attributed, according to local tradition, to the Caliph Hârun al-Rashid who died here in 809. The shape of the building, however, suggests a rather later date, perhaps 14th century.

From Mashhad, it is possible to continue by road either to the north-, and on to the Caspian coast, or south along the Afghan border into Sistân and Baluchestân. Those taking the first of these routes can make a short detour to the village of **Râdkân** (before reaching Quchân, turn right off the main road at Sayyed Abâd), to see a 13th-century Mongol funerary tower. It is 25 metres (82 feet) tall, and decorated on the outside with brick and tile designs.

(following pages) *Three quatrains from* The Rubaiyat of Omar Khayyám, *an 11th-century Persian work popularized in the West by Edward Fitzgerald's translation.*

PERSIAN POETRY

Poetry has always been considered the most noble form of literature in Iran and is certainly one of the richest expressions of Persian creativity. Strongly influenced in its composition and vocabulary by Arabic poetry, Persian poetry is also the heir to a very ancient literary verse tradition, recorded in part in the *Avesta*, the sacred book of the Zoroastrians. The first verses written in literary Persian appear in the ninth century in Khorâssân; in the tenth century, the official encouragement of the use of Persian at the Samanid court, rather than Pehlevi (Middle Persian) or Arabic, stimulated the development of a literature in that language. From that time on, the use of Persian spread to the entire plateau, gradually replacing the local dialects.

The official role played by poetry in the royal courts explains the appearance very early on of the panegyric, written as *qasida*, and which proclaimed, according to well-defined models, the virtues and courage of the ruler or of a patron. Among the numerous poets of panegyric *qasida* were Anvari (died around 1187) and Khaqani (died in 1199), known for the subtlety of their images and the originality of the themes presented.

Another lyric form was developed from the *qasida*, the *ghazal*, a much shorter form used mainly to express love, both mystic and human. The *ghazal* flourished from the 12th century, and many *qasida* poets, including Anvari and Khaqani, are also known for their *ghazal*. But the uncontested masters of this form are Saadi (died around 1290) and Hâfez (died in 1389), whose use of language and subtlety of thought are unrivalled.

The *ruba'i*, which became famous in Europe in the 19th century with Edward Fitzgerald's translation of Omar Khayyâm's poetry, and the *dobay* are both four-line poems which differ from one another in their rhythm. They deal with mystical, philosophical or romantic themes, and their form imparts the impression of both spontaneity and elegant precision. There are few Persian men of letters who have not written at least one *ruba'i*, but the very number of these poems, which were rarely signed, makes it difficult to attribute them with any accuracy to a specific poet.

Apart from these short, precise poetic forms, there exists also a narrative tradition, known as *masnavi*, used for epic poetry or for various forms of didactic works ranging from history to medicine. The epic dates back to the pre-Islamic period in Iran; the *Avesta* contains fragments of epic poetry and Ferdusi was inspired by older epic works when he wrote his *Shâhnâmeh*. After Ferdusi, the epic poem was replaced by verse narratives. This genre was best developed by Nizâmi (1141–1209), the author of five long dramatic *masnavi*, among which is *The Book of Alexander*, which tells of the heroic feats of the Macedonian conqueror, and *Khosrow and Chirine*, which narrates the lifes and love of the Sassanian king and an Armenian princess. But the *masnavi* was also used with great success by Sufi poets, in particular by Farid od-Din Attâr (died around 1220) in his *Conference of the Birds*, which is considered one of the masterpieces of Persian literature, and by Djalâl od-Din Rumi (1207–1273) in his *Masnavi Manawi*.

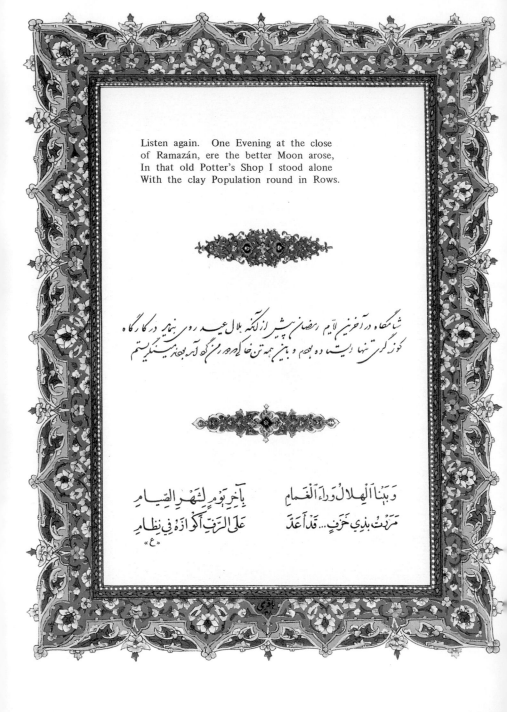

Listen again. One Evening at the close
of Ramazán, ere the better Moon arose,
In that old Potter's Shop I stood alone
With the clay Population round in Rows.

شامگاه در آخرین لیّام رمضان پیش از آنکه هلال عید روی بنماید در کارگاه
کوزه گری تنها ایستاده بودم و بین جمع تن خاک مردمان که آنرو بعد میسنگلدیستم

وَبُنَّا الْهِلَالَ وَرَاءَ الْغَمَامِ
بِآخِرِ يَوْمٍ لِشَهْرِ الصِّيَامِ
مَرَبْتُ بِذِي خَرَفٍ... قَدْ أَعَدَّ
عَلَى الرَّفِّ أَكْوَازَهُ فِي نِظَامِ
«ع»

Then said another—"Surely not in vain
My substance from the common Earth was ta'en,
That He who subtly wrought me into Shape
Should stamp me back to common Earth again."

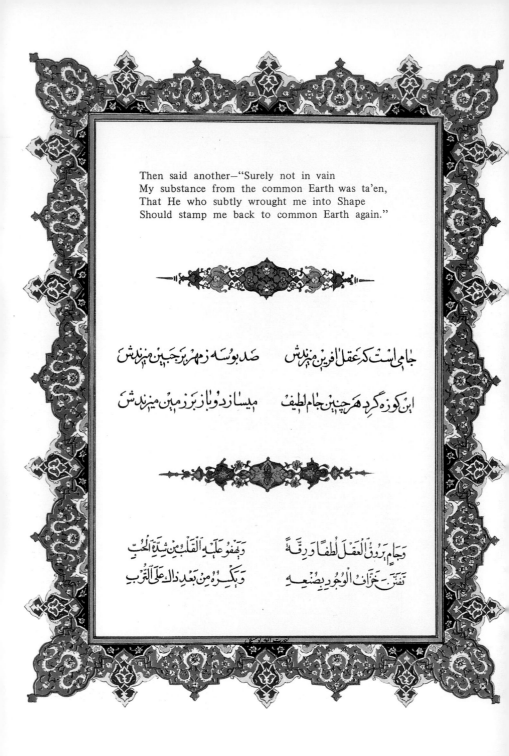

جامی است کہ عقل آفرین میزندش   صد بوسہ زمہر برجبین میزندش

این کوزہ گرد ہر چنین جام لطیف   میسازد و باز برزمین میزندش

وجام برون القل لطفا ورقة   وهفو علیه القلب من شدة الحب

تفنن خزان الوجود بصنعه   وبکرہ من بعد ذاک علی الترب

And, strange to tell, among that Earthen Lot
Some could articulate, while others not:
And Suddenly one more impatient cried—
"Who is the Potter, pray, and who the Pot?"

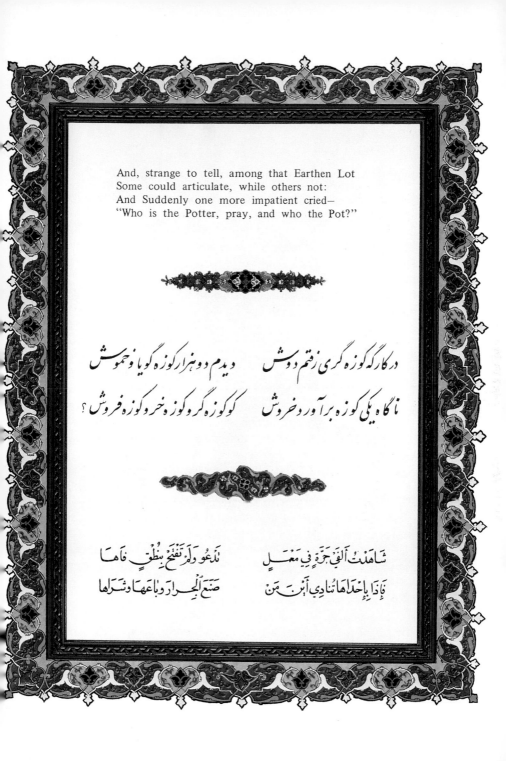

دیدم دو هزار کوزه گویا و خموش   در کارگه کوزه گری رفتم دوش

کو کوزه گر و کوزه خر و کوزه فروش؟   ناگاه یکی کوزه برآورد خروش

نَدْعُو وَلَوْ نَفْتَحُ بِنُطْقٍ فَاهَا   شَاهَدْتُ أَلْفَيْ جَرَّةٍ فِي مَعْمَلٍ

صَنَعَ الْجِرَارَ وَبَاعَهَا وَشَرَاهَا   فَإِذَا بِإِحْدَاهَا تُنَادِي أَيْنَ مَنْ

The Northwest: Zanjân and Azerbaijân

Zanjân Province

For the sightseer, the most interesting town in the province of Zanjân is **Qazvin**, 125 kilometres (78 miles) west of Tehran, at the junction of the roads leading north to Rasht and the Caspian Sea, northwest to Tabriz and Turkey, and southwest to Hamedân and—until recently—Baghdad. Qazvin was probably founded by the Sassanian ruler Shâpur I in the third century AD. It was for a short time capital of the Safavid Dynasty when Tahmâsp I (1524–1576) transferred his court, fearing that the previous capital, Tabriz, could be endangered by its proximity to the Ottoman Empire. The Safavids remained in Qazvin until 1598 when, in the reign of Shâh Abbâs I, the capital was once again moved, this time to Isfahan.

Today Qazvin is a medium-sized town of some 300,000 inhabitants. Despite the numerous earthquakes which have plagued its history, it still has something to show of its former glory. The oldest sections of the **Friday Mosque** (masjed-e Jomeh) date from the beginning of the Islamic period, although the mosque was largely rebuilt during the reign of the Seljuq ruler Malik Shâh (1072–1092). The very simple decoration of the arches surrounding the central court is particularly fine. The south *eivân* and the prayer room with its marble *mehrab* date to the 12th century. Various sections of the mosque have been restored at different periods, including the eastern *eivân* (Safavid) and the minarets (Qâjâr).

The **Haidariye** *madresseh*, just east of the town centre, was originally a 12th century Seljuq mosque. During the Qâjâr Dynasty, it was incorporated into a *madresseh,* but the very attractive original Seljuq *mehrab* can still be seen. The Seljuq mosque was a kiosque mosque, a square-domed chamber (now no longer visible) facing towards Mecca. The decoration on the walls (stucco inscriptions and floral designs) are very fine and remarkably well preserved; the carved stucco decoration of the *mehrab* is one of the richest examples of this period to be seen in Iran.

Little is left in Qazvin of the Safavid period other than a small palace, the **Chehel Sotun**, located in a park in the centre of town (Azâdi Square). It is a two-storeyed building, characteristic of the arcaded pavilions of the period, such as those of Isfahan. Inside, fragments of paintings on the walls and ceiling are still visible and the interior is currently being restored. In places, one can clearly see several layers of paint, the result of a common feature of Iranian interior decoration which was to plaster and then paint over existing designs without removing them. A superb wooden Safavid coffin has been placed in the corridor near the entrance. On the first floor is the regional museum which contains a variety of objects, including Neolithic pottery and bronzes from tombs in the Alamut area, calligraphy, decorated tilework and Qâjâr handicrafts.

Behind Azâdi Square, at the other end of the avenue leading to the Friday Mosque, is another Safavid building, the **Ali Qâpu Palace**, of which only the entrance gate is left and which is now occupied by the police.

In the east of town is a small **funerary tower**, of late Mongol date (15th century) built for the Persian geographer and scholar Hamdollâh Mostofi, minister to Sultan Uljaitu. The square building has a conical roof decorated with turquoise tiles.

The *imâmzâdeh* **Hussein**, on Boulevard Jomhuri-ye Eslâmi near the Friday Mosque, is a characteristic example of late Iranian art. Founded in the 16th century by Shâh Tahmâsp, it was restored during the Qâjâr Dynasty. The entrance gate, in front of which is a small park, is typically Qâjâr, decorated with geometric tile motifs; it supports six narrow minarets with floral designs. Behind this gate is the mausoleum itself with its turquoise dome. The outer façade of the sanctuary, at the back of the terrace, is entirely covered in small, shining mirrors.

There are two more Qâjâr constructions in Qazvin, both monumental gateways. The first, the **darb-e Kushk**, in the north of town on Avenue Hafez, was built in 1917. It is richly decorated in blue, yellow and white tilework; above the central arch is the old emblem of Iran, the lion and the sun (the crowns of the lions have now been removed). The second gateway, known as the **Gateway to Tehran** (darvâzeh Qalem-e Tehrân), can be seen at the eastern exit of town, on the road to Tehran. It was restored in the 1960s.

The Castles of the Assassins

Several roads from Qazvin lead into the Alborz Mountains, and more specifically into the Rudbâr, Alamut and Dailam massifs which separate Zanjân from the Caspian coast. By the Sassanian period, the inhabitants of these isolated and harsh regions had a reputation as tough and independent-minded fighters, and a series of strong fortresses were built in the hills to keep them at bay. From the ninth century, the Dailam area became a Shi'ite refuge, particularly for the Zaidi, a sect which recognized a separate lineage of Imams from the Twelver Shi'ite majority. A local dynasty, the Buyids (945–1055), which originally came from the Dailam, even succeeded in extending its domination over much of Iran, reaching as far as Baghdad. Dailamite domination ended with the arrival of the Seljuqs in the 11th century but the region remained open to Shi'ism. When Hassan Sabbâh undertook, around 1090, to establish the headquarters of his Ismaelian followers (known in the West as the Assassins) in the area, he was faced with only limited opposition (see page 142). The most famous of the Rudbâr castles is that of Alamut, which Hassan Sabbâh occupied, but others have been identified in the region, among them Lamassar and Meimundiz which were the last to surrender to the Mongols after the fall of Alamut in 1256. The ruins of Alamut (which today consist only of a few piles of stones) are perched at 1,800 metres (5,905 feet) above sea-level, on top of a rocky outcrop dominating the village of Gazor Khân, in a fertile but narrow valley. According to a local legend, a ruler of Dailam out hunting saw his trained eagle on top of the rock. Realizing the strategic value of the location, the ruler had a castle built there which he called Aluh Amut, or the 'lesson of the eagle'.

Although the trip to **Alamut** is slightly less arduous today than it was 20 years ago, when it took several days on horseback to reach the castle, it is still difficult. It is a full-day's excursion from Qazvin, and requires an early start, particularly in autumn when the sun sets early, in order to allow sufficient time at the castle itself and to avoid negotiating the mountain roads in the dark. The pass which leads to the valley below the castle is generally closed by snow until May. The road from the pass is slow and in bad condition; it winds first through Mo'allem Kalâye and then goes on to the village of Gâzor Khân from where a steep path leads up to the rock itself (a good half-hour's walk up).

In cloudy or very windy weather it is worth thinking twice about whether you really want to go up the last stretch: the path is very narrow and the clouds may block the view off completely. In good weather, however, the trip is well worth the effort and allows one to glimpse a rural mountain life that would otherwise remain hidden.

Qazvin is linked directly by road to Hamedân, 234 kilometres (145 miles) to the southwest, one of the oldest towns in Iran. Near the border between the provinces of Zanjân and Hamedân, in the district of Avaj, are two brick funerary towers, known as the **towers of Kharaqân**. Built in 1067 and 1093 by an architect from Zanjân, Mohammed ibn Makki, they are similar in shape and very sophisticated decoration to the tomb of Ismâil the Samanid at Bukhara (built 914–943). Built on an octagonal plan with eight corner pillars (one of which contains an internal staircase) they are the oldest dated monuments to possess double-shelled domes and among the first to have been decorated with coloured glazed tiles.

The road from Qazvin to Tabriz goes through the town of **Zanjân** (180 kilometres or 112 miles), the provincial capital, which has no monuments of particular interest. However, about 40 kilometres (25 miles) before Zanjân, a large blue dome stands out at the foot of the hills. This is **Soltânieh**, once the capital of the Il-khan Mongols and now a small village. The dome is that of the mausoleum of Sultan Uljaitu Khodâbendeh and is the only remaining building of a once splendid capital. In 1384, Soltânieh was destroyed by Tamerlane's armies and only the mausoleum, a famous pilgrimage site, was spared.

In 1306, Sultan Uljaitu (1304–1317) began the construction of his new city, Soltânieh, the 'Imperial one', to replace Tabriz as the capital of the Il-khans. It would appear that the building of his own mausoleum started at around the same time. Having converted to Shi'ism, Uljaitu decided to alter the building so that it could house the bodies of the Imams Ali and Hussein, buried in Kerbala and Najaf, in Iraq. But both towns refused to part with the Imams, and the mausoleum was used for the sultan himself. A number of other buildings linked to the mausoleum have been found recently as well as the base of the semi-circular walls, now partly restored, that surrounded it.

The mausoleum is an octagonal domed construction, built of brick. In shape it is more reminiscent of certain mausoleums in Central Asia, such as the tomb of Sultan Sanjar at Merv (1157), than of buildings in nearby Azerbaijân. When the decision was made to turn it into a mausoleum for the Imams, a *mehrab* was added to the southern side and a funerary chapel to the west. This gives the impression from the outside that the building was either left unfinished or has been partly destroyed. A vaulted gallery runs around the top of the building and opens into a series of triple arcades; above this is a *muqarna* cornice. The remains of eight minarets are visible around the dome, one at each corner. The latter, completely covered in turquoise glazed tiles, is 52 metres (171 feet) tall and very elegant with its rather pointed shape. The minarets and the dome, currently being restored, were originally decorated in blue and black tiles, while the vaults of the gallery still bear the very fine painted mouldings executed during the period after Uljaitu's conversion to Shi'ism (the gallery is not usually open to the public). Beneath the gallery the brick of the exterior walls was left plain except on the south side, facing towards Mecca, where there are still traces of glazed decoration. The interior of the mausoleum was also originally richly decorated in tilework, which was plastered over at a later date, either when Uljaitu decided to turn the building into his own mausoleum or as part of Safavid restoration work.

The Provinces of Azerbaijân

Iranian Azerbaijân is now divided into two separate provinces (*ostân*), a Western and an Eastern one, which occupy the northwest corner of the country. The frontier with the Republic of Azerbaijân follows the course of the Aras (or Araxes) River; in the east, the Turkish frontier runs through the Zaki Mountains. Geographically, this region is very varied as it contains a succession of mountain massifs and basins, the largest of which contains Lake Orumieh. The mountain ranges are of volcanic origin and have an average height of about 2,500 metres (8,200 feet); the Sahand, between Tabriz and Marâgheh, reaches 3,710 metres (12,170 feet) and the Sabalân, to the west of Ardabil, culminates at 4,811 metres (15,780 feet). The climate of Azerbaijân

THE ISMAILITES AND THE ASSASSINS

The term 'assassin', used in Europe from the 13th century to describe a hired killer, is said to be derived from the Arabic *hashishiyun*, or 'hashish eater'. This expression, probably a pejorative one from the very beginning, was used to design the Ismailites who had the reputation of intoxicating themselves with hashish before their politically- or religiously-motivated murders. The Assassins were feared as much in the Muslim world as in the Christian one for their daring and their practice of unexpectedly attacking even the most prominent men despite the protection that might surround them.

The Ismailites emerged from the scission which occurred in the Shi'ite community on the death of the Sixth Imam, in 765 (see page 91). They refused to accept as successor a younger son of the Imam and recognized as legitimate heir his elder half-brother Ismail. Like the Twelver Shi'ites, the Ismailites believe in the return of the Mahdi, the messianic Imam. In order to prepare for his return, the *dâi*, or propagandists, were entrusted with the duty of preaching to the faithful. Pursued for their beliefs as much by the Sunnis as by other Shi'ites, the *dâi* were frequently compelled to carry out their task in hiding.

Taking advantage of the collapse of the power of the Abbassid caliphs in Baghdad towards the end of the ninth century, Ismailite missions were sent out to the Yemen, India, and North Africa. Their success was such that in 909, the hidden Imam proclaimed himself caliph and founded the Fatimid Dynasty. In 937, after the conquest of Egypt, the Fatimid Caliphate moved to the newly-built city of Cairo. But this first Ismailite state was short-lived; after repeated attacks from Sunni armies it finally fell to the Kurd Saladin who restored the Abbassid caliphate in Egypt in 1171.

During the 11th century, Ismailism was shaken by a deep ideological crisis. In 1017, the Druze proclaimed the divine nature of the Fatimid caliph al-Hâkim, an unacceptable promotion in the eyes of other Ismailites. Many intellectuals were led to re-examine the very foundations of their own beliefs.

In this climate of political and moral uncertainty, one man, possessed of a very strong personality and determined to defend his Ismailite faith against the aggression of the Sunni Seljuq rulers, came to the fore: Hassan Sabbâh. Born towards the middle of the 11th century in Qom, Hassan Sabbâh was brought up in Ray in the Shi'ite faith. Having converted to Ismailism, he spent several years in Egypt before returning to Iran. There he joined the Nizarites and militated against the Seljuqs first in the Dâmghân area and then later around Qazvin where he gathered together a band of dedicated followers. In September of

1090, his men captured the castle of Alamut through trickery. An isolated and practically inaccessible fortress, it was to become the headquarters of the Ismailites. Until his death in May 1124, Hassan Sabbâh never left Alamut again, and directed all his operations against the Seljuq Empire from there. The capture of Alamut was followed by the seizure of a series of other castles, first of all nearby in the Rudbar, an area which had long been a Shi'ite stronghold, and then further afield near Dâmghân, Isfahan and in the mountains of Kuhestân, near present-day Afghanistan.

In 1092, the Seljuq sultan Malik Shâh attacked the Ismailite fortresses at Alamut and in Kuhestân. Faced by an enemy far superior in number, Hassan Sabbâh decided to remain entrenched, relying on his most fearsome weapon: assassination. It was at Alamut that the first *fidâ'i*, or 'those who devote themselves', were formed. After a very strict doctrinal and military training, the *fidâ'i* were prepared to sacrifice their own lives to carry out any task they might be given, in the belief that their actions would grant them entry to Paradise. Then began a series of carefully executed attacks against high-ranking or prominent men—princes, governors, generals, theologians—all of whom had condemned Ismailism. One of the first victims was the vizier of Sultan Malik Shâh, Nizâm al-Mulk, killed in 1092.

Ismailite missions which had been set up outside Iran adopted the same methods as their fellow believers, and with great success, most notably in Syria where their armies for the first time faced the Crusaders. The assassination of Conrad de Montferrat, the king of Jerusalem, caused a great stir throughout the Christian world.

The heir to Hassan Sabbâh at Alamut, Bozorg-Umid (ruled 1124–1138), succeeded in maintaining the strength of the Ismailites, but their power declined after his death, particularly after the appearance of the Mongols at the beginning of the 13th century. The final blow was delivered by Hulagu, Genghis Khan's grandson, who arrived in Iran in 1256 and launched a series of attacks against the Ismailite castles in the Rudbar and Kuhestân. In order to obtain the best possible conditions for surrender from Hulagu, the Ismailite Imam Rokn od-Din ordered his fortresses to give themselves up without a fight. Most of them obeyed, although Alamut and Lamassar refused. In December 1256, Alamut finally surrendered and the once proud castle was burned down. Its library, which contained the Ismailite chronicles and Hassan Sabbâh's autobiography, was destroyed, and only a few fragments were saved from the flames.

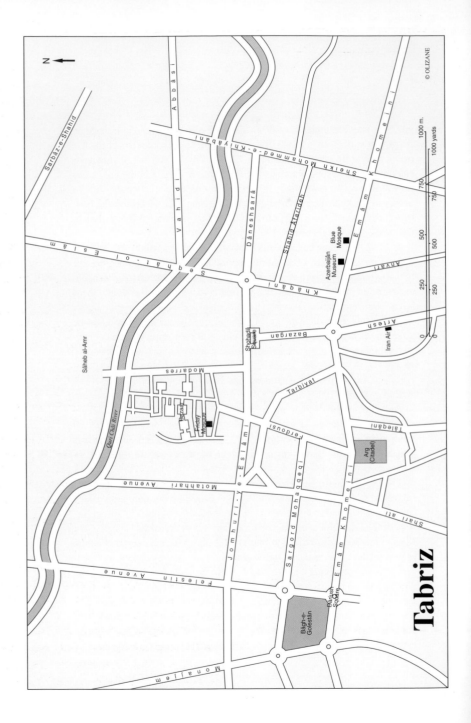

N

Sarbāz-e-Shahīd

A b b ā s i

Sheikh Mohammed-e-Khiyābāni

V a h i d i

Dāneshsarā

Shahīd Atariān

S e q h â t - o l   e s l ā m

Azerbaijān Museum

Blue Mosque

E m ā m   K h o m e i n i

Anvari

Khaqāni

Bazargan

Artesh

1000 m.
1000 yards
750
750
500
500
250
250
0
0

Iran Air

© OLIZANE

Sāheb al-Amr

Qūri Chāi River

Shohadā Square

Modarres

Tarbiyat

Bāzār

Friday Mosque

Ferdousi

Tāleqāni

Arg (Citadel)

Mottahari   Avenue

Jomhuri-ye-Eslāmi

Sargord Mohaqeqi

E m ā m   K h o m e i n i

Sharīati

Felestin   Avenue

Bāgh-e-Golestān

Bārush Square

Monajjem

Tabriz

is very dry and most of the basins are sheltered from rainfall by the surrounding mountains. The plains of the Araxes and Tabriz, as well as the Orumieh Basin, only receive an average of 200 to 300 millimetres of rainfall a year, hardly more than Tehran. As a result, crops can only be grown on the sides of the hills, except where the land is irrigated too. Azerbaijân is much colder than the Iranian Plateau, with average temperatures around 27° C (80° F) in summer (21° C, 68° F at Ardabil, closer to the Caspian Sea), and -2° C (30° F) in winter (-20° C in Ardabil).

Once inhabited by mountain peoples of Indo-European origin, Azerbaijân has undergone a slow but thorough ethno-linguistic change since the arrival of Turkish tribes from Central Asia. This process, which probably began in the seventh century, increased considerably in the 11th and 12th centuries after the Seljuq rulers sent Turkish tribes to Azerbaijân to defend it against the Christian state of Georgia and the empire of Trabzond. The Turks settled for the most part in the north and in Anatolia, and in somewhat smaller numbers around Tabriz and Marâgheh. The adoption of Shi'ism by the Safavids was followed by the return to Iran from Anatolia of many of these Shi'ite Turks, fleeing the Sunni Ottoman Empire. The decision by Shâh Abbâs (1571–1629) to form the Shâhsevan confederation from several different Turkish tribes also attracted a large number of nomads to the region, and Azeri, a Turkish dialect, became widely used, spreading as far as Qazvin. Today, Azeri is spoken by around 9.5 million people in Iran, mostly in the two Azerbaijâns, as well as in parts of Zanjân and Gilan.

The geographic and climatic conditions prevalent in Azerbaijân are ideal for a nomadic lifestyle, and the Turkish tribes who settled there had little trouble adapting to their new home. However, in the past hundred years, this traditional way of life has been profoundly modified. The closure of the frontier with Russia in 1886 cut off the Shâhsevan in East Azerbaijân from their winter pastures in the Araxes Plain, and the policies of Shâh Rezâ in the 1930s led to the enforced settlement of many nomads in villages. Today, although there still exists a semi-nomadic population in Azerbaijân, large-scale nomadism has completely disappeared.

TABRIZ

Tabriz, the capital of East Azerbaijân, is set in a valley at the foot of the Sahand Mountains, 294 kilometres (183 miles) northwest of Zanjân. The second biggest town in Iran, it has a population at present of almost one million and has become an important industrial and trade centre for business between Tehran and Turkey. Tabriz is said to have been founded in Sassanian times, and by the tenth century was by all accounts a major centre. It was promoted to the rank of capital by the Mongol Il-khân ruler Ghazan Khân (1295–1304) and retained that status almost without interruption until the 16th century, when the Safavids transferred the court first to

Qazvin and then to Isfahan, which was less prone to attack from Ottoman forces. Tabriz suffered in the wars between the Safavid and Ottoman empires, as well as from the clashes with Russian troops which began in the 18th century, and was occupied several times by foreign armies. Earthquakes and epidemics also took their toll, to such an extent that at the beginning of the 19th century the population of the town was reduced to one third of what it had been a hundred years earlier. Today only a few historical monuments remain in Tabriz.

The most important of these is the **Blue Mosque** (masjed-e Kabud), sometimes considered a masterpiece of Iranian decorative tilework. Built towards the end of the reign of the Timurid ruler Jahan Shâh (1436–1467), it was seriously damaged by an earthquake; today only a few pillars, parts of the outer wall and the main gate, and sections of the vaulted ceiling and a dome remain. The mosque plan is a variant on the usual Iranian four-*eivân* courtyard style: the courtyard has been replaced by a large domed chamber with an entrance on each of the four sides. The *mehrab* is in a smaller room, also domed. On three sides of the main chamber are further vaulted rooms. This rather original plan may be a result of local adaptation to cope with the colder, harsher climate of Azerbaijân.

The decoration of this mosque is justly renowned for the exceptional quality of the work, the finesse of the designs and the harmony of the overall composition. The range of colours used is more varied than previously, with the addition of an olive green, an ochre and a brown to the more usual blues and whites. The best examples are to be found on the gateway, especially on the inside walls of the porch where the magnificent mosaics really do warrant closer inspection. Inside the mosque, the decoration has been less well preserved but is equally rich and reproduces the same designs as outside (medallions, flower arabesques and inscriptions).

Apart from the mosque, there are few other buildings to visit in Tabriz. The **Azerbaijân Museum**, next door to the mosque (Imam Khomeini Avenue), has a rather mixed collection of archaeological and ethnographical objects. Further west along the same avenue are the remains—two solid towers and a wall—of the **citadel**, or *Arg*, which dates back to the Mongol occupation at the beginning of the 14th century.

The covered **bazaar** and the **Friday Mosque** are to be found in the old quarter between Jomhuri-ye Eslâmi Avenue and the Quri Châi River. On the other side of the river is a more modern mosque, the **masjed-e Sâheb ol-Amr**, surrounded by a wall, and surmounted by a low dome set on a tall drum.

From Tabriz it is possible to make day excursions (some of which will be long days) to visit other major sites in both provinces of Azerbaijân. The road that goes to Astara and the Caspian Sea passes through the old town of **Ardabil** (235 kilometres, 146 miles), once an important Sufi centre and famous for being the place of origin of

Ruins of the Blue Mosque in Tabriz, 1881 engraving by Jane Dieulafoy

the Safavid rulers. The mausoleum of Sheikh Safi al-Din (1252-1334), an ancestor of Shâh Ismâil, the founder of the Safavid Dynasty in the 16th century, is located here. Shâh Ismâil himself is also buried in the same tomb. The mausoleum is a domed circular tower decorated with large glazed brick designs (those around the door were added after the construction of the building). At the base of the dome is a short Kufic inscription. Inside, behind a silver grille, are the tombs of the Sheikh and his two sons. The walls are richly decorated in tilework, with stalactite niches and fretwork panelling, similar in style to that of the Ali Qapu Palace in Isfahan. The mosque beside the mausoleum has been rather badly preserved but its stalactite gateway is still very fine.

The **Church of Saint Thaddaeus** (Ghara Kelisâ, or Black Church) is one of the most interesting buildings in Azerbaijân. It is located about 140 kilometres (87 miles) away from Tabriz, near Mâku and the Turkish border (take the road west to Qareh Ziyâ od-Din on the Tabriz–Mâku road). The earliest church on this site is said to have been built by the apostle Thaddaeus soon after his arrival in this part of Armenia in 66 AD. He later died as a martyr and was buried in the church. The oldest part of the existing church is the chevet, dating from the tenth or 11th century, which has a conical roof of black stone. The rest of the building is more recent and underwent some changes in the 19th century. The very finely carved stones on the outer walls decorated with floral designs and figures are worth having a close look at. Rarely visited, this church is busy only for a few days every year on the anniversary of the death of Saint Thaddaeus, when Armenians from all over the country attend special services.

Another interesting church in the region is that of **Saint Stephen** (Kelisâ Darre Shâm) built in the hills near Jolfâ, once a prosperous Armenian town on the frontier with the Republic of Azerbaijân. At the beginning of the 17th century, it was from here that whole families of Armenians were deported to Isfahan by Shâh Abbâs. The church of Saint Stephen was founded at the same time as that of Saint Thaddaeus, but the present building dates mainly from the 16th century, although a few sections are older (14th century). Here again, the carved decoration of the stones on the outer walls are very fine.

Due to a favourable location in a fertile plain, near the roads linking the Iranian Plateau, Turkey and Armenia, **Marâgheh** (143 kilometres, 89 miles, from Tabriz) became an important city, first under Arab and then under Kurdish domination. During the reign of Hulagu (1217–1265), it was briefly made the capital of the Il-khân Mongols. This period was its heyday and Hulagu's policy of religious tolerance encouraged the settlement there of large numbers of foreigners, including Nestorian Christians and Buddhists. Today, very little is left of Marâgheh's early history: Hulagu's famous observatory and the old Friday Mosque are in ruins, and only a series of

St Stephen's Church, Jôlfa

remarkably well preserved mausoleums, dating back to the 12th century, remain.

The oldest of these, built in 1147, is the **Gonbad-e Sorkh**, or Red Tomb, which owes its name to the deep red colour of its bricks. It is a square building with a conical, eight-sided roof and a stalactite ceiling. The decoration of the exterior walls is limited to Kufic inscriptions above the door and in a niche, geometric brick designs and some discreet touches of turquoise tilework, particularly on the half-columns set at each corner.

This mausoleum was one of the earliest in Iran to use glazed tiles in its decoration, a technique which had advanced greatly by the time of the second circular mausoleum was built nearby in 1167. Here the geometric patterns and the Kufic inscriptions formed by the red bricks are enhanced with turquoise tiles.

The octagonal **Gonbad-e Kabud** (1197) is the most ornate of the Marâgheh mausoleums. Each side of the building is decorated as if it were a *mehrab*, with a *muqarna* arch above it. Only the stone base is left plain. The flat panels, and the half-columns at the corners, are decorated with an interlaced polygon pattern made of bricks. The arches above the panels, Kufic inscriptions, stalactite cornice and roof were all once entirely decorated with turquoise tiles of which a few traces still remain.

The **Gonbad-e Khafariyeh** is the mausoleum of a Mameluk emir, Shams od-din Karasunkur, viceroy of Egypt and then of Syria, who fled to Iran in 1311. Sultan

Uljaitu Khodâbendeh (whose own mausoleum can be seen at Soltânieh) gave Marâgheh to the emir where he lived until he died. His mausoleum, completed in 1328, is also built of red brick but is decorated with black, blue and white tiles, colours which also appear at Soltânieh, built a few years earlier. The fifth mausoleum at Marâgheh, known as Khoi Burj and which was probably a Timurid building, collapsed in 1938.

Lake Orumieh, very near to Marâgheh, is Iran's largest lake. Its average surface area is some 4,500 kilometres^2 (1,737 miles^2), and may expand to 6,100 kilometres^2 (2,355 miles^2) in particularly wet years. Because of its high salt content there is only a very limited marine life and flora, but its waters are famous for their therapeutic value, especially in easing rheumatisms, and several spas have been built along the shores of the lake. **Orumieh** (1,300 metres, 427 feet), set in a very fertile plain on the west side of the lake, is the main city of West Azerbaijân. Its inhabitants are a mixed population of Kurds, Azeris, Armenians and Chaldeans, with a relatively large Christian community (Protestant, Catholic and Russian Orthodox). The **Friday Mosque**, built in the Seljuq period (12–13th century) has been restored several times but the *mehrab* still retains its very fine original carved stucco decoration. The **Se Gonbad** (Three Towers), located in the southern quarter of town, is a circular funerary tower similar to those at Marâgheh. Built in the late 12th century, it is another attractive example of Seljuq decorative art.

Just south of Lake Orumieh, near Naqadeh and Mohammad Yâr, is the archaeological site of **Hasanlu**. According to Assyrian administrative documents, the region south of Lake Orumieh was known as 'Mannai' in the ninth century BC and the remains of a fortified citadel at Hasanlu have thus been attributed to the Manneans, an Iranian people who formed a small principality in the area. Surrounded by powerful neighbours, (Assyrians, Urarteans and Medes), the Manneans took part in the changing political and military alliances struck between these nations, finally becoming vassals of the Scythians. At Hasanlu, the administrative town and the temples were located within the citadel, protected by walls nine metres (30 feet) high. Excavations have yielded a number of gold and silver objects, including the famous Hasanlu gold cup, now in the Archaeological Museum of Tehran, decorated with engraved mythological scenes, tentatively identified as representations of the Hurrian god Kummabi. Around 800 BC, the town was completely destroyed by invading Urartians who had settled near Lake Van.

The site of Hasanlu provides us not only with important information on Mannean culture, still very badly understood, but also on the early development of architecture in Iran and particularly of the hypostyle hall. Although limited in size—the largest room has two rows of four columns—the halls at Hasanlu do appear to represent an early stage in the evolution of the Achaemenian *apadanas* of Susa and Persepolis.

In the south of Azerbaijân is a second important archaeological site, **Takht-e Soleiman** (Solomon's Throne), or Shiz, the great Sassanian religious centre where the Warriors' Fire, one of the three most sacred fires of Zoroastrianism, was kept. The walls and the remains of 38 towers built around a crater lake are still standing; within them are the ruins of a palace and the fire temple. Access to the site is more difficult than Hasanlu and involves a long detour (take a secondary road near Takab, on the Miyândoab–Bijâr road).

Farsi for Silk

I arrived in Osku with an effective Persian vocabulary of one word. I got out of the bus and said it. 'Abricham'. Around me were scenes of mid-afternoon torpor. Old men lay sprawled about in the shade of a tree. Some sipped tea through sugar lumps held in their teeth. It was very hot. A few of the old men looked up, but no one answered me. I took a glass of tea from a ragged chai-khana boy, and slumped down against the bark. Now was no time for battling against language problems.

An hour later the sun had sunk a little lower and I tried again.

'Abricham', I said.

The old man next to me shrugged his shoulders.

'Abricham', I said again.

This time, for some reason, it worked.

'Abricham'? said the Persian.

'Abricham', I replied.

The old man muttered to his neighbor and a Chinese whisper passed around the tree. One of the younger old men on the far side of the trunk was deputed to guide me. The man got up, shook the dust from his flap cap, and led on through a maze of mud walls. I followed. After a few minutes we arrived at a small wicket gate set low in the wall. The old man knocked, waited, then knocked again. There was the sound of footsteps and the gate opened. A tall man in his late thirties came out. The old man rattled away in guttural dialect, pointed at me, shurgged his shoulders then grunted. The tall man smiled and extended his hand.

'How do you do'? he said. 'My name is Salim. I am the village schoolmaster. This old man says that you are a crazy foreigner who keeps repeating the same word over and over again. What do you want'?

'I am looking for the silk farm. The word I kept repeating was Abricham'.

'Abricham. Farsi for silk.'

'Oh I see. I am sorry. You see most people around Tabriz speak Turkish. No one here understands a word of Farsi'.

Velvet cloth with silver on a gold background, probably used as a decorative hanging or intended to be cut for a coat, c. 1600, courtesy of the Board of Trustees of the Victoria & Albert Museum.

154

Salim took me to the silk farm. It was another backyard affair, although by necessity a silk loom was a more complicated machine than the simple carpet loom we had seen outside Sivas. It lay in a small semi-subterranean mud-brick hut, attached to a courtyard house in a distant part of the maze. The silk was already wound onto seven weighted spindle whorls which Salim said came from a village nearby. The silk was spun across the full five-foot width of the loom frame into a sheet of separate threads. At the far end a single man sat on a bench. He operated the entire machine. Two pedals alternately lifted and lowered two frames of tightly strung cross-threads. A chain shot a shuttlecock in between, across the width of the loom, carrying a line of silk alternately under and over the spread of silk threads. A comb then pulled the woven material towards the operator where it wound itself around a wooden roll.

The machine was completely unmotorized and apparently homemade. Its existence near Tabriz, where Polo talks of the weaving of 'many kinds of beautiful and valuable stuffs of silk and gold', again proves Polo's accuracy in all matters mercantile, although since the time of the Yule that has never really been in doubt. I was shown the finished dyed silks and to the inexpert eye they looked exceptionally fine.

I was on the verge of haggling for a piece but, looking at my watch, I saw the time and rushed back to the square to catch the next bus back into town.

William Dalrymple, In Xanadu, 1990

William Dalrymple followed on foot the route of crusader Robert Curthose from Rouen to Jerusalem, and then in the footsteps of Marco Polo from there to Ghenghis Khan's palace of Xanadu in China. Guided by his explorer and historian predecessors, Dalrymple chronicles his journey in In Xanadu.

Western Iran

The western part of Iran, which covers the five modern provinces of Kordestân, Bâkhtarân, Hamedân, Ilâm and Lurestân, is dominated by the Zagros mountains with its deep valleys, its high cols and some surprisingly varied mountain scenery which is among the most beautiful in the country. Winters here are very cold with heavy snow falls, but summers are much more pleasant than on the plateau or near the Persian Gulf. At the beginning of this century, these provinces were still considered wild and dangerous, and even today they are underdeveloped, particularly Kordestân and Ilâm. There is no rail link, for example, between western Iran and the rest of the country except for one line that passes through southern Lurestân without even reaching the provincial capital. Despite this, the area has been one of vital strategic importance since antiquity because of its position between the Mesopotamian Basin and the Iranian Plateau. In the third millennium BC, the Kassites, Lullubi and Guti fought here against the Babylonian dynasties and the Akkadian Empire, causing the fall of the latter around 2200 BC. The Kassites, who had come from Lurestân, succeeded in establishing their own dynasty in Babylon between the 16th and 12th centuries BC. The Medes, who had settled in the modern province of Hamedân, fought for centuries against the Assyrian Empire, based in the Upper Tigris Basin, finally capturing its capital, Niniva, in 612 BC. With the formation of the huge Achaemenian and Sassanian empires, western Iran retained strategic importance, located as it was between the imperial capitals (Babylon, Ctesiphon) and the Iranian Plateau.

The mountainous nature of the region and its cultural links with Mesopotamia lead to the development in this part of Iran of a very specific form of artistic expression, rock-carved bas reliefs. Until the seventh century BC, these carvings were relatively few in number, but increased considerably once the Achaemenian rulers used them for political and religious reasons, combining figurative representations with inscriptions. This practice continued, with greater or lesser success depending on the period, during the Parthian, Seleucid and Sassanian dynasties. These carvings, often remarkably well preserved despite their age and the harshness of the climate, are historical documents of exceptional importance and form a large part of the cultural visits in the region. However, some of the sites require long detours by road and may therefore be difficult to include in a tour.

Today, western Iran is still the land of the Kurds and the Lurs, two of the main Iranian-speaking minorities. The precise identification of these ethnic groups through the centuries is difficult. It would appear that Kurdish mercenaries, known as Kardukoi, formed part of the army that attacked Xenophon's Ten Thousand in 400 BC. But the Arab geographers who later described the region used the term 'Kurd' for

156

Bas-relief showing the investiture of Ardeshir II, centre, receiving the sacred crown from the god Ahura Mazda, Taq-e Bostan, Bâkhtarân

all the nomadic tribes in the area, regardless of their ethnic or cultural background. It was only after the Mongol invasions in the 13th century that the name Kurdistan was used to designate the whole northwestern zone of the Zagros. The central government of Iran never really had much direct administrative control over this region until 1865, during the Qâjâr Dynasty, when the last Kurdish prince was dismissed from his post.

During the 1920s and '30s, the separatist demands of the Kurds, which had emerged as much in Iran as in Turkey and Iraq, were suppressed by Rezâ Shâh. In 1946, however, taking advantage of the Russian occupation of northern Iran, the small Kurdish Republic of Mahabad was founded around Lake Orumieh. Isolated from other, more predominantly Kurdish areas further south, the republic lasted only a few months. Since then, the Kurdish question has been a continued presence on the political scene and has influenced many of the decisions taken by the central government. The problem of Iranian support for Kurd autonomists in Iraq, for example, was one of the key points in the negotiations that lead to the signing, in 1975, of the Algiers Agreement between Iran and Iraq.

The Lurs live mainly in the provinces of Bâkhtarân and Lurestân. The capital of the latter, **Khoram Abâd**, has for centuries been identified with Lur regional power. It was here that the *atabek*, the Lur chieftains, built their citadel, the Dez-e Siâh or Black Fortress. For nearly four centuries, they controlled the region from this fortress and were only subdued when Shâh Abbâs stormed it at the beginning of the 17th century and had the last *atabek* put to death. The ruins of the fort, set atop a rocky outcrop, can still be visited today.

Bâkhtarân

Bâkhtarân (also known as Kermânshâh), is an important city of about half a million inhabitants. Less ancient than Hamedân, it is thought to have been founded during the reign of the Sassanian king Bahram IV, at the end of the fourth century AD. Because of its location on the main roads leading to Baghdad and Kirkuk and its proximity to the Mesopotamian border, it has been repeatedly attacked during its history. It suffered badly during the wars between the Ottoman and Safavid empires (the last occupation of the town by the Turks was in 1915) and more recently in the war with Iraq. From September 1980, the border region around Qasr-e Shirin, Sar-e Pol-e Zahâb and Gilân-e Gharb (less than 200 kilometres, 125 miles, from Bâkhtarân) became one of the two main fronts of the war, and Bâkhtarân, with its large oil refinery, was a prime target for Iraqi shelling. As a result, much of the town has needed rebuiling recently.

One of the trilingual inscriptions at Ganjnâmeh (Hamedân), carved by the Achaemenian kings Darius I and Xerxes

A few kilometres northeast of Bâkhtarân, nestled at the foot of the Paru Mountains, is the Sassanian site of Tâq-e Bostân (the Arc of the Garden), where a series of bas-reliefs and grottoes have been carved into the cliff face. The first of these reliefs can be seen just after the entrance to the garden, before reaching the grottoes. It represents the investiture of Ardeshir II (379–383), with the king in the centre, standing over a Roman soldier (or Ahriman, the god of Evil), and receiving the royal crown from the hands of the god Ahura Mazda, on the right. Mithra is shown standing on the left, holding the sacred *barsom* which symbolizes the power of plant life.

The grottoes of Tâq-e Bostân are unique in Sassanian art. It is probable that three grottoes were originally intended, with two smaller ones flanking a larger, central one. For reasons which remain unknown, the left-hand cave was never dug. The right-hand cave, the later of the two existing ones, is decorated on the back wall with representations of Shâpur III (383–388) and his grandfather, Shâpur II (310–379), shown leaning on their swords. Beside each of them is an inscription in Pehlevi which identifies them.

The left-hand grotto, the larger and most complex one, is generally dated either to the reign of Peroz (457–484) or to Khosroe II (590–628). Unlike the previous grotto, there is no inscription here to identify the figures with certainty. The outer wall around the entrance is decorated with floral motifs, similar to the designs found on fragments of carved stucco from Sassanian palaces, and with two winged figures holding a royal crown. The back wall is divided into two registers. The upper one shows another royal investiture with the king standing between the gods Ahura Mazda and Anahita. Beneath this is a remarkable sculpture of a knight on horseback, dressed in full armour with jousting lance raised. This warrior is thought by some scholars to represent Khosroe II and his horse Shabdiz. Close examination of the astonishing detail, particularly of the chain mail, will reveal the sculptor's skill. In the large hunting scenes on the side walls, the king is again shown as the principal figure, successfully shooting the game driven towards him by his beaters. The scene at the top of the left wall, which still bears some of the original paint, is a much later addition which dates to the reign of the Qâjâr ruler Fath Ali Shâh (1798–1834). Near the entrance to the site are several fragments of Sassanian columns and capitals which were found in the area.

The road which leaves Bâkhtarân for the Iraqi border (and which used to continue to Baghdad) goes through Sar-e Pol-e Zahâb (120 kilometres, 75 miles) where some of the earliest rock carvings in Iran may be seen. The most important one dates back to the end of the third millennium BC and shows the victorious king Annubanini of the Lullubi, a mountain people who controlled the trade routes between Babylon and the Iranian Plateau. The king is portrayed standing with one foot on a slain enemy while the goddess Inanna presents him with a royal ring. Beneath the figures, an inscription in Akkadian invokes the help of the gods against the enemy. It is this bas-relief, whose composition is said to have inspired the Achaemenian artists who carved Darius' bas-relief at Bisotun (see below).

Bisotun

About 40 kilometres (25 miles) from Bâkhtarân, in the direction of Hamedân, the road passes under a tall cliff which bears one of the most famous bas-reliefs in Iran. This is the site of **Bisotun** (or Behistun). In addition to the Achaemenian carving for which the site is best known, there are several later sculptures scattered around the foot of the cliff next to the road. Among these are two Parthian carvings accompanied by Greek inscriptions. The left one, unfortunately badly damaged by a 17th century Persian inscription, represents king Mithridates II (123–87 BC) receiving four dignitaries. This is the oldest known Parthian carving and still reflects the traditional Achaemenian manner of presenting figures in profile rather than face on. The right-hand carving commemorates the victory of Gotarzes II (38–51 AD) over his rival Meherdates and shows the king on horseback brandishing a spear and accompanied by a winged Victory. The style in this much later sculpture is closer to the Roman.

On the far right of the site, protected by a metal covering, is a Seleucid carving (148 BC) in high relief showing a reclining Heracles. Nearby, on an isolated block of stone, is a further Parthian carving showing a priest or a nobleman carrying out a ritual at an altar. The inscription accompanying it mentions the name of Vologeses, the name of five Parthian kings who ruled between 51 and 228 AD.

The most famous carving at Bisotun is set about sixty metres above the road. It was sculpted by order of the Achaemenian king Darius I in 520 BC to commemorate his victory over the Magus Gaumata and the subsequent consolidation of his power. In 522 BC, Gaumata rebelled against Cambyses II and usurped the throne. He was executed a few months later by Darius who then proclaimed himself king. However, his legitimacy to the throne was contested by eight other pretenders who began a series of rebellions. In this relief, Darius is represented on the left, standing over the body of Gaumata. Facing him are the eight rebel chiefs chained together. The last figure, wearing a pointed hat, is Skunkha, king of the Scythians, whose portrait was added to the bas-relief at a later date after Darius' victory against the Scythians in 518 BC. Behind Darius, on the left, stand his allies, Gobryas and Artaphernes. Above the prisoners hangs the winged symbol of Ahura Mazda, the all-powerful god, in whose name the Achaemenian kings ruled. Although this relief of Darius is the first great art work of his reign, the representation of the figures surpasses that of the time of Cyrus the Great. The inspiration for this carving appears to have come from the Lullubi

Kalagan summit, Alvand Mountains

relief at Sar-e Pol-e Zahâb (see above): the composition is very similar and makes use of size to indicate the relative importance of the figures.

Around the relief are inscriptions in three languages, Elamite, Neo-Babylonian (or Akkadian) and Old Persian, which give the official version of Darius' fight for power and his final triumph. The importance of this text lies in the fact that it is the only one by an Achaemenian ruler to relate the historical events of his reign and those that preceded it. Darius recounts Gaumata's rebellion against Cambyses II in detail, followed by the rebellions of each of the eight provinces and their final defeats. He ends with an acknowledgement of Ahura Mazda's invaluable assistance in his struggle—thereby justifying the legitimacy of his claim to the throne—and appeals to future rulers to preserve the monument and spread his message. The Elamite text, which appears to have been carved first, is in two sections, one to the right of the relief and the other below, to the left. The Babylonian text is carved on the left, and the Old Persian text directly below, the figures. It was thanks to these inscriptions, which are comparable in value to the Rosetta stone, that a British officer, Henry Rawlinson, was able, in 1838, to decipher Old Persian cuneiform.

Darius' decision to carve his message to the world on the Bisotun cliff was hardly an arbitrary one: the cliff is directly above the road that lead from his capital, Ecbatana, to Babylon. The message itself was addressed as much to posterity as to his subjects. Indeed, the inscriptions are placed too high to be read from the road and access to them was deliberately rendered almost impossible, on the king's orders, by smoothing down the surface of the rock beneath them. But copies of the inscriptions—of which several fragments have been found—were sent to each province of the empire, including Babylon, thus ensuring that the king's message was made known to all.

Further along the same road is the small town of **Kangâvar**, about 90 kilometres (56 miles) from Hamedân. Excavations here have revealed the remains of a temple dedicated to Anahita, the goddess of water and abundance, which dates back to Seleucid or Parthian times. The site was first described in 1840 by two Frenchmen, Eugène Flandin and Pascal Coste, although the presence of modern houses on the site at the time lead to inaccuracies in the drawing of their temple plan. Excavations were carried out in the 1960s and 1970s, but have been interrupted since. Today, the main remains are the platform on which the temple was built and a large staircase on the south side leading up to it. The best preserved part of the temple is in the western corner where several sections of columns are visible (the best view of them is to be had from the side road parallel to that part of the temple). Fragments of columns and building blocks have been assembled in front of the staircase and, despite the work that has already been carried out, it is still rather difficult to imagine the overall layout of the temple complex.

Hamedân

The city of **Hamedân**, the provincial capital, is equidistant from Sanandaj, Bâkhtarân and Arâk at the foot of the Alvand Mountains (3,565 metres, 11,696 feet) in the Zagros, at an altitude of 1,700 metres (5,577 feet). It occupies a key site on the road which, even in antiquity, linked Mesopotamia to the Iranian Plateau. It is here that the first Median capital, Ecbatana, was founded. The Medes, who formed a loose federation of warlike tribes of Indo-European origin, settled on the plateau around the ninth century BC. In 673 BC, the chieftain of one of these tribes, Phraortes, succeeded in unifying the various Median groups under his command and established his capital at Ecbatana, the 'Place of Assembly'. In 550 BC, Cyrus the Great defeated the last Median king, Astyages, and Ecbatana became the summer residence of the Achaemenian court, well away from the torrid heat of Susa. After Alexander the Great's conquest (331 BC), Ecbatana lost much of its former importance although it remained a staging post between the plateau and Mesopotamia. In the 12th century, Hamedân briefly became the capital of the Seljuq Dynasty, but it was destroyed a century later during the Mongol invasion, and again by Tamerlane's armies in 1386.

Because of its position, Hamedân was also severely hit by the wars between the Ottoman and Safavid empires—the Turks occupied the city from 1724 to 1730—to the extent that when the English writer James Morier visited it in 1813, he found little more than a mass of ruins.

These successive sackings have spared few of Hamedân's ancient monuments. In addition, part of the modern town around the small hill known as Tappeh-ye Hekmatâneh, near Ekbâtân Square, is built over the site of Ecbatana and no large-scale excavations have yet been carried out on the ancient Median capital. For the moment, almost the only visible remains of the pre-Islamic era is the **Sang-e Shir**, or Stone Lion, a statue tentatively dated to the Parthian Dynasty which has been set up in a park in the southeast of town. With a little imagination one can just make out the form of a lion in the now shapeless rock, badly eroded by time and weather, and smoothed down by the thousands of women's hands which have patted it in the hope that their wishes would be fulfilled.

In the very centre of Hamedân is Imam Khomeini Square (once Pahlavi Square), from which radiate six large avenues connected to each other by a ring road. The main monuments in town are to be found within or just outside this ring road. The oldest monument is undoubtedly the **mausoleum of Esther and Mardochius**, located in a small side street off Shari'ati Avenue, near Khomeini Square. This is an important Jewish pilgrimage site and Hamedân still has a large Jewish community. According to tradition, Esther, the Jewish wife of the Achaemenian king Xerxes (485–465 BC), succeeded in securing royal protection for the followers of her faith and organized, with the help of her uncle Mardochius, the establishment of Jewish colonies throughout the Persian Empire. However, the tomb is also attributed to a Sassanian queen who died in the early fifth century AD. Inside, are two wooden cenotaphs draped with cloth; the bones have been buried in the crypt.

Near the ring road stands the **Gonbad-e Alaviân**, a well-preserved 12th century Seljuq tomb (the original dome has disappeared, replaced by a modern roof). The *mehrab*, as well as the walls inside and out, are decorated with geometric and floral designs in carved stucco. In the crypt, which can also be visited, is a table covered in various votive offerings, including knotted pieces of green cloth and safetypins. To get to the tomb, follow Bâbâ Tâher Avenue from Khomeini Square to Imâmzâdeh Abdollah Square, and turn right onto Alaviân Boulevard. The tomb is located in the courtyard of a school (the entrance door is in a small street to the right of the boulevard).

The two other mausoleums in Hamedân are modern constructions which are reminiscent, each in their own way, of the tall Gonbad-e Kâvus in Mâzanderân Province, which dates back to the 11th century (see page 119). The first tomb is that of **Avicenna**, located south of Khomeini Square on Bu Ali Sinâ Avenue. Built in 1952,

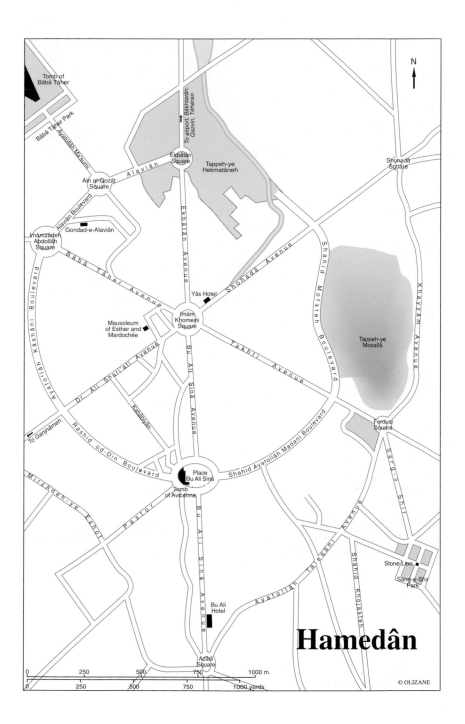

Tomb of
Bâbâ Tâher

Bâbâ Tâher Park

Ayatollâh Masumi

To airport, Bâkhtarân,
Qazvin, Tehrân

Ekbâtân
Square

Tappeh-ye
Hekmatâneh

Shohadâ
Square

A l a v i â n

Ain al-Qozât
Square

Alaviân Boulevard

Imâmzâdeh
Abdollâh
Square

Gondad-e-Alaviân

Bâbâ Tâher Avenue

Ekbâtân Avenue

Shohadâ Avenue

Shahid Morateh Boulevard

Khayyâm Avenue

Ayatollâh Kâshâni Boulevard

Yâs Hotel

Imâm
Khomeini
Square

Mausoleum
of Esther and
Mardochée

Dr. Ali Shari'ati Avenue

Bu Ali Sinâ Avenue

Takhti Avenue

Tappeh-ye
Mosallâ

To Ganjnâmeh

Rashid od-Din Boulevard

Kababiyân

Shahid Ayatollâh Madani Boulevard

Ferdusi
Square

Sarg-e Shir

Mirzâden-ye Eshot

Pastor

Bu Ali Sinâ Avenue

Place
Bu Ali Sinâ

Tomb
of Avicenna

Ayatollâh Taleqani Avenue

Shahid Khojasteh

Stone Lion

Sang-e-Shir
Park

Bu Ali
Hotel

Hamedân

Azâdi
Square

0   250   500   750   1000 m.

0   250   500   750   1000 yards

© OLIZANE

N

this tower is composed of a conical roof held up by twelve tall pillars around an empty central space. A small museum at the foot of the tower contains copies of Avicenna's works.

Born in Bukhara around 980, Abu Ali Hussein ibn Abdallah ibn Sinâ, or Avicenna, was one of the most influential—and criticized—scholars both in the Islamic world and in the West. One hundred and fifty-seven works have been attributed to him on such diverse subjects as metaphysics, mechanics, acoustics, astronomy, and geometry. In Europe, Avicenna is best known for his al-Qânum fit'tibb, or Canon of Medicine, translated into Latin by Gerard of Cremona in the 12th century. This encyclopaedic work in five volumes is the sum total of all Islamic medical knowledge at the time; its scope, clarity, layout and particularly its synthesis of ideas from Galen and Aristotle were to make it one of the most important texts in European medical faculties until the 17th century.

Avicenna took up Aristotle's ideas on logic and metaphysics, including the importance of scientific observation. But such peripatetic philosophy and logic were criticized by many schools of thought, and Avicenna's writings in particular were strongly attacked by the great Sufi scholar al-Ghazâli (1058–1111). Even in Europe, Avicenna did not escape criticism: in 1526, Paracelsus is said to have burnt a copy of the Canon at Basle University.

The second tomb is that of **Bâbâ Tâher**, built in the north of the town in a small park. Like Avicenna's tomb, it has twelve external pillars, but here the central space is filled by the tower itself. Very little is known about the life of Bâbâ Tâher, a famous Sufi poet who lived between the tenth and 13th centuries and who gained his reputation for his do-bayti, four-line poems of a simpler metre than the rubâ'i. In these poems, Bâbâ Tâher presents himself as a humble dervish, filled with passion and love for God yet deeply aware of Man's insignificance and loneliness. To resolve these problems, the poet seeks the way to absorption and annihilation within God.

A dozen kilometres southwest of town, in the Alvand Hills, is the site of **Ganj-nâmeh**. At the end of a narrow valley, two Achaemenian inscriptions have been carved into the rock face, the first one by Darius I (522–486 BC) and the second by his son Xerxes (486–465 BC). Both are written in three languages, Old Persian, Neo-Elamite and Neo-Babylonian, and are practically identical in wording to one another, differing only in the name and genealogy of each ruler. The inscriptions begin by praising the god Ahura Mazda, creator of the world, of Paradise, of Man and of the Great King of the Achaemenians and end with the titles of the ruler, including that of King of Kings (Shâhinshâh), and with the name of his father.

Word Pictures

Teheran (3,900 ft), October 2nd . . . The day's journey had a wild exhilaration. Up and down the mountains, over the endless flats, we bumped and swooped. The sun flayed us. Great spirals of dust, dancing like demons over the desert, stopped our dashing Chevrolet and choked us. Suddenly, from far across a valley, came the flash of a turquoise jar, bobbing along on a donkey. Its owner walked beside it, clad in a duller blue. And seeing the two lost in that gigantic stony waste, I understood why blue is the Persian colour, and why the Persian word for it means water as well.

We reached the capital by night. Not a glimmer of light on the horizon warned us of it. Trees, then houses, suddenly enveloped us. By day it is a Balkan sort of place. But the Elburz mountains, which usurp half the sky, give a surprising interest to the streets that face them.

Shahrud (4,400 ft), November 13th. A bus arrived next morning at Ayn Varzan, full of lady pilgrims on their way to Meshed. Their chatter in the yard below woke me up. Five minutes later I was beside the driver, and my luggage underneath the ladies.

From the pass above Amiriya we looked back over a mounting array of peaks, ranges, and buttresses to the white cone of Demavend in the top of the sky; and forward over a plain of boundless distances, where mountains rippled up and sighed away like the wash of a tide, dark here, shining there, while shadow and sunshine followed their masters the clouds across the earth's arena. Trees of autumn yellow embowered the lonely villages. Elsewhere, desert; the stony black-lustred desert of eastern Persia. At Samnan, while the ladies drank tea in a brick caravanserai, I heard of an old minaret, which I found before the police found me. When they did, I ate sorrow, as the expression is, that I could stay no longer in their beautiful city, and we drove away into the dusk. . . .

Robert Byron, The Road to Oxiana, 1937

Byron, born in 1905, was part of a generation of young travellers who set off to far flung places between the two World Wars. Out of their travels arose a literary genre, that of the literary travel book, of which The Road to Oxiana *is one of the finest.*

Khuzestân Province

The Khuzestân Plain which lies at the foot of the Zagros and Bakhtiâri mountains is a prolongation of the Mesopotamian Plain in Iraq, through which flow the Tigris and Euphrates rivers. The southeastern frontier of the province, near Abâdân and Khoram Shahr, is formed by the Shatt el-Arab (or Arvand-rud in Persian), the confluence of these two great rivers. The Khuzestân Plain, which has a surface area of some 40,000 kilometres^2 (15,444 miles^2), is the largest expanse of low-level land in Iran, rising, at the foot of the mountains, to a height of only 170 metres (558 feet) above sea level. Just like Mesopotamia, Khuzestân is a fertile plain, particularly along its main rivers, the Dez, Karkheh and Karun. Thanks to the construction, in the 1960s, of a large dam on the Karkheh, it has been possible to provide better irrigation for the plain. This in turn has lead to the cultivation of an entirely new range of crops in the region, including sugar cane. Today, the province's wealth comes mainly from its oil deposits, concentrated in Lower Khuzestân (south of Ahvâz) where large-scale salination of the soil has rendered vast expanses of land completely sterile, preventing the agricultural development of the area.

The population of Khuzestân is ethnically very mixed and includes a high proportion of Arabs. The Safavid Dynasty had named the region Arabistan, recognizing the ethnic origin of the majority of its inhabitants. In the 17th and 18th centuries, Arabistan was claimed as much by Persia as by the Ottoman Empire. Local authority was in the hands of two Bedouin tribes, first the Bani Kaab and then the Bu Kassab who, in 1812, founded the emirate and town of Mohammara (now Khoram Shahr). Caught between two powerful empires, the emirs of Mohammara succeeded nevertheless, through careful politics, in keeping their autonomy. In 1905, the emirate even benefited from military assistance from the British, who were keen to protect the oil wells and refineries that they controlled in the area. However, the foundation of the Pahlavi Dynasty in 1925 marked the end of the emirate. The Persian army invaded Arabistan and captured the emir. Then began a movement to counter the strong Arab identity in the province: Arabistan was renamed Khuzestân (Country of Towers), Mohammara became Khoram Shahr, the Persian language replaced Arabic and the immigration of non-Arab families was encouraged. Spontaneous revolts, which became more and more organized, began and continued until the 1970s.

THE IRAN–IRAQ WAR

Of all the Iranian provinces, Khuzestân suffered the most from the war between Iran and Iraq and was the scene of some of the bloodiest and hardest-fought battles. The Iraqi high command had hoped to cash in on the historical and cultural links be-

Fragments of columns at Susa, c. 1881 engraving by Jane Dieulafoy

tween the populations living on either side of the Shatt el-Arab, Iraq's only access to
the Persian Gulf, but the expected uprising against the Iranian government failed to
materialize. The strategic and economic importance of the oil-rich lands in Iran
directly to the east of the Shatt el-Arab explain in large part the Iraqi aggression and
the concentration of their attacks on the urban centres of Ahvâz, Khoram Shahr and
Abâdân.

Abâdân, originally an island in the Arvand-rud with a population of a few hundred villagers, became, in 1913, the site of an oil refinery. It was chosen partly
because of its proximity to the port of **Khoram Shahr**, the old emirate of Mohammara, located at the confluence of the Arvand-rud and the Kârun. The latter, which is
navigable as far as Ahvâz, the capital of Khuzestân, 160 kilometres (99 miles) further

north, allowed relatively easy communication with the hinterland. A town rapidly developed around the Abâdân refinery, and, in the 1970s, had grown to over 300,000. In 1980, the refinery was the largest in the world and was therefore of vital economic importance to Iran.

All three towns have been largely rebuilt since the end of the war with Iraq. At one point Khoram Shahr became a ghost town and was all but razed to the ground. In May 1982, the Iranian army launched an offensive to recover Khoram Shahr, with the reported loss of some 50,000 lives. The shelling of the towns of Khuzestân, and particularly of Dezful in the north, lead to an exodus of the population, with nearly two million refugees forced to settle in camps set up well inland. Today, oil drilling and processing is well under way again and the port of Khoram Shahr is functional once more, although work at the Abâdân refinery is not yet back to its pre-war level.

Susa and the Susian Plain

The province of Khuzestân can be divided into two separate zones, Upper and Lower Khuzestân. The former, which includes the Susian Plain, has a higher rainfall than Lower Khuzestân (south of Ahvâz). Thanks to this and a good understanding of irrigation techniques, Susiana has been, at various times in its history, an extremely fertile plain. While the climate in winter is very pleasant, with temperatures rarely below 20° C (68° F), summers are scorching, and temperatures regularly reach over 50° C (120° F). It is this climate which drove the Achaemenian rulers to leave their administrative capital of Susa in summer for Ecbatana (Hamedân), situated more than 500 kilometres (311 miles) further north in the mountains.

The Susian Plain owes much of its historical importance to its geographic location, which resulted in the introduction of the Sumerian and Babylonian cultures into this part of Iran from the fourth millennium BC. This location also contributed to the development of Elamite civilization.

About 30 kilometres (19 miles) from Dezful, and 115 kilometres (71 miles) north of Ahvâz, is the small town of Shush, the site of the ancient city of **Susa** and a pilgrimage centre for the faithful who come to pray at the tomb of Daniel. Despite the importance and long history of Susa, there is very little left of the monuments today, and the visitor will have to make quite a considerable effort to picture what this glorious city might have looked like at the different stages of its development.

Pre-Elamite Susa
There are several distinct periods of human settlement at Susa. A first religious and administrative centre was built at the beginning of the fourth millennium BC. This

very early period is not well understood, but the discovery of numerous seals and high quality vessels suggests links with Lurestan and the Iranian Plateau, not just with Mesopotamia. During the fourth millennium BC, Susa turned away from the Iranian world and drew closer to Sumer, centred around the city of Uruk in Mesopotamia. This swing between two civilizations, from Mesopotamia to Iran and back again, became a characteristic feature of Susian Plain history.

Gradually, a new culture with its own script, sometimes called proto-Elamite, developed around Susa. The city became an important trading centre, and the excavation of the stratigraphical layers of this epoch have revealed a large number of seals, inscribed tablets which deal mainly with accounts and small marble statues. This period appears to have ended rather abruptly for reasons that are still unclear, and Susa turned once again to Mesopotamia, becoming a medium-sized town of Sumerian type (c. 2800–2300 BC). Around 2300 BC, Susa was annexed by the Semite Akkad Empire and elevated to the rank of main city of one of the empire's administrative regions. After going through a period of peace and prosperity which ended with the fall of Akkad in 2150 BC, Susa was captured by the new, independent state of Elam, which had formed in the nearby mountains.

The Elamite Empire

It was as capital of the Elamite empire (2000–500 BC) that Susa was to know its period of greatest glory, particularly during the 12th century BC after the destruction of the Babylonian Kassite Empire by Elam. An impressive amount of treasure was brought back from Babylon to Susa, including the famous Code of Hammurabi (now in the Louvre Museum in Paris), victory statues of the kings of Akkad and royal charters. However, at the end of the 12th century, during the reign of Nebuchadnezzar I, Babylon took its revenge. Susa was sacked and burned to the ground.

Practically nothing is known about the four centuries following the destruction of Susa, but it would appear that the city was rebuilt and prospered once again. One date is certain, that of the sack of Susa in 646 BC by the Assyrian king Assurbanipal after the Elamites suffered a severe defeat in 653 BC. Elamite power was broken, but the Assyrian Empire was to last only a few more years itself, and Susa was integrated into the Persian Achaemenian Empire.

Achaemenian Susa

Susa under Achaemenian rule produced another brilliant period in its history. In 521 or 520 BC, Darius I decided to make the city his administrative capital. Its geographical location halfway between Babylon and Pasargadae was very favorable. The reconstruction and embellishment of Susa continued throughout Darius' reign, and Artaxerxes II later added a new palace to the south. Unlike Persepolis, which appears not to have been known to the Greeks before Alexander the Great's conquest, Susa's reputation as a great city had already travelled far beyond the borders of the empire. But the breakup of Alexander's empire marked the end of Susa's role as capital. Under the Seleucids, the town was renamed Seleucia on the Eulaeos, and the objects found there from this period suggest a certain Hellenization of the town. During the Parthian period, Susa prospered but its population declined dramatically under the Sassanians. In the 13th century, the town developed again to some extent, due in part to the number of pilgrims visiting Daniel's tomb, but it then declined again thereafter.

It was not until the 19th century that the West rediscovered Susa; the first archaeological surveys were carried out in 1851 by a British mission, and were followed by excavations directed by William Loftus. From 1884 to 1896, Marcel and Jane Dieulafoy unearthed part of the Achaemenian palace and found the famous glazed brick lion and archer friezes which are now on show in the Louvre Museum in Paris. Several French archaeologists then worked at Susa from the late 19th century to the mid-1960s: Jacques de Morgan; Roger de Mecquenem; and finally Roman Ghirshman who spent twenty-one years there, working his way down the various stratigraphic levels. In the late 1960s and 1970s, the excavations were taken over by joint Iranian and American teams.

Visit of the Site
■ THE ACROPOLIS
The main remains at Susa date back to the Achaemenian period and are dispersed on two of the four hills of the site. The most imposing monument, and one which no visitor can fail to notice on arrival, is in fact a modern one: it is the castle, built at the end of the 19th century by the French director of excavations, Jacques de Morgan, as the team's headquarters. It is built on the tell of the acropolis and has the advantage of allowing the visitor to get his bearings as it is visible from a great distance in this plain whose small hills are otherwise devoid of other distinguishing marks. The acropolis was the site of the Elamite royal city, although excavations have also revealed stratigraphic layers dating back to the Neolithic, proto-Elamite, Achaemenian, Parthian and Sassanian periods. At present, there are few visible remains of the acropolis and any earth walls still surviving are rapidly being eroded by the elements.

■ THE APADANA
The foundations of the palace of Darius I are to be seen on the tell of the *apadana* to the northeast of the acropolis. The palace was built on a partly artificial terrace; the only access to it was from the eastern side, by a ramp that led to Darius' Gate. The palace was composed of a series of courtyards aligned on the same axis and flanked by smaller chambers which probably served as apartments. To the north of the ter-

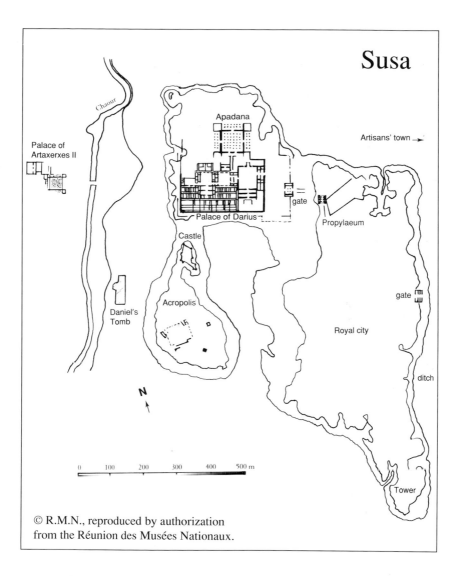

Susa

Chaour

Palace of
Artaxerxes II

Apadana

Artisans' town →

gate

Palace of Darius

Propylaeum

Castle

Daniel's
Tomb

Acropolis

gate

Royal city

ditch

N

0   100   200   300   400   500 m

Tower

race was the *apadana*, a hypostyle room of 36 columns, each topped by a capital in
the shape of animals set back to back. Three of the sides of the *apadana* opened out
onto columned porticos.

Modern access to the hill is from the west, through the apartments surrounding
the courtyards. The latter are still easily recognizable by their paved floors and the
walls separating the various rooms have been partly rebuilt in brick and clay so that
the overall plan of the palace is visible. The famous glazed brick lion frieze that Dieu-

lafoy took back to Paris was found at the foot of the north wall in the east courtyard. In the *apadana* a few fragments of columns and capitals have been left on the ground.

■ OTHER VISITS
To the east of the *apadana* was the **royal city** with the residential quarters of the court and officials; this site was also occupied in the Parthian, Sassanian and Islamic periods. In the 1970s, a second palace, which is thought to date from the reign of Artaxerxes II, was discovered on the other bank of the Shaour behind Daniel's tomb. Near the entrance to the site of Susa, on the main road of the village, a small **museum** exhibits some of the objects found during the excavations (the opening hours here are rather erratic, particularly in the afternoon).

Near the museum is the **tomb of the prophet Daniel** (ârâmgâh-e Dânyâl), recognizable by its white sugar loaf dome, which still attracts large numbers of pilgrims every year. The honeycomb appearance of the 13th-century dome is characteristic of Khuzestân. The front of the tomb, with its central *eivân* flanked by two short minarets, is decorated in blue tiles. Men and women enter the building by separate doors (*châdors* must be worn by women and may be hired at the entrance) and remain apart during the entire visit. Like many mausoleums, this one is richly decorated inside with small mirrors.

Choqâ Zanbil

Forty-five kilometres (28 miles) from Susa, on the road to Ahvâz, stand the ruins of the ziggurat of Choqâ Zanbil, by far the best preserved of the few Elamite monuments to have survived. The ziggurat, a pyramidal stepped temple, evolved from the early Sumerian temple platforms and became characteristic of Mesopotamia. Choqâ Zanbil, however, is so far a unique example of this form of architecture in Elam. Investigatory excavations were first carried out on the site in the 1930s by the Frenchman Roger de Mecquenem, and systematic excavations followed between 1951 and 1962, directed by Roman Ghirshman. These unearthed the earliest glazed tiles to be used in Iran for decorative purposes. Although still simple in shape and design, they are the precursors of the later Achaemenian murals from Susa.

In 1330 BC, a change of dynasty in the Elamite kingdom marked the beginning of a new period of territorial expansion. In the 13th century BC, the king Untash-Napirisha (or Untash-Gal according to the old method of transcription) founded a religious capital, Dur Untash, on the road from Susa to Anshân, the main city of Elam. The centre of this new town was the temple, dedicated to the Sumerian god Inshushinak, which was surrounded by the walled religious city.

At this period, the temple consisted only a vast square courtyard enclosed within walls. The ziggurat was built later when the king decided to dedicate the temple not just to Inshushinak, the god of Susa, but also to Napirisha, the god of Anshân. The original construction became the ground floor of the ziggurat and the upper four floors were built one inside the other (rather than one on top of the other as was the case in Mesopotamia) until the entire surface of the old central courtyard was covered over. A small temple was erected at the summit. Today, the ziggurat stands only 25 metres (82 feet) tall but would have reached over 60 metres (197 feet) originally. Unlike the Mesopotamian ziggurats which are squatter and have three outer staircases, this has only a single covered staircase which is invisible from the outside.

On the northwest side of the ziggurat stood a group of temples dedicated to the secondary divinities (Ishnikarab and Kiririsha). An oval wall surrounded these temples and the ziggurat; a second larger wall enclosed yet more temples, and a third and final one protected the city of Al-Untash. It appears that houses were never actually built in the city, but a royal quarter has been identified in the southeast which included residential buildings and a funerary palace equipped with vaults to hold the royal ashes. A nearby temple was dedicated to Nusku, the fire god.

Al-Untash was abandoned in the 12th century BC when the Elamite kings moved to Susa, taking with them the treasures of Choqâ Zanbil which were to decorate the newly-restored temples of Susa. In 640 BC, Al-Untash was completely destroyed by the Assyrian king Ashurbanipal a few years after his conquest of Susa.

Choqâ Zanbil is still located within a military zone and it is necessary to get written permission from the Shush Archaeological Bureau to visit it. Photography is not allowed at the site.

The capital of Khuzestân, **Ahvâz**, is located almost in the centre of the province, 140 kilometres (87 miles) south of Shush and 130 kilometres (81 miles) north of Khoram Shahr. It is an industrial town, largely rebuilt after the war with Iraq, but is useful as a stopover for people visiting Susa and the region. Note that distances by road between Ahvâz and the major tourist sites outside the province, such as Shiraz or Hamedân, are quite considerable, and that at the moment there are few air links with other cities, except Tehran.

For those with free time on their hands and who are particularly interested in the ancient history of Iran, there are several possible excursions to be made around Masjed-e Suleiman and Izeh (the roads are not always very good in this area, and distances are quite great, between 160 and 240 kilometres (99 and 149 miles) from Ahvâz). Near **Masjed-e Suleiman**, now a large industrial centre, are the remains of several terraces, thought to be of Achaemenian date and which may be the forerunners of the terraces at Pasargadae and Persepolis. About 25 kilometres (16 miles) north, at **Bard-e Neshandeh**, is yet another terrace. Parthian statues and carvings

Noruz

The most important festival in Iran is undoubtedly Noruz, the New Year celebration. This very ancient festival, which is closely tied to Mazdean beliefs, has its origins already celebrated in the Archaemenian period, when the kings marked the return of Spring each year with great festivities held at Persepolis.

The preparations for Noruz begin long before the actual day: this is mainly a family holiday or one to be spent with close friends and which lasts thirteen days in all. It is not only an occasion for feasting but also for certain traditions and practices that have remained essentially unchanged for millennia. On the last Wednesday before the New Year, known as *chahârshambeh-ye suri*, for example, small bonfires are lit on streets and people, both old and young, jump over them to bring happiness in the coming year.

In every house, a special New Year's table is set, known as the *haft sin* table, or 'seven S's', seven symbolic objects beginning with the letter 'S'. In the centre are the *sabzi*, germinating seeds of wheat or lentils, symbols of renewal. Around these are placed garlic (*sir*), apples (*sib*), jujubes (*senjed*), vinegar (*serke*), a type of halva made from walnuts (*samanu*) and a gold coin (*sekeh*). A mirror, a Koran, bread, a goldfish, a bowl of water with leaves floating in it, coloured hard-boiled eggs and various sweets finish off the table around which the family sit to see in the New Year.

The twelve days that follow New Year's Day are traditionally spent visiting friends and acquaintances, with much eating and exchanging of presents. The thirteenth day after Noruz, known as *sizdah bedar* or 'thirteenth outside', is spent on a large family picnic. Custom has it that on this day the *sabzi*, the germinating seeds that had been kept in the house since New Year's Day, are thrown out to ward off evil. On this day, everyone leaves their houses in a massive exodus into the country and parks.

Isfahan Province

The province of Isfahan (pronounced Esfahân), is located almost in the centre of Iran between Tehran and Fârs. It is mainly a province of mountains and desert with an arid climate, but despite this, it has quite a large population, living mostly in the numerous oases that mark the old caravan routes. These routes linked not only the northwest and southeast of Iran, but crossed the mountain cols to the south, towards Shiraz and the ports on the Persian Gulf. For most tourists, the main destination in this province is the city of Isfahan itself but it would be a shame to miss some of the smaller towns, many of which are still very traditional, and which can easily be visited from Isfahan or on the way to one of the neighbouring provinces.

Kâshân

About 100 kilometres (62 miles) south of Qom on the secondary road to Isfahan, is the town of **Kâshân**, once one of the most prosperous oases in Iran. Known since Seljuq times for the quality of its ceramics (the Persian word *kâshi* for glazed tiles is derived from the name of the town), Kâshân was also, until the 18th century, an important centre for the manufacture of carpets, silk and other textiles. During the Safavid Dynasty, the town benefited greatly from the patronage of Shâh Abbâs I (1587–1629) who set out to embellish it further, notably by laying out a garden, the Bâgh-e Fin, and who even requested to be buried there. Given the grandiose construction projects that mark his reign, one might expect the **mausoleum of Shâh Abbâs** to be a sumptuous building, but it is in fact remarkably modest in size and appearance. It consists at present of a black tombstone, placed in the crypt of the *imâmzâdeh* Habib ibn Musâ, now a mosque. This mosque (on Zeyârat Habib Street, off Imâm Khomeini Avenue, just north of Khomeini Square) is currently being entirely rebuilt but the tomb is still visible in a corner.

In the centre of Kâshân are the mosque and the *madresseh* **Aghâ Bozorg** (turn right off Fâzel-e Narâqi Avenue, towards Kemâl ol-Mulk Square). The traditional plan of Iranian mosques has been adapted here and comprises only two large *eivân*, each flanked by two rows of arcades, one on the north side, by the entrance, and the other on the south side, in front of the *mehrab*. The courtyard, surrounded by single arcades, contains a second, sunken court in the centre which has been turned into a garden with trees and a fountain. The south *eivân* with its two minarets gives onto the *mehrab* chamber, which is covered with a brick dome (there is a good view from the entrance over the courtyard and this *eivân*). The decoration of the arcades and *eivân*, which is restricted to blue, red or yellow touches against a brick ground, is very simple but elegant.

Among the other mosques in Kâshân are the **Friday Mosque** (masjed-e Jomeh), built under the Seljuqs and restored several times since, and the Meidân-e Fays Mosque, built during the Timurid Dynasty (15th century). The bazaar, located between Bâbâ Afzal and Mohtasham avenues, is very interesting for the architecture of its old caravansarais, with their domed roofs and painted walls.

Another recommended visit is the **Borujerdi House** (khâneh-ye Borujerdihâ; the entrance is on a street right off Alavi Avenue, in the southern part of town; open mornings only). This is an old private house, now open to the public, and which retains a very original six-sided wind tower, pierced with window-like openings which create a draft for cooling the house.

A few kilometres southwest of Kâshân, in the small village of Fin, is one of Iran's most famous gardens, the **Bâgh-e Fin** (or Bâgh-e Shâh,the King's Garden), which was designed for Shâh Abbâs. The original Safavid buildings have now all been replaced by Qâjâr ones, but the layout of the trees, canals and marble basins is still very close to the original. It is difficult to find a more pleasant spot to relax in the shade after a long trip through the sand and heat of the desert.

The road that goes out to Bâgh-e Fin (Amir Kebir Street) passes by an important prehistoric site, **Tappeh-ye Sialk**, one of the first and most rewarding sites ever excavated in Iran. Sialk was occupied almost continuously from the fourth millennium BC until the eighth century BC; it has yielded, layer by layer, a hoard of cultural artefacts, particularly painted pottery, from which it has been possible to work out in remarkable detail the chronology of the cultural development of this part of the Iranian Plateau. The objects excavated are now in the Louvre Museum in Paris and the Archaeological Museum in Tehran. There are only a few very modest remains left to be seen today on the two badly eroded hills at Tappeh-ye Sialk, including the odd shard and the outline of a few houses.

On the other side of the road, about a kilometre in the direction of Kâshân, is the *imâmzâdeh* **Abu Lolo**, built during the Safavid Dynasty and recognizable by its pointed roof decorated with very fine turquoise and yellow tiles.

From Kâshân, the road to Isfahan goes to **Natanz** (80 kilometres or 50 miles from Kâshân), where one can visit the funerary complex of Abd al-Samad, also called the Friday Mosque. Abd al-Samad is thought to have been a disciple of the Sufi sheikh Abu Sa'id, who died in 1049. The building of the complex took several years. The oldest section is a mosque in the shape of an octagonal Seljuq pavilion which was turned into a four-*eivân* mosque between 1304 and 1309. The tomb itself is dated to 1307. It is a cruciform chamber with a pyramidal eight-sided roof, decorated outside with blue ceramics. Inside is a superb *muqarna* dome. Between 1316 and 1317, a

Mehrab of Sultan Uljaitu Khodâbendeh in the Friday Mosque, Isfahan

khânehqâh, or dervish monastery, was added to the southwest of the complex. Today, only its gateway still stands, richly decorated in blue ceramics.

From Natanz, it is possible to make a wide detour to the northeast along the Yazd road to pass through the villages of Ardestân and Nâin. Within a very short distance, one finds a remarkable concentration of some of the oldest mosques in the country, all of which have been spared destruction or rebuilding in later styles. These small and relatively simple buildings, completely devoid of colourful glazed tile decoration, will be of particular interest to the student of early Islamic architecture in Iran. Fifteen kilometres (9 miles) north of Ardestân is **Zavâreh**, a village which possesses the oldest dated mosque in Iran to have been built with four *eivân* around a central courtyard (the mosque was finished in 1136). It is this plan which became that most frequently used for Iranian mosques, replacing the older hypostyle mosque such as the one at Nâin (see below). The Zavâreh mosque is small and simple in structure. Its decoration is limited to a single Kufic inscription, even the *mehrab* is plain. Zavâreh has a second mosque, the masjed-e Pamonar, built during the Seljuq period (11th century). It is in a bad state of preservation and only very little of the original stucco decoration remains.

The Friday Mosque at **Ardestân** is another of the very earliest four-*eivân* mosques, but unlike Zavâreh it was built over an older hypostyle mosque. This small mosque is characterized by wide pillars and low vaults. The dome of the main *eivân* still bear traces of its very fine decoration, and the *mehrab* are covered in carved stucco. The remains of a Seljuq *madresseh* can be seen in the northwest corner.

The small town of **Nâin**, located at the crossroads to Yazd (162 kilometres, 101 miles), Isfahan (145 kilometres, 90 miles), and Tehran, was once famous for its carpets. The oldest sections of its Friday Mosque date from the Abbâssid period (tenth century); it is a hypostyle mosque, with a courtyard surrounded by porticos but with no *eivân*. The columns of the porticos are rather squat and set close together, but their rich stucco decoration, and that of the *mehrab*, hides a certain structural heaviness. This tenth-century stucco decoration at Nâin is still in exceptional condition and is renowned for the great variety of its geometric and floral motifs as well as the quality of its calligraphic inscriptions. The wooden *mimbar* to the right of the *mehrab* is 14th century.

At Nâin it is also possible to visit a private house of the Safavid period, built in a style once typical of town houses here but which has become only too rare today. The centre of the house is its rectangular courtyard, planted with trees and in which stands a water fountain. Around it, are two floors of vaulted chambers some of which (on the first floor) still bear the original painted decorations: panels with hunting scenes; miniature-style representations of garden parties with dancers and musicians; and star-shaped medallions of phoenixes and dragons. The latter are a good example of the way in which painting styles in Persia were modified after the Mongol invasion and the introduction of Chinese designs. The dragon and the phoenix are ancient motifs in China where they are frequently represented together, as they are here, with coiled bodies.

The City of Isfahan

Esfahân nesf-e jahân, 'Isfahan is half the world': this well-known saying was originally coined to describe Isfahan in Safavid times, when the city was at the height of its glory. Even today, Isfahan remains one of the Iran's most beautiful cities and its monuments can be ranked among the most splendid of the Islamic world. The atmosphere in town is a relaxed one: this is a place to wander in, to get to know slowly, with its gardens, its river side and its shopping streets. It is a town that contains a multitude of hidden treasures and a quick visit, even if it takes in the main monuments, will hardly do it justice. However, many Iranians do not share these feelings about Isfahan and will tell you that its inhabitants are mean and unpleasant people; best to see for yourself and make up your own mind.

The main monuments of Isfahan are essentially the work of one man, Shâh Abbâs the Great, who made the town his capital in 1598 and had it rebuilt according to a precise plan, with large avenues, magnificent gardens and a royal palace. Isfahan's history is considerably older than the Safavid Dynasty; some scholars have even identified it with the Achaemenian city of Gaba mentioned by Strabon. The remains of two Sassanian fire temples suggest that an important centre existed here at that time, a centre which may well have been the city of Djay. The earliest detailed information about Isfahan is from the beginning of the Islamic period. The town was then composed of two sections, one of which was the old city of Djay, called the *shahrestân*, that is the 'town' itself. Outside its walls was a Jewish colony, the Yahoudiyeh, founded, according to local tradition by Jews deported from Jerusalem by Nebuchadnezzar (it is, however, more likely that the Yahoudiyeh dates from Sassanian times).

From 935, Isfahan was governed by the Buyid Dynasty, and after that, at the beginning of the 11th century, by a local dynasty, the Kakuyids. The urban development which had begun under the Buyids continued under the Seljuqs, in particular during the reigns of Alp Arslan and Malik Shâh, when Isfahan briefly became the capital. It was at this period that work on the Friday Mosque began. In 1228, the town was captured by Genghis Khân's Mongol troops but seems not to have suffered. In 1338, however, at the time of Tamerlane's invasion, the inhabitants of the city rebelled rather than pay ransom money to the conqueror. As a result, the entire population was massacred.

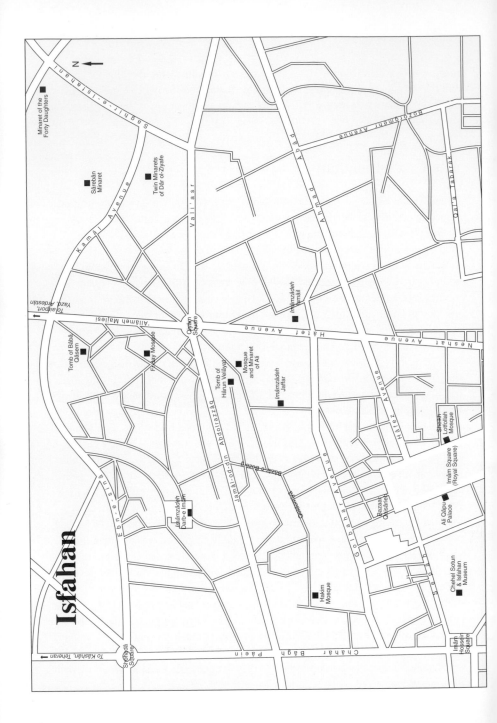

Isfahan

Minaret of the
Forty Daughters

Sārebān
Minaret

Twin Minarets
of Dār ol-Ziyafe

Sāghir-e-Isfahāni

Kamāl Avenue

Vali'asr

Abād

Ahmad

Bozorgmani Avenue

Qala Tabalak

N

Imāmzādeh
Ismāïl

To Ardport,
Yazd, Ardestān

'Allāmeh Majlesi

Qeyām
Square

Hatef Avenue

Neshat Avenue

Tomb of Bābā
Qāsem

Friday Mosque

Tomb of
Hārun Velāyat

Mosque
and Minaret
of Ali

Imāmzādeh
Jaffar

Hafez Avenue

Ebn-e-sinā

Abdolrazzāq

Jamāl-od-din

Bāzār Bozorg

Qeisāriyeh

Bāzār-e Bozorg

Imāmzādeh
Darb-e Imām

Bazaar
Oheisārieh

Golbahār Avenue

Sheikh
Lotfollah
Mosque

Imām Square
(Royal Square)

Ali Qāpu
Palace

Chehel Sotun
& Isfahan
Museum

To Kāshān, Teheran

Shohadā
Square

Chahār Bāgh Pāein

Hakim
Mosque

Imām
Hossein
Square

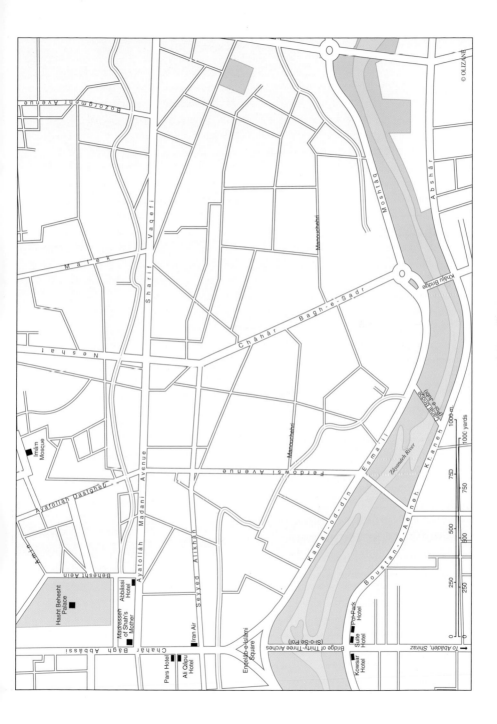

© OLIZANE

Bozorgmehr Avenue

Sharif Vaqefi

Malek

Neshat

Moshtāq

Abshār

Manouchehri

Khaju Bridge

Chāhār Bāgh-e-Sadr

Imam Mosque

Ayatollah Dastgheib

Madani Avenue

Ferdowsi Avenue

Manouchehri

Kamal-od-din

Esmaîl

Zāyandeh River

Khaneh

Aein e Ahmad Bridge

1000 m.

1000 yards

750

750

500

500

Beheshti Aein

Ahmad

Hasht Behesht Palace

Madrasseh of Shah's Mother

Abbássi Hotel

Seyyed Alikhán

Boustan-e-Aeineh

250

250

Chāhār Bāgh Abbássi

Pars Hotel

Ali Qápu Hotel

Iran Air

Engeláb-e-Islami Square

Bridge of Thirty-Three Arches (Si-o-Se Pol)

Suite Hotel

Pol-Park Hotel

To Abdadeh, Shiraz

Kowsar Hotel

0

0

The transfer of the Safavid capital to Isfahan by Shâh Abbâs in 1598 marks the beginning of the city's most glorious period. The decision to move the capital was a strategic one, prompted by fear for the safety of the old capitals, Tabriz and Qazvin, which were considered too close to the Ottoman Empire. Shâh Ismâil (1501-1524) had already begun work on several gardens and palaces in Isfahan, but it was during Shâh Abbâs' reign that the city finally took the form that it still partly visible today, centred around the Royal Square and Chahâr Bâgh Avenue. Concerned about developing trade in his new capital, Shâh Abbâs ordered the deportation of entire Armenian families from Jolfa, in Azerbaijân, to the southern suburbs of Isfahan. Due to the presence at the Safavid court of a large number of foreigners—English and Dutch merchants from the East India Companies, European artists, and diplomats hoping to secure alliances against the common Ottoman enemy—Isfahan was opened up to the outside world, and became one of the most glorious cities of its time.

This splendour and magnificence lasted only just over a century. Isfahan was ruined by the Afghan invasion at the beginning of the 18th century and by Nâder Shah's decision to transfer the capital to Mashhad in 1736, a move which relegated the city to the role of a provincial town. During the 18th and 19th centuries, Isfahan had a half-abandoned look to it; when the French writer Pierre Loti visited it at the beginning of this century, he wrote : 'Approaching, one is struck by the sad state of these buildings that promised such splendor from afar! ... Where they are exposed to the winter winds, the domes and minarets, all but stripped of their long-patient mosaics, seem eaten away by a grey leprosy.'

Isfahan's main monuments are centred around the following areas: the Royal Square and Chahâr Bâgh Avenue, the Friday Mosque, and on the other bank of the river, Jolfâ. Most of the buildings are from the Safavid period, although a few monuments from the Seljuq Dynasty (the Friday Mosque, the Sareban and Forty Daughters minarets, the Shahrestan Bridge) and the Mongol Dynasty (the tomb of Bâbâ Qâsim, imâmzâdeh Jaffar) still remain.

NORTH OF THE BAZAAR: THE PRE-SAFAVID MONUMENTS

Just north of Qiyam Square, on Allâmeh Majlesi Avenue, is the Friday Mosque (masjed-e Jomeh), one of the most venerable and magnificent of all the buildings in Isfahan. Compared to the great Safavid mosques, this one is very sobre: its dome is of undecorated brick, and the vaulted halls around the central courtyard have also been left plain. But it is this austerity which is part of its beauty and which allows one to appreciate all the more the elegance and finesse of the tilework decoration of the courtyard and eivân.

From an architectural point of view, the mosque is extremely complex, both because of its size (it has 476 separate domes), and because of the number of different periods of construction it has known. Excavations carried out in 1977 have brought to light the remains of a very early mosque at this site which dates back to the eighth century (according to the Arab historian Abu Nu'âim the mosque was founded in 771–772). Rebuilt around 841, it was, in the tenth century, a hypostyle mosque with porticos surrounding the central courtyard. Inscriptions dated to the 11th and early 12th centuries, and which correspond to the oldest sections of the present mosque, have shed some light on the various changes which occurred during the Seljuq period. A large dome was first built in front of the *mehrab* by the vizier Nizâm al-Mulk between 1072 and 1092 (the same dome in place today), and a second one, known as the Gonbad-e Khaki, was added in 1088 at the northern end of the complex, opposite the *mehrab*, by Taj al-Mulk, Nizâm's sworn enemy. It is often said that the Gonbad-e Khaki was built by Taj al-Mulk in an attempt to outdo Nizâm's construction, but its exact function remains unclear (it has been suggested that it was a ceremonial chamber of some sort or an observatory).

An inscription on a door in the northeast façade mentions the reconstruction of the mosque after a fire in 1121 which spared only the few sections described above. The complex that one visits today is therefore in large part a mosaic from different periods, the result of all the renovations and modifications carried out since the fire: a 14th century *mehrab*; a winter hall which is probably Timurid; minarets built by the 'Black Sheep'; and interior decoration of the Safavid period.

The **entrance** to the mosque is through the southeast door which gives out onto one of the streets of the bazaar (the position of the Gonbad-e Khaki in the north of the mosque prevents one from entering from that direction although it would be more usual to do so). This door, of Seljuq date, is very simply decorated with turquoise tilework. A corridor leads directly to the central courtyard; on the right, is an entrance to a *madresseh*.

The courtyard is a classical one with four *eivân* and a marble fountain in the centre. The façades of double arcades which join the *eivân* are entirely decorated with mosaic tilework, mostly from the 15th century. The **south** *eivân*, flanked by two minarets, is the most richly decorated, the blue and turquoise shades which dominate the exterior contrasting with the ochres on the inside of the dome. The latter is an exquisite piece of work for the harmony of its colours and forms: the entire surface of the ceiling is covered in large cells (the stalactites used by the Safavids had not yet been developed at this period) decorated with very simple, dotted geometric motifs. Although this ceiling is Timurid (15th century) the inscriptions on the outside, as well as the white and blue tiles of the arch, are somewhat later (16th and 17th centuries).

Behind the *eivân* is the **mehrab hall** built under Malek Shâh by Nizâm al-Mulk, one of the few sections of the old mosque to have survived the fire in 1121. This

The Friday Mosque

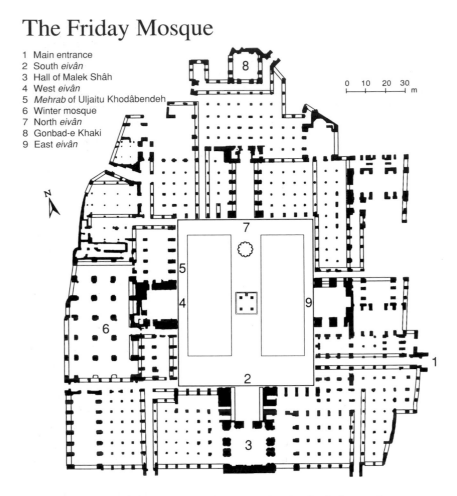

1 Main entrance
2 South *eivân*
3 Hall of Malek Shâh
4 West *eivân*
5 *Mehrab* of Uljaitu Khodâbendeh
6 Winter mosque
7 North *eivân*
8 Gonbad-e Khaki
9 East *eivân*

0   10   20   30
└────┴────┴────┴──┤ m

huge chamber, beautifully proportioned, is covered with a brick dome. The inscription at the base of the dome dates to the 11th century. The *mehrab* is not original but was added in the 16th or 17th century.

The **north** *eivân*, built during the Seljuq period, has seen very little change since Safavid times and is characterized by its rather discreet decoration. It leads on to the **Gonbad-e Khaki**, the domed chamber built by Taj al-Mulk in 1088. Despite its small size (10 metres [33 feet] wide and 20 metres [66 feet] high) and its sobriety, this room is nevertheless one of the most perfect and most elegant examples of the transition from a square plan to a circular one in Persian architecture. The solution chosen here was to use a succession of arches ever decreasing in size, ending up with a circle of sixteen arches on which the dome is set. There is no tilework decoration and the star patterns inside the dome are created by the brick alone.

The **west** *eivân*, recognizable by the small tower at its top and which is used for calling the faithful to prayer, is also a Seljuq construction. It was largely redecorated during the Safavid period but the *eivân* has retained the original shape of the stalactites. To the right of the *eivân* are the **mehrab chamber of sultan Uljaitu Khodâbendeh** and the winter mosque (these rooms are usually kept locked; ask one of the guardians to open them for you). This famous *mehrab*, built in 1310 and remarkably well preserved, was made for the Mongol sultan Uljaitu Khodâbendeh, whose tomb is at Soltânieh. The floral motifs and the exquisite calligraphy in carved stucco of the *mehrab* are unusually fine. The inlaid *mimbar* (14th century) to the right of the *mehrab* is another work of great quality.

A door at the back leads to the **winter mosque**, a large bare low-ceilinged room with intersecting arches that run down from the ceiling to the floor as thick pillars. The lighting, which today is artificial, used to be limited to the glow that filtered through the translucid alabaster windows in the ceiling. This winter hall is thought to have been built during the transformations carried out around 1447.

Mention must also be made of the remarkable **vaulted rooms** all around the central courtyard which are built entirely of brick and date from the 12th–14th centuries. Here again, there is no decoration other than that of the brick itself, but the result is never monotonous, and it is said that no two vaults in the entire mosque have exactly the same design.

Just to the north of the mosque is the **tomb of Bâbâ Qâsim** (ârâmgâh-e Bâbâ Qâsim), built in memory of a Persian theologian by one of his students, in 1340. Restored in the 17th century, it has an attractive stalactite gateway decorated in blue and white tiles. Next to the mausoleum stands the *madresseh-ye* Emâmi, also built in honour of Bâbâ Qâsim. Here again, the use of glazed tiles is relatively limited and the colour of the natural brick plays an important role in the decoration.

To the west of the Friday Mosque is the *imâmzâdeh* **Darb-e Emâm**. This monument, finished in 1453, was built over the tombs of two descendants of Imams, Ibrahim Batha and Zain al-Abedin. It is unusual in having two domes, but its fame is mainly due to the quality of the tilework on the main *eivân*, considered a worthy rival of the Blue Mosque in Tabriz. The tilework on the exterior of the domes, also very fine, is later than that of the *eivân*. The dome over the main chamber was restored during the reign of Shâh Abbâs (1642–1666) and the one over the *eivân* was added as part of modifications carried out (1670–1671) during the reign of Shâh Suleiman.

Several old minarets still remain in the quarters between Vali-e Asr and Sorush avenues. The first, the **twin minarets** of Dâr ol-Ziyafe, were once part of the entrance gate to a Mongol *madresseh*. They are to be found just south of Kamâl Avenue. Slightly further north is the **Sârebân Minaret** (menâr-e Sârebân), or Minaret of the Camel Driver, perhaps the most beautiful of all Isfahan's surviving minarets with its decor in natural brick and its glazed stalactite cornices. It was built towards the end of the 12th century during the Seljuq period. The mosque to which it was originally attached has now disappeared. The **Minaret of the Forty Daughters** (menâr-e Chehel Dokhtarân) on Sorush Avenue is of the same period (1108) but is squatter and less slender than the former one. It has one unusual feature, a window set two-thirds of the way up which looks south, the direction of Mecca.

THE SAFAVID ROYAL CITY

The centre of Isfahan during the Seljuq period was the Friday Mosque and the *meidan-e* Kuhneh, to the north of the present Royal Square. In 1598, Shâh Abbâs decided to shift this centre—according to some, in order to annoy a rich merchant who was reluctant to part with his property—and turned to the Naqsh-e Jahân (Image of the World), a vast palatial park designed by Shâh Tahmâsp (1524–1576). The palace in the park was enlarged to become the Ali Qâpu Palace, and additional buildings were erected in other areas of the park. Between 1589 and 1606, work began on the square itself and on the buildings around it, as well as on a large avenue called Chahâr Bâgh which was to link the square to the river. The Allâhverdi Khân Bridge at the end of this avenue also dates to this period. Work was interrupted for a few years and only started again in 1612 with the construction of the Imam Mosque. At this time, the finishing touches were added to the other monuments around the Royal Square. Today, a large part of the gardens, pavilions and palaces from this early Safavid period have disappeared, in particular along the banks of the Zâyandeh-rud.

THE ROYAL SQUARE (MEIDAN-E IMAM, EX-MEIDAN-E SHÂH)

The **Royal Square** of Isfahan was the symbolic centre of the Safavid Dynasty and of its empire. Usually filled with a crowd of street-sellers and entertainers, the square was also used for a variety of celebrations and festivals, for polo matches—the stone goal posts are still visible at either end of the square—and for public executions. The Shâh and his court watched the festivities from the balcony of the Ali Qâpu Palace.

The square is surrounded on all four sides by long walls with double arcades, interrupted at intervals by the main monuments: the Imam Mosque (ex-Shah's Mosque) in the south, the Mosque of Sheikh Lotfollah in the west, the Ali Qâpu Palace in the east, and the entrance to the Great Bazaar in the north. The centre of the Square has been laid out with fountains and water basins and recently planted with trees. It is a very popular spot on summer evenings when the Isfahanis settle down on carpets on the lawn and bring out their picnics and samovars. The shops under the arcades sell a variety of tourist souvenirs, textiles and handicrafts (compare prices and quality from shop to shop before buying and bargain hard).

At the end of the Royal Square is the huge gateway to the **Imam Mosque** (ex-masjed-e Shâh, the King's Mosque), flanked by two turquoise minarets. Behind it and slightly to the right are the main *eivân* and the dome of the prayer hall. The construction of the mosque, commissioned by Shâh Abbâs, began in 1611 but the work was probably still unfinished at the time of the ruler's death in 1628. This monument is the largest of those attributed to Shâh Abbâs, and he considered it his masterpiece. In his impatience to see it finished, he attempted to hurry up the work by adopting a new method of glazed tilework decoration, known as *haft rangi* (see page 77). As a result, some sections of the mosque are decorated with the older technique of tile mosaics and others with polychrome painted tiles.

The **gateway** to the mosque has a mainly ornamental role and serves to balance the entrance gate to the bazaar at the other end of the square. Finished in 1616, this is one of the largest *pishtaq* in Iran (about 27 metres [89 feet] high). It is also one of the most richly decorated with its triple-twisted columns around the arch and its half-dome covered on the inside with a cascade of stalactites. These stalactites are repeated in the niches to each side of the entrance. The large inscription around the arch is the work of the great Safavid calligrapher from Tabriz, Ali Rezâ Abbâssi, who joined the entourage of Shâh Abbâs around 1593. He quickly became one of the best-known court calligraphers and his work can be seen on all Shâh Abbâs' great monuments in Isfahan and Mashhad. His style is characterized by great clarity and a sharp sense of proportion and was often imitated by later artists. Some scholars have even attributed to him the technique used here of writing a text on two superimposed lines, a technique frequently used for the decoration of mosques and tombs during the Safavid period.

One of the peculiarities of this mosque is that it is not built on the same axis as the gateway which gives onto the square. Because of the necessity of orienting the *mehrab* towards the southeast and Mecca, and of keeping the *pishtaq* aligned with the walls of the square, there is a 45° angle between the gate and the north *eivân*. Instead of being rectangular, the back of the north *eivân* is triangular. One of the sides of the triangle gives onto the domed vestibule which one enters on passing through the gate. From here, the visitor has a first glimpse of the central courtyard, although the way in is deliberately blocked by a bench. To gain entrance, go round the *eivân*, either on the right or the left, along an angled corridor.

As soon as one enters the **central court**, attention is drawn by the south façade and its *eivân*, minarets and the dome of the prayer hall. The outer wall of the *eivân* is decorated with white and gold arabesques set on a blue ground, while the minarets are predominantly turquoise. The dome which rises up behind retains this turquoise

188

colour in its very regular design of thin white and yellow scrolls. The outside of the dome rises to a height of 52 metres (171 feet), but the ceiling inside is only 38 metres (125 feet) tall, a discrepancy produced by the use of a double shell. This construction technique allows the architect to design a dome of entirely different shapes outside and in. Here, the outer dome is onion-shaped while the inner one is squat, with proportions better adapted to the limited space of the prayer hall. Unlike the dome of the Mosque of Sheikh Lotfollah, where both shells are built parallel to one another and begin at the same level, here the shells start at different heights; thus the windows which, on the outside, are set in the drum, are to be found in the curve of the dome itself on the inside.

The Imam Mosque

1 Gateway
2 North *eivân*
3 South *eivân*
4 *Mehrab* Hall
5 *Madresseh*

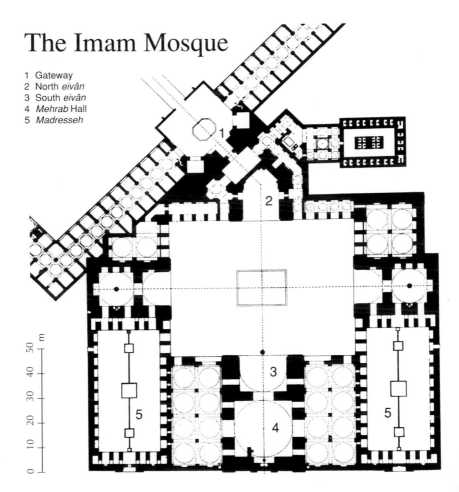

The decoration inside the dome is remarkably elegant and repeats the same blue, white and gold shades seen outside. The *mehrab* and the *mimbar* are both made of marble. On either side of the prayer hall is a rectangular room with two bays of wide vaults set on stone pillars. Except for the pillars, the entire surface of the vaults and the walls is covered in glazed designs. The floral motifs at the centre of each vault echo the design inside the dome.

The east and west walls of the central court are strictly symmetrical, with a small prayer hall behind each *eivân*, and three arcades to either side of it, one of which opens onto a *madresseh*. These *madresseh* are composed of a central rectangular court surrounded by rooms for the students. As in the main courtyard, the entire surface of the walls is decorated with glazed tiles; the motifs in the southeast court, in cobalt blue and bright yellow, are particularly fine.

Despite its more modest size, the **Mosque of Sheikh Lotfollah**, on the eastern side of the Royal Square, is nonetheless a worthy rival of the Imam Mosque. Probably begun by Shâh Abbâs in 1602, it was finished in 1619 and was named after a famous theologian of the period. Its dome is a masterpiece of Persian tilework with its extremely fine arabesques and harmonious shades of colour: the dome is decorated with blue and black flowers with white scrolls set against a creamy-coloured ground, while the drum is predominantly blue. The entrance gate is a rich mosaic of blue and yellow floral motifs with a particularly fine stalactite vault.

From the square, one notices that the dome is not aligned with the entrance gate. Unlike the Imam Mosque, the reason for this here is not linked to the orientation of the *mehrab* towards Mecca (this mosque has no courtyard so that the problem of orientation does not arise). Instead, it should be understood as an attempt to create an impression of increased volume to compensate for the small size of the building.

The asymmetry of the gate is not the only architectural peculiarity here. There is no four-*eivân* courtyard nor any minarets, only a single domed prayer room which is entered along a narrow corridor. At the end of this dark passageway is a sharp turn, and one emerges suddenly into a sumptuously decorated chamber so rich that some visitors experience a sensation of claustrophobia. The large panels of floral scrolls on the walls are surrounded by inscriptions by Ali Rezâ Abbâssi, the famous calligrapher of the reign of Shâh Abbâs.

The transition from a square plan to a circular one in this room is one of the simplest but also the most successful that exists: the four corner squinches extend to the ground and alternate with four blind arches of the same size to form a regular octagon. Small faceted pendentives, each corresponding to one of the windows in the drum, form the transition to a sixteen-sided polygon.

Opposite the Mosque of Sheikh Lotfallah is the **Ali Qâpu Palace** (emârat-e Ali Qâpu) or High Gate. Originally a small Timurid palace, it was enlarged by Shâh

Abbâs to become the monumental entrance to the palatial complex located in the huge park which extended as far as Chahâr Bâgh Avenue. It served also as a reception pavilion for foreign dignitaries and embassies and is said to have been one of Shâh Abbâs' favourite residences. The *talâr* on the first floor which overlooks the square served in summer as a throne room from where the ruler could watch the polo matches below or review the troops (there is a good view from there over the square and the town).

The Ali Qâpu Palace has six floors which are reached via a series of small twisting staircases and low doors. The rooms are empty today but the walls and ceilings still bear their original fresco and glazed tile decoration. The painted wooden ceilings of the *talâr* and *eivân* are particularly fine. It would be impossible to give a detailed description here of the incredible variety of motifs in these rooms, but it is well worth taking a little time to discover them. Be sure to go as far as the top floor, to the music room, for the fretwork panelling on the walls and vaults cut into vase-shaped niches which would originally have held porcelain vessels. The decoration on the inside of the dome in this room is also extremely fine.

THE BAZAAR AND OLD QUARTERS TO THE NORTH OF THE ROYAL SQUARE

On the north side of the Royal Square is the **Bazaar Qaisârieh** or Imperial Bazaar (also known as the Great Bazaar, bazar-e Bozorg), a veritable labyrinth of domed streets which stretches into the old town. The gateway to the bazaar, built in the reign of Shâh Abbâs, is decorated with tilework mosaic; its main motif represents Sagittarius, the town's astrological sign, shown here as a chimera, half-man and half-tiger. It was just to the west of this area that the trading posts of the English and Dutch East India Companies were located in the second half of the 17th century.

Inside the bazaar, past Golbahar Street, is the **Hakim Mosque**, founded in the 12th century and rebuilt in 1654. According to local tradition, the royal physician, Hakim Dâoud, was forced to flee the country after a quarrel with his ruler. The latter pleaded for him to return but Hakim Dâoud would agree only on the condition that a mosque be built and named after him (another, more credible version of the story states that the mosque was built with the money that the physician sent back to his family from India). The decoration of this four-*eivân* mosque, although modest, has been carefully executed. The upper row of arcades around the courtyard was never finished.

Further east in the bazaar, near Hâruniyeh Street, stands the *imâmzâdeh* Jaffar. This small octagonal tower built in 1325 during the Mongol period is one in a series of tombs of Jaffar, a Companion of the Prophet. Its fine blue and white tilework mosaic was restored in the 1950s.

Further north towards Jamal ol-din Abdolrazâq Avenue is the **Mosque of Ali**, whose **minaret** (menâr-e masjed-e Ali) is said to be the oldest in Isfahan, built between 1131 and 1155. Now restored, it is 50 metres (164 feet) tall and has a plain brick decoration. The present mosque is later than the minaret and dates back to 1521.

Nearby is the **tomb of Harun Velâyat** (boqe-ye Harun Velâyat). Nothing at all is known about the person for whom this tomb was built in 1513, during Shâh Ismâil's reign. The gateway which leads to the courtyard is one of the finest examples of early Safavid tilework, with delicate scrolls and rich complex designs.

Just to the east of Hâtef Avenue, which joins Qiyâm Square and Neshât Avenue, is the *imâmzâdeh* Ismâil, started in the reign of Shâh Abbâs and finished in 1634. The entrance to the *imâmzâdeh* is through a superb domed brick hall, now occupied by shops.

CHAHÂR BÂGH AVENUE

Chahâr Bâgh Avenue once led from the Safavid city to the royal gardens at Hezâr Jerib and Jolfâ on the other bank of the Zâyandeh River. Shâh Abbâs chose not to connect the avenue directly with the Royal Square, and it therefore began slightly to the west of the palatial complex. It was planted with trees, and a canal ran down the centre of it in a series of little waterfalls. It was a favourite promenade of the people of Isfahan, and still is today: Chahâr Bâgh has become one of the main shopping streets of the city with tea rooms, cinemas and fashionable clothes shops.

The main monuments around Chahâr Bâgh were built in the reigns of Shâh Abbâs' successors and are equally great works of art as the constructions of that great ruler. Unfortunately, all too often, the only remains we have today of the innumerable houses, palaces and pavilions of Safavid Isfahan are the descriptions left by 17th- and 18th-century travellers. Among the few buildings still standing is the **Chehel Sotun** (or Forty Columns), set in the old royal park between the Ali Qâpu Palace and Chahâr Bâgh Avenue (the entrance is on Sepah Avenue). Used for official ceremonies and particularly for receiving foreign embassies, the palace was finished in 1647 during the reign of Shâh Abbâs II; it was later largely rebuilt after a fire in 1706. The palace opens out onto a *talâr* with tall, narrow wooden columns set on carved stone bases. The name of the palace—which in reality has only twenty columns—is an allusion to their reflection in the water of the large pool in front of the *talâr*. One of the characteristic features of Safavid palatial architecture is the integration of buildings into a natural environment such as a park or a garden. Here, water plays a very important role in the spatial relationship between inside and out. In addition to the large ornamental pool at the Chehel Sotun, the architects laid out fountains in front of the throne and on the terrace, as well as canals linking the pools in the garden.

The *talâr* is covered with a flat wooden roof, whose ceiling and eaves are painted with very fine motifs, while the walls of the *eivân* are decorated with floral frescoes. Originally, the entire exterior façade was covered in stalactites set with mirrors, but these now remain only in the *eivân* which gives onto the *talâr*, where the throne was placed.

This throne room leads into the great audience hall with its three domes and which now houses the **Isfahan Museum** (at present only one of the halls of the building is open to the public). Here again, the ceiling is painted with sumptuous designs in blues, reds and golds. The six large historical murals on the upper part of the walls represent Safavid court life or military exploits of Safavid rulers; they are painted in a style which reflects a certain European influence. The battle scenes above the entrance have been identified as the campaigns of Shâh Ismâil I (1501–1524) against the Uzbeks, and those of Nâder Shâh in India (1739–1740); next to them is a reception held by Shâh Abbâs II (1642–1666) in honour of a king of Turkestan. On the opposite wall is a scene of a sumptuous banquet given by Shâh Abbâs I (1587–1629), and a representation of a battle between Shâh Ismâil and the Ottoman Janissaries of Sultan Suleiman; last of all is a painting showing Shâh Tahmâsp (1524–1576) receiving the Indian prince Humayun.

Beneath these great scenes are smaller paintings, closer in style and subject matter to Persian miniatures. Covered in plaster during the Qâjâr period, they have recently been carefully restored. All around the room are a series of exhibits, mostly Safavid objects from the 17th and 18th centuries, including carpets, armour, porcelain and coins (the dates given in the cases are those of the Islamic calendar).

Just south of Imam Hossein Square is Park Shahid Rajâi (ex-Bâgh-e Bolbol) and the small **Hasht Behesht Palace** (Palace of the Eight Paradises). Built in 1699 by Shâh Suleiman, this pleasure pavilion was later renovated by the Qâjâr ruler Fath Ali Shâh around 1880, and again under the Pahlavis. It is a more or less octagonal building with a large central domed hall which gives onto a series of small chambers. The paintings on the walls, and the stalactite ceiling decorated with small mirrors, are particularly interesting.

Just past the park, at the corner of Chahâr Bâgh Avenue and Shâhid Ayatollah Madani Street, is the *madresseh* **of the Shah's Mother** (once the madresseh-ye Madar-e Shâh, now known as madresseh-ye Chahâr Bâgh), built between 1706 and 1714 during the reign of the last Safavid ruler, Shâh Soltan Hussein. It is an enormous complex which includes, in addition to the *madresseh* itself, a caravansarai (khân-e Madar-e Shâh) of the same date, now turned into a luxury hotel. Today the *madresseh* functions as a theology school and visits are therefore limited to the entrance hall.

The entrance gate of the *madresseh*, on Chahâr Bâgh Avenue, stands out sharply from the rather austere arcaded façade of the building. The gate, which has a richly decorated stalactite vault, has wooden doors covered in partly-gilded silver sheets decorated with floral motifs and inscriptions. Once past the gate, one enters a domed vestibule with a superb design of polished bricks and blue and white tiles.

Unlike the courtyards of the mosques which are large, empty areas, the central courtyard here resembles a garden with its tall plane trees and central canal-fed marble basin. Doors at each corner of the courtyard lead to smaller yards. All around are the rooms of the students, set on two floors, each one opening out onto a vaulted niche, sparingly decorated with black and blue lines. The outer surface of the walls around the court is covered in glazed tiles.

The north and east *eivân* of the court, decorated with scrolls and inscriptions, serve as classrooms. As is the case in mosques, the south *eivân* is the most ornate. It is flanked by two quite short minarets, very richly decorated, particularly on the balcony and stalactite cornices. Behind the *eivân* is the domed prayer hall. From the exterior, the dome is reminiscent of the dome on the Imam Mosque in the Royal Square, with a calligraphic inscription around the drum, broken at intervals by the windows, and a floral design on the dome itself. This elegant decoration has been executed with a skill hardly equalled in any other building in the city, and there is no sign here of decadence, despite the late date of its construction. The inside of the dome is covered with a very rich design of arabesques. Next to the *mehrab* is a very fine *mimbar* carved out of a single block of marble.

The income from the caravansarai next to the *madresseh* was intended to pay for the upkeep of the theological college. Built along classical lines with rooms giving out onto the central courtyard, the caravansarai was turned into a luxury hotel (Hotel Abbâssi, ex-Hotel Shâh Abbâs) under the last shâh. Even if you are not staying there, the garden is a very pleasant, quiet place for afternoon tea. In the street behind the caravansarai is the Honar Bazaar (bazar-e Boland).

THE ZÂYANDEH-RUD AND ISFAHAN'S BRIDGES

The bridges over the Zâyandeh-rud, the river that separates Isfahan from its southern suburbs, include some of the most important constructions in the city. The oldest bridge is the **pol-e Shahrestân**, which was probably built in the 12th century during the Seljuq period. Until recently, it was still located

Chahar Bagh School, Isfahan

outside the town limits. This ten-arch bridge of stone and brick is the simplest of the old bridges and was originally defended on one side by a tower.

Further upstream is the **pol-e Khâju**, perhaps the most famous of Isfahan's bridges, and which has the unusual feature of serving as a sluice gate. In this desert climate, ensuring a sufficient and constant supply of water is of vital importance to the survival of a settlement. The problem was solved in various ways in Iran over the centuries, most notably by building the famous *qanât*. In Isfahan this sluice gate was devised to allow the accumulation, in times of changes in the level of the river, of reservoirs of water. The gates are set in the water channels which run between the pillars of the bridge.

The pol-e Khâju was built by Shâh Abbâs II in 1650 on the site of an older bridge. It has 24 arches and is 132 metres (433 feet) long. The monotony of the arches is lightened by the presence of semi-octagonal pavilions on each side of the bridge. With its two storeys of arcades and its stone steps over which the water flows, the pol-e Khâju is certainly one of the most picturesque spots in the city.

The next bridge is the **pol-e Jubi**, or Canal Bridge, 147 metres (482 feet) in length and formed of twenty-one arches, which was originally an aqueduct (now covered over) which supplied the gardens on the north bank of the river.

Slightly further upstream, at the end of Chahâr Bâgh Avenue and Enqelab-e Eslâm Square, is the Allâhverdi Khân Bridge, named after one of Shâh Abbâs' generals who was responsible for its construction. It is more commonly known as **Si-o-Se pol**, or Bridge of Thirty-Three Arches. Built around 1600 during the reign of Shâh Abbâs I, it linked Isfahan with the Armenian suburb of Jolfâ. At 295 metres (968 feet) long it is by far the longest bridge in town. It has two levels of arcades and resembles the pol-e Khâju without being as architecturally complex. The small *châikhâneh* (tea house) under the bridge on the south is a fun place to have tea or an ice cream, or to smoke a *qaliân*.

The last of the old bridges is the **pol-e Mârnân** in the far west of town. It was partly destroyed by floods a few years ago and has been rebuilt recently.

ON THE SOUTH BANK: JOLFÂ

Jolfâ, the Armenian and Christian quarter of Isfahan, was established in 1603 on the south bank of the Zâyandeh and was linked to the Muslim town by Si-o-Se pol. As all the caravans that arrived from Shiraz and the south of the country passed through Jolfâ on their way to the Royal Square, it rapidly became a flourishing trading quarter. Shâh Abbâs had been counting on this prosperity when, despite strong opposition on their part, he imported entire Armenian families from the town of Jolfâ on the Araxes River in Azerbaijân. During Shâh Abbâs' reign, Jolfâ was given complete religious freedom as well as a certain administrative autonomy, and was, for example, permitted to name an Armenian mayor. A cathedral, churches and even a convent were built and the Armenian community soon numbered some 30,000—and almost twice that figure according to some estimates. The first 100 years following the founding of the town were its most prosperous, and visiting European travellers have left us descriptions of luxurious houses whose beauty rivalled the Safavid palaces on the other bank of the river. Christian missionaries also settled at Jolfâ, first the Portuguese and then, from 1653, the Jesuits. But during the reigns of Shâh Abbâs' successors, life became more difficult for the Armenian community because of heavy taxation and, during Shâh Soltan Hussein's reign (1694–1722), persecutions and confiscations of property and belongings.

Today, Jolfâ is a rather quiet suburb, with none of the great bustle of activity which it once knew. Because of modern urban development and extensive reconstructions, it has lost much of its earlier character. To appreciate the importance of the Armenian community and what it has represented since its arrival in Isfahan at the beginning of the 17th century, a visit the **Cathedral of the Holy Saviour** (kelisâye Vânk) is recommended.

The entrance to the cathedral, indicated by a tilework plaque showing the cathedral and inscribed in Armenian, is in a small side street (Kelisa Street) off Nazar-e Sharqi Avenue. In the inside courtyard, on the right, stands the belfry, a sort of square tower open on all sides. The cathedral itself is domed in the same manner as the mosques. Its outer walls, which are covered in protective bricks, have a very modern appearance. However, some of the original paintings, now badly damaged, can still be seen near the door.

Work on the cathedral began in 1606 but very soon it became obvious that the building would be too small for the needs of the rapidly-expanding Christian community, and it was rebuilt in 1655. If you have just visited one of Isfahan's mosques, the contrast upon entering this cathedral will be striking: there is none of the brightness and tranquillity of the mosque with its vivid colours and purely geometric or floral designs. Here, the interior space is very restricted, despite the height of the dome, and dark. Around the base of the walls is a wide band of glazed tiles. Above this, the walls are covered in paintings of European inspiration, blackened by candle smoke, representing endlessly repeated scenes of martyrdom, notably that of Saint Gregory. These paintings, as well as the scene of the Last Judgement above the entrance door, were given to the cathedral by an Armenian merchant named Avadich who is said to have had great difficulty in getting them accepted by the rest of the community. The interior of the dome, on the other hand, is painted in Persian style with very elegant blue and gold designs.

A **museum** of Armenian culture has been set up in a building next to the cathedral. It contains a variety of objects related to the Armenian community in Isfahan, including Safavid costumes, embroidery, tapestries, European paintings brought back by Armenian merchants and a remarkable collection of illuminated manuscripts dating mainly from the 12th to the 17th centuries. Just outside the museum are several carved stones representing scenes from the Bible.

A second Christian church, the **Church of Bethlehem** (kelisâ-ye Bethlehem), is on Nazar-e Sharqi Avenue, near the junction with Haft-e Tir Avenue. It dates back to the 17th century and contains paintings of little artistic value, including a martyrdom of Saint Gregory.

EXCURSIONS AROUND ISFAHAN

On Azâdegân Avenue, which forms part of the ring road around the south of the city (just before Basij-e Mostazafin Square, is the **tomb of Bâbâ Rokn od-Din** (ârâmgâh-e Bâbâ Rokn od-Din). This mausoleum, with its rather original ten-sided conical roof and drum, was built in 1629 by Shâh Abbâs to commemorate a theologian who died in the 14th century. Unfortunately a large part of the tilework, both inside and outside, has now disappeared.

In the western suburbs of Isfahan, on the main road out to Najaf Abâd and Hamedân, are the famous **Shaking Minarets** (menâr-e Jonbân) which belong to a small 14th-century Mongol mosque. As their name suggests, these minarets have the unusual feature of moving from side to side when shaken vigorously: as soon as one of them shifts, the movement is transmitted to its twin. Several theories have been put forward to explain this phenomenon but none are completely satisfactory. Although the minarets themselves date to the 18th century and have little artistic value, the *eivân* (1317) beneath them is more interesting and contains the tomb of a Sufi sheikh who died in 1338.

A few kilometres further on along the same road one can see the remains of a **Zoroastrian fire temple** (*ateshgâh*) of the Sassanian Dynasty on top of a hill to the right of the road. The climb up to the ruins from the road is quite steep and requires good shoes.

Fârs Province

The province of Fârs, in southwestern Iran near the Persian Gulf, has played such a major role in the country's ancient history that it is considered the centre of Iranian identity. It is this province that gave its name to the Persian language spoken today, Fârsi.

In the first millennium BC, when the Persian Indo-European tribes arrived in Iran after a long migration from the Caucasus, they settled in the Bakhtiari Mountains, to the northeast of present-day Fârs, in a region then known as Parsumash. King Teispes (675–640 BC) of Parsumash annexed the kingdoms of Parsa and Anshân, which correspond roughly to the modern province of Fârs. The city of Anshân, about 40 kilometres (25 miles) north of Shiraz, had been one of the capitals of the Elamite Empire, along with Susa. Anshân became the seat of one of the two branches of the Achaemenian royal family, founded by Cyrus I, and it was from there that Cyrus II (559–530 BC) set out on his conquest of the Median and Assyrian empires. Later, the Achaemenian rulers were to establish their capitals in newly-conquered cities such as Susa and Ecbatana, but Fârs appears to have held a special significance. The construction of Pasargadae and Persepolis, which served for the main politico-religious ceremonies, and of the royal tombs at Naqsh-e Rostam, reflects the sacred character of the whole region.

During the Parthian and Seleucid dynasties, many foreign cultural influences entered Iran, but one region in particular kept the old traditions alive: Fârs. When the Sassanian Ardeshir I, whose family came from Istakhr near Persepolis, set out against Artabanus V, the last Seleucid ruler, he presented himself as the legitimate heir of the Achaemenians, the restorer of Persian values. For the Sassanians too, Fârs appears to have held particular religious and political significance, and some of their most important bas-reliefs were carved near Persepolis. As for Istakhr, where the temple dedicated to the goddess Anahita was located, it was one of the main Zoroastrian centres of the empire.

In the north of the province, the Zagros Mountains rise steeply to over 3,000 metres (9,000 feet) in height, but south of Shiraz they become progressively lower, eventually forming basins which are well adapted to cultivating crops such as cereals, cotton and vines. To the south and east lie the *garmsirat*, or warm lands, once winter pastures used by the nomadic tribes and which mark the transition between the inland plateau and the coastal region along the Persian Gulf. Until the second half of this century, nomadism was the main way of life for a large proportion of the population of Fârs, particularly in the east and north of the province. The largest nomadic group were the Qashqâi, who travelled seasonally between the *garmsirat* and the mountains to the north of Shiraz. Organized into a tribal confederation, they held considerable power at regional level but were disarmed and forced to settle by Rezâ Shâh in the 1960s. A second confederation, the Khamseh, which was artificially created in the 19th century from groups of diverse ethnic origins, used to live in the region between Shiraz and the Persian Gulf.

Shiraz

To an Iranian, the very mention of the name of Shiraz will evoke an elegy to a unique sophistication, an art of living present nowhere else in the world, the product of an ancient and learned civilization. Shiraz is an opulent oasis of greenery and culture in an otherwise barren landscape; it is the town of roses, of nightingales, of love and, at one time, of wine. But above all, Shiraz is the town of poetry, of Saadi and of Hâfez. The popularity of these poets is such that their verse provokes tears and sighs of admiration, and most Iranians carry collections of their poetry and are able to recite lines pertinent to every aspect of daily life. Their writings have been immortalized in the form of innumerable proverbs and aphorisms.

The foreign visitor who arrives in Shiraz today, and for whom the town is not as evocative as it is for an Iranian, may wonder at its reputation. Most of its famous gardens have long since disappeared and, while Shiraz was spared destruction during the Mongol invasions, few of its buildings pre-date the 18th century. There are none of the imposing mosques of Isfahan here, no Chahâr Bâgh and no fairytale bridges. The charm of Shiraz is much more subtle, more poetic, more insubstantial.

Shiraz was founded in the Achaemenian Dynasty; under the Sassanians it became one of the main cities of the province, without ever rivalling Istakhr in importance. It was only after the Arab invasion that Shiraz emerged as the major town of the region and was used as a base for the Arab armies attacking Istakhr (684). Shiraz benefited from the decline of Istakhr and, in 693, became the provincial capital. Under the Saffarid Dynasty (867–963), and later under the Buyids (945–1055), Shiraz played an important political role. It was at this period that its fortifications, which it was to keep until the 20th century, were first built. Unlike so many other towns in Iran which suffered from the invasions of Genghis Khân (1220) and Tamerlane (1387), Shiraz was left unharmed, its rulers having preferred to surrender rather than fight. From the 13th century, the town became the literary centre of all Persia, thanks in large part to the reputation of two of its most famous citizens, the poets Saadi (c.1207–1291) and Hâfez (c.1324–1389). Shiraz already had a long tradition of painting and this flourished further in the 14th century with the development of its own style and school.

During the reign of Shâh Abbâs (1587–1629), the governor of Fârs, Emâm Qoli Khân, set out to transform the town. Taking as a model the recent work that had been carried out in Isfahan, he had a wide avenue built flanked by pavilions, palaces and *madresseh*. Few of these buildings can be seen today as Shiraz later fell into decline, a situation aggravated by a series of natural and unnatural disasters. For example, in 1729 the town was sacked by the Afghan army, then again in 1744 by Nâder Shâh as a reprisal for the rebellion of the province's governor. But from 1750, Karim Khân, the ruler of the new Zend Dynasty, transferred his capital to Shiraz and set about making extensive changes, including the building of a royal quarter and the Regent's Mosque and Bazaar. Zend rule was short-lived and after the death of the last ruler, Loft Ali Khân, his successors, the Qâjâr, moved to Tehran. Shiraz remained an important stop on the caravan routes from the port of Bushher on the Persian Gulf but this role declined in the 20th century with the modernization of the country, and as rail and motorized road transport gradually replaced donkeys and camels. Today, Shiraz is still not linked to the national railway system and the town is mainly an administrative centre.

The main monuments in Shiraz are to be found in the centre of town, on the south bank of the Khoshk River. The old royal quarter of the Zend, built in the 18th century, has been cut in two by the Karim Khân Zend Avenue which crosses town from east to west, and only a few of the original buildings can still be seen today. The imposing **citadel of Karim Khân** is at Shohada Square; today it houses the municipal offices (*shahrdâri*) and is not open to visitors. Opposite the citadel, Karim Khân laid out a landscaped garden; one of its pavilions has been turned into a **museum** (muzeh-ye Pârs). Once a reception hall, this small octagonal building was also briefly Karim Khân's mausoleum until Aghâ Mohammed Qâjâr ordered the body removed. The *haft rangi* decoration on the outer walls with its floral motifs and hunting scenes in shades of blue, beige, green and pink, is typical of the period. Inside is a small, mixed collection of objects relating to the life of Karim Khân.

Another building from the same period is the **Regent's Mosque** (masjed-e Vakil), further east on Zend Avenue, next to the Regent's Bazaar. Both buildings are named after the title of Regent, or 'Vakil', which Karim Khân took when he came to the throne and which he preferred to the more usual title of Shâh. The mosque was restored in the 19th century and its main interest lies in its *haft rangi* decoration, done in the same style as that of the Pars museum, with the distinctive pink and green used by the Shiraz school. The *mehrab* hall is quite remarkable with its 48 cabled columns, and its *mimbar* carved out of a single block of white marble.

The old Regent's Bazaar was cut in two when Zend Avenue was built. The larger of the two halves, covered with a series of very fine brick vaults, is to the south of the avenue; the northern section has been renamed bâzâr-e No (the New Bazaar).

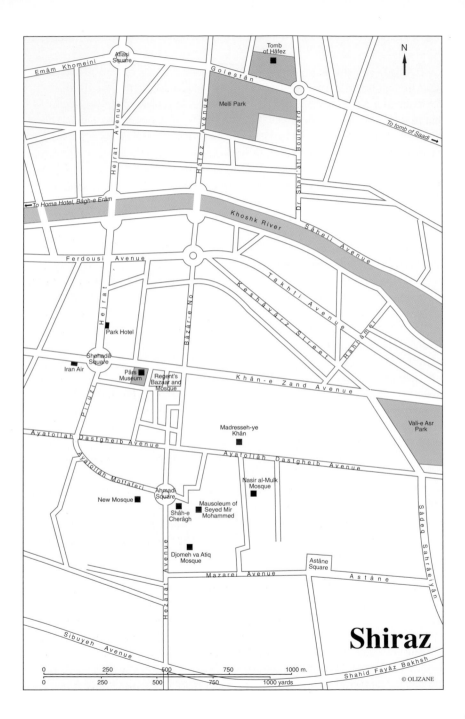

Shiraz

A second group of monuments, older than the ones mentioned above, can be seen around Ayatollâh Dastgheib Avenue. North of the avenue is the **madresseh-ye Khân**, built in 1615 by Emâm Qoli Khân, the Safavid governor of the province who hoped to reproduce in Shiraz the type of large-scale transformations that Shâh Abbâs had carried out in Isfahan. The *madresseh* has been heavily restored and only the octagonal hall that can be seen from the entrance is original. The interior is designed in traditional style with a central court surrounded by arcades which lead into the students' rooms. The south *eivân* is decorated with blue and pink tiles in stylized designs of flowers and birds.

The **New Mosque** (masjed-e Nov or masjed-e Shohadâ, the Martyrs' Mosque), on Dastgheib Avenue, was built by the local ruler Sa'd ibn Zangi, patron of the poet Saadi, at the end of the 12th century (it was finished in 1218). Its plan is the usual four-*eivân* one but with a much larger courtyard. The mosque was renovated in the 16th century but was quite extensively damaged by earthquakes in the 18th and 19th centuries.

Not far away on the other side of Ahmadi Square (Hezarat Street) is the **Mausoleum of Shâh Cherâgh** (ârâmgâh-e Shâh Cherâgh), which has a bulbous dome set on a tall thin drum and a small golden-roofed minaret. Inside is the cenotaph of Ahmed ibn Musâ, brother of Imam Rezâ, who died in Shiraz in 835. The first buildings erected here in his honour were built in the 13th century and modified later. In the 19th century an earthquake destroyed the original dome which was rebuilt as it is today, decorated with large beige and turquoise floral designs. This mausoleum is an important pilgrimage site for Shi'ite Muslims.

Nearby is a second mausoleum, built in the Qâjâr period, that of **Seyed Mir Muhammed**, another brother of Imam Rezâ. Again, the dome is set on a very narrow drum and is decorated with a lozenge design.

Further east is the **Nasir al-Mulk Mosque**, one of the most successful Qâjâr buildings of the 19th century. Its outer walls, and in particular the south *eivân*, are decorated with the characteristic predominantly pink flower motifs of the period. Inside, under the arches of the winter mosque, the vaults are decorated with geometric patterns and the twisted pillars with stylized palmettes. From the roof of the mosque one has a good view over the above-mentioned tombs.

Further south, the old Friday Mosque or **masjed-e Atiq** was built on the site of a Saffarid mosque (ninth century) of which a few remains can be seen in the *mehrab* hall (part of the decoration and brickwork). The present buildings are much more recent and were heavily renovated in the 17th century. The mosaics on the western walls are 16th century. One interesting feature of this mosque is its House of Korans (bayt al-Mushaf) or House of God (Khodah-ye khâneh), a square building with a tower at each corner, set in the centre of the courtyard. Built in the 14th century and

On His Travels

The world to me has been a home;
Wherever knowledge could be sought,
Through differing climes I loved to roam,
And every shade of feeling caught
From minds, whose varied fruits supply
The food of my philosophy.
And still the treasures of my store
Have made my wanderings less severe;
From every spot some prize I bore,
From every harvest gleaned an ear,
but find no land can ever vie
With bright Shirâz in purity;
And blest for ever be the spot
Which makes all other climes forgot!

Hâfez, from The Rose Garden of Persia, translated by Sir William
Jones, 1895

Shams al-Din Muhammad Hâfez, native of Shirâz, who lived c. 1324–
1389, led a life of poverty, considering it the companion of poetic genius.
The brilliance, energy and originality of his poems have carried his fame
throughout the world

*Sir William Jones, one of the great scholars and translators of
Islamic literature in the 19th century*

restored in the 20th century, it is said to have housed copies of the holy book. The very fine relief inscription around it is attributed to Yahyâ al-Jamali, a famous 14th-century calligrapher.

Even if the gardens for which Shiraz was once famous are now long gone, the town still has a number of parks and gardens which are particularly pleasant to wander through in summer or after a long drive through the desert. However, it must be said that unless they are visited under the very best of conditions, some of these gardens may be a disappointment, particularly because of the rather garish aspects of the pavilions. One of the most popular gardens is the **Bâgh-e Eram** in the northwest part of town, which is known for its cypress trees. In the middle of the garden, reflected in the pool in front of it, stands a Qâjâr palace (19th century) decorated with figurative scenes and animals.

The tombs of the poets Saadi and Hâfez are also on the north bank of the river. To most Iranians, these are the most important monuments in Shiraz. The **tomb of Hâfez** is the closest to the centre of town (entrance on Golestan Boulevard, opposite Melli Park). Built in 1953 in a garden, the mausoleum is a small open pavilion; inside it is a marble tombstone on which are carved several of the poet's verses. Shams od-Din Muhammad—or Hâfez, 'he who knows the Koran by heart'—was born in Shiraz between 1317 and 1326. He spent most of his life in his native town and died there in

Bâgh-e Erâm Palace, Shiraz

1389. As a court poet, Hâfez was subjected to the vagaries of political life, going through periods of disgrace, and even once of exile. His poems have been collected in a *Divân*, or anthology, of some 500 *ghazal*, a particularly diffi-cult poetic form because of the complexity of the metre and the requirement to keep to a single rhyme. Hafez is considered the undisputed master of the *ghazal*, and his poems reflect a richness and a subtlety unequalled even by that other great talent, Saadi. Despite its apparent simplicity, Hâfez' work has lead to very diverse inter-pretations; in his *Divân*, mystical poems associated with a profound symbolism

Mausoleum of Hâfez, Shiraz

are found with others, more mundane in appearance, which deal with love and wine. But should one to read the literal meaning of the words, or should an attempt be made to uncover the poet's esoteric message? When does the word 'love' refer to carnal love, and when is it the ideal love of God, union with the Divine? The freedom given to the reader to make his own interpretation and the simplicity of the language go a long way to explain the great popularity of Hâfez' poetry. Indeed, his *Divân* has even become a book of prophecy: when opened at random, it allows one to predict the future—providing that the verses are correctly interpreted, of course!

Do not miss the opportunity to visit the little *châikhâneh* in the park for a cup of tea and a rose water ice cream. The entrance to the teahouse is in the back wall of the garden.

Saadi's tomb, also set in a pleasant garden, is in the northeast of Shiraz, at the end of Bustân Boulevard. The present tomb was built in 1952 and replaces an earlier, much simpler construction. Unlike Hafez, Musleh od-Din Saadi, born in Shiraz in

1189, travelled extensively in Iraq and Syria, where he was even taken prisoner by the Crusaders. After his travels, he returned to his native Shiraz where he finished his two most famous works, the *Bustân* (*The Orchard*) and the *Golestân* (*The Rose Garden*), didactic collections of moral tales in the form of maxims and written either in verse or in a mixture of prose and verse. Saadi also wrote a number of *qasida* and *ghazal*; although the latter may not quite reach the perfection of those by Hâfez, they are undoubtedly worthy precursors. The main theme of his *ghazal* is love, both physical and mystical, which he treats in an elegant manner, in simple but expressive terms. Saadi is said to have died in 1290 at the age of over 100 years old.

Persepolis (Takht-e Jamshid)

Persepolis is undoubtedly the most impressive of all the archaeological sites in Iran, not only because of its sheer size but by the nature of the ruins themselves which display some of the finest examples of Achaemenian carving to be seen anywhere. Unlike Susa and Pasargadae, where a considerable mental effort on the part of the visitor is required to grasp the original layout of the palaces, it is possible here to picture a part of the Achaemenian world.

The site of Persepolis is extensive and a good two hours are needed for the visit. Allow at least a half-day's excursion from Shiraz (120 kilometres [75 miles] there and back) and more if you want to visit the other sites nearby. Be careful in summer as the sun is very hot and the ruins offer little shade.

Around 518 BC, as soon as work on Susa was finished, Darius I began the construction of a new capital in the plain of Marv-e Dasht, near Pasargadae, Cyrus the Great's capital. Parsa (better known in the West by its Greek name, Persepolis) never had an administrative or commercial role but is generally thought to have served for the New Year celebrations. These were the most important festivities in the Mazdean calendar when envoys from all the vassal states of the Achaemenian Empire came to present tribute to the King of Kings. (It should be pointed out, however, that this interpretation is not unanimously accepted and that some scholars prefer to see Persepolis simply as a residence and treasury located near the royal tombs at Naqsh-e Rostam.)

The site of Persepolis was carefully chosen: the palatial complex was built to impress those who came to it and symbolized the power of the Achaemenian rulers. The trip each year from Susa, the administrative capital some 500 kilometres (311 miles) away, would have been a long and difficult one, and this isolated position would have accentuated the prestige and glory of the king. Indeed, beginning with the reign of Darius, the whole region of Fârs appears to have taken on a sacred character linked to the religious beliefs which lay behind the very principle of royalty: the

Achaemenian kings held their power directly from the god Ahura Mazda, and the political and religious aspects of the coronation ceremonies, held nearby at Pasargadae, and of the New Year ceremonies are therefore difficult to separate from one another. It is in this context that the decision to build the royal cemetery at Naqsh-e Rostam, a few kilometres away from Persepolis, must be seen.

Thanks to the numerous inscribed tablets that have been found, it has been possible to establish a detailed chronology of the construction of Persepolis, which lasted over 60 years. The terrace, *apadana*, monumental staircases and Darius' palace (*tachara*) were all built during Darius' reign (522–486 BC). Xerxes I (486–465 BC) added the great Gate of All Nations and his own palace (*hadish*); he also began work on the Hall of a Hundred Columns which was finished in the reign of Artaxerxes I (465–423 BC). But the construction of Persepolis was never really completed and several buildings, including Artaxerxes II's palace (359–338 BC) were left unfinished. The term 'palace' given to some of the buildings may be somewhat misleading as it is debatable whether the Achaemenian rulers ever actually lived at Persepolis except during the New Year celebrations. Excavations carried out in the plain at the foot of the terrace have uncovered buildings belonging to a lower city. Even in the king's absence, a minimum staff of priests and soldiers would most probably have remained at Persepolis all year round to protect the buildings and ensure their upkeep.

Alexander the Great entered Persepolis in January 330 AD. The town had surrendered without a fight but it was sacked and the royal treasure taken away, although the buildings appear to have been left intact and were guarded by Macedonian soldiers. Much controversy has arisen over the destruction of Persepolis: were the palaces deliberately burnt on Alexander's orders, or was the fire that destroyed them accidental, a consequence of one of the conqueror's orgies? The event is interpreted by some as Greek revenge for the destruction of the temples of Athens by the Persians in 480 BC, but it has rightly been pointed out that Alexander, who was not in the habit of destroying the cities he conquered, had absolutely nothing to gain from the burning of Persepolis. Whatever the real reasons behind the fire, the city was entirely destroyed and abandoned thereafter.

Europe rediscovered Persepolis at the beginning of the 17th century when travellers brought back descriptions of the ruins, but it was not until the early 19th century that the first excavations were carried out. The Oriental Institute of Chicago began systematic digs under the direction of Ernst Herzfeld from 1931 to 1934. These excavations were continued by Erich Schmidt until 1939, and then taken over by the Iranian Archaeological Service.

VISITING PERSEPOLIS

On arrival at Persepolis one is confronted by an impressive wall, completely smooth

A Lydian, Persepolis

Procession of tributary
nations:
   The Scythians,
   recognizable by their
pointed hats, lived near the
Black Sea and were gifted
horsemen and blacksmiths.
   Very few vassal nations
   retained the privilege of
   bearing weapons in the
   prescence of the .
Achaemenian King of Kings

Lydia (present-day Western
Turkey), the land of King
Croesus, owed its proverbial
   wealth to trade and gold
   mines. The bowls and vases
   carried here in tribute
closely resemble exhibits in
the Rezâ Abbâssi Museum in
                      Tehran

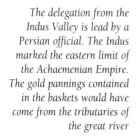

The delegation from the
Indus Valley is lead by a
Persian official. The Indus
marked the eastern limit of
the Achaemenian Empire.
The gold pannings contained
   in the baskets would have
come from the tributaries of
               the great river

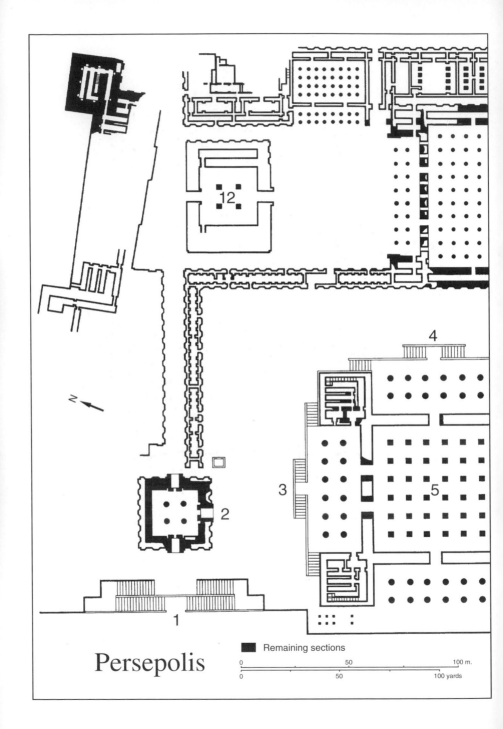

N

12

4

3

2

5

1

Persepolis

Remaining sections

0   50   100 m.
0   50   100 yards

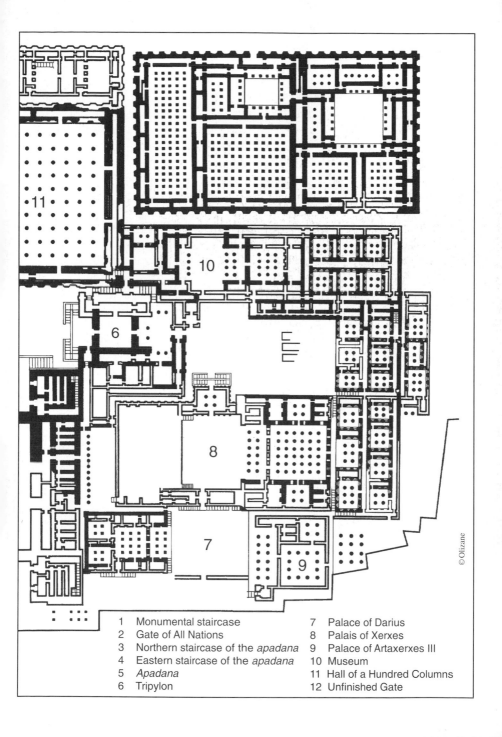

1	Monumental staircase	7	Palace of Darius
2	Gate of All Nations	8	Palais of Xerxes
3	Northern staircase of the *apadana*	9	Palace of Artaxerxes III
4	Eastern staircase of the *apadana*	10	Museum
5	*Apadana*	11	Hall of a Hundred Columns
6	Tripylon	12	Unfinished Gate

©Olizane

and plain, about 15 metres (49 feet) tall: this is the artificial terrace on which the palaces were built. From the ground, the ruins can hardly be seen except for the very tallest columns and the Gate of All Nations. It is only as one climbs the monumental staircase that the rest of the site is progressively revealed in all its splendour.

This vast terrace of Persepolis, some 450 metres (1,476 feet) long and 300 metres (984 feet) wide, was originally fortified on three sides by a tall wall. The only access was from the **monumental staircase** which leads to the **Gate of All Nations**. This gate, built by Xerxes I, is a square room, open on three sides. The east and west door-jambs are decorated with large sculptures of guardian bulls and winged bulls with human heads, strongly influenced by Assyrian sculpture (in Assyria, however, the bulls have five legs whereas here the Achaemenian artist has only given them four). From the south door of the Gate of All Nations one can proceed directly to the *apadana*, while the west door leads to a broad avenue and a second monumental gate (left unfinished).

The *apadana*, begun by Darius but finished only in Xerxes' reign, was the great audience hall where the King of Kings received delegations from the vassal nations. In this immense hall, measuring 75 metres^2 (807 feet^2) stood six rows of six columns. Each column, some 20 metres (66 feet) tall, ended in a capital in the shape of grif-fons, bulls or lions set back to back. The *apadana* was flanked on three sides by porti-cos and on the fourth side by small chambers.

Two **monumental staircases** on the north and east sides lead up to the *apadana*. Both are decorated with carvings which, in the case of the east staircase, are in excep-tional condition through having been buried for centuries under layers of ash and earth. This staircase is without a doubt one of the most remarkable works of art left to us from the Achaemenian period. It presents a summary of one of the ceremonies held during the New Year festivities: the great procession before the Achaemenian ruler of the delegations from the various vassal nations and the presentation of their tribute. It is well worth taking a little time to look at the details of some of these carvings: carpets and chairs being carried on servants' backs; the expression on the face of a young lion or ram; the sometimes touching way in which the men are shown talking among themselves or holding hands; and everywhere a wealth of detail of clothes and hats which represent better than anything the great diversity of peoples that formed the empire.

In the centre, between the two ramps of the staircase, stand eight guards facing each other. Above them is the symbol of the god Ahura Mazda, the winged sun, and, to each side, a fight between a lion and a bull. The surface of the side walls is divided into three horizontal rows: to the right of the stairs are long lines of Persian and Median guards accompanied by cavalry, infantry and archers; to the left is the proces-sion of the vassal states, each group accompanied by a Persian or Median official. The

Persepolis was built in c. 518 BC by Darius I

exact identity of some of the nations represented is still unclear but the generally accepted interpretation is the following (from right to left): in the top row are the Medes, who were given the honour of leading the procession, followed by the Elamites, bringing lions; the Parthians with camels and pelts; the Sogdians from Central Asia (or the Arachosians from Afghanistan) also bringing camels and pelts; the Egyptians with a bull; possible Bactrians with a camel and vessels; and finally probably the Sagartians with clothes and a horse.

In the second row, still from right to left, are the Armenians leading a horse and carrying a large vase; the Babylonians with a bull, lengths of cloth and cups; the Cilicians (or a Central Asian people) with rams, pelts and cups; the Scythians, wearing pointed hats, with a horse and armbands; the Assyrians with a bull and spears;

and the Chorasmians of Central Asia with a horse, armbands and axes.

In the bottom row are the Lydians with vases and a chariot; the Cappadocians with a horse and clothes; the Ionians with lengths of cloth and plates; the Bactrians (or the Arachosians of Afghanistan) leading a camel; and the Indians carrying baskets with vases and leading a donkey.

The staircase to the left of the central stairs is decorated, from the bottom up, with Ethiopians, or Kushites, carrying an elephant's tusk and leading an okapi or a giraffe; the Somalis with an antilope and a chariot; the Arabs with a dromedary and cloth; and the Thracians with shields, spears and a horse. The figures with a bull, shield and lance are perhaps Drangianians from Sistân and Afghanistan.

To the left of the east staircase of the *apadana* is another smaller set of stairs, which leads to the **tripylon**. Here, the carvings include a variation on the theme of the lion and bull fight, a sphinx and processions of guards and dignitaries, but there are no representations of the vassal nations. The doorjambs of the north and south doors of the tripylon show King Darius followed by two servants holding a fan and a parasol, while the opening of the east door shows the king seated on his throne under the winged symbol of Ahura Mazda, and held up by the twenty-eight vassal nations.

From the south corner of the *apadana*, one enters **Darius' palace**, or *tachara*. This building, composed of a central hall with columns surrounded by smaller rooms, was also finished by Xerxes. The central hall is sometimes called the Hall of Mirrors because of the highly polished surface of the stones. The doorjambs that lead into it are decorated with large bas-reliefs of the king fighting a lion, a bull and a chimera, as well as servants carrying various objects. The west and south stairs to the palace are decorated with representations of the Immortals (the royal guard) and of vassals bringing tribute.

The south staircase of the *tachara* leads to the unfinished **palace of Artaxerxes III**, which is in bad condition, and to **Xerxes' palace**, the *hadish*, built on the highest terrace of the site. This is once again a square room with 36 columns, surrounded by side chambers and with a portico on the north side. A few bas-reliefs still remain on the door jambs showing the king followed by servants carrying parasols, vases and incense burners.From the *hadish* one goes on to the so-called harem, built by Xerxes and left incomplete (the exact function of the building is not clear, it may have been a storage area for the treasury but most probably was not a harem). A small **museum** here exhibits various objects found at the site as well as Islamic ceramics and glassware from Istakhr nearby.

The largest hall at Persepolis is known as the **Hall of a Hundred Columns**, or Throne Room. It is very likely that an important ceremony was held here as the north portico gives onto a vast courtyard of some 4,000 metres^2 (43,056 feet^2) behind which is an unfinished monumental gate and the avenue which leads to the Gate of

All Nations. Several theories have been put forward as to the function of this hall, including that of a storage room for the tribute brought at the New Year celebrations: after a procession in the courtyard, the vassal delegations would have placed their tribute at the feet of the King of Kings, seated in the hall.

A path leads from the ruins to two **tombs** dug in the cliff face behind the terrace. On the left is the tomb of Artaxerxes II (405–361 BC) and on the right that of Artaxerxes III (361–338 BC). Both tombs are shaped like those at Naqsh-e Rostam (see below) and are decorated on the outer façade with bas-reliefs of the king held up by the twenty-eight vassal nations and worshipping before a fire altar; above him are the winged symbol of Ahura Mazda, the sun and the moon. To the extreme south of the terrace a third tomb, that of Darius III Codomanus (336–330 BC) was left unfinished.

Very near the site of Persepolis are the carvings of **Naqsh-e Rajab**, which date to the Sassanian period. The province of Fârs is particularly rich in Sassanian rock carvings, the most famous of which are those at Naqsh-e Rostam and Bishâpur. Here, at Naqsh-e Rajab, are two investiture scenes, those of Ardeshir I (224–241 AD) and of Shâpur I (241–272 AD), as well as a bas-relief of Shâpur I on horseback, followed by a group of noblemen and foot soldiers. This last scene is accompanied by an inscription in Pehlevi and Greek. The investiture scene is one of the most frequently represented subjects in Sassanian bas-reliefs, and although the details vary from one example to another, the basic composition is always the same: the ruler receiving a crown, symbol of royalty, from the hands of a god, usually Ahura Mazda. The figures are shown either standing, as in the case of Ardeshir here, or on horseback, as in the case of Shâpur. Secondary figures may also appear: Ardeshir is accompanied here by his son Shâpur and by a page carrying a fan (standing behind him) as well as by two children, set between the king and the god.

The last carving at Naqsh-e Rajab is of a man with his face turned sideways, raising a finger. Under it is an inscription in Pehlevi, a shorter version of a text which appears at four other sites, including Naqsh-e Rostam, and which is attributed to a certain Kartir, a Zoroastrian Magus who lived during the reigns of Bahram I (273–276) and Bahram II (276–293) and who was in large part responsable for the setting up of a religious state orthodoxy under the Sassanians. These inscriptions relate the main events in Kartir's life, describing his ascension through the clerical hierarchy and his attacks on heretic religions, in particular Manicheism, Christianity and Judaism. The figure shown next to the inscription is believed to represent Kartir.

Naqsh-e Rostam

Naqsh-e Rostam, about four kilometres (2.5 miles) north of Persepolis, is one of the

Two Faces of Fear

Now the most important moment, the moment that will determine the fate of the country, the Shah, and the revolution, is the moment when one policeman walks from his post toward one man on the edge of the crowd, raises his voice, and orders the man to go home. The policeman and the man on the edge of the crowd are ordinary, anonymous people, but their meeting has historic significance. They are both adults, they have both lived through certain events, they have both had their individual experiences. The policeman's experience: If I shout at someone and raise my truncheon, he will first go numb with terror and then take to his heels. The experience of the man at the edge of the crowd: At the sight of an approaching policeman I am seized by fear and start running. On the basis of these experiences we can elaborate a scenario: The policeman shouts, the man runs, others take flight, the square empties. But this time everything turns out differently. The policeman shouts, but the man doesn't run. He just stands there, looking at the policeman. It's a cautious look, still tinged with fear, but at the same time tough and insolent. So that's the way it is! The man on the edge of the crowd is looking insolently at uniformed authority. He doesn't budge. He glances around and sees the same look on other faces. Like his, their faces are watchful, still a bit fearful, but already firm and unrelenting. Nobody runs though the policeman has gone on shouting; at last he stops. There is a moment of silence. We don't know whether the policeman and the man on the edge of the crowd already realize what has happened. The man has stopped being afraid—and this is precisely the beginning of the revolution. Here it starts. Until now, whenever these two men approached each other, a third figure instantly intervened between them. That third figure was fear. Fear was the policeman's ally and the man in the crowd's foe. Fear interposed its rules and decided everything. Now the two men find themselves alone, facing each other, and fear has disappeared into thin air. Until now their relationship was charged with emotion, a mixture of aggression, scorn, rage, terror. But now that fear has retreated, this perverse, hateful union has suddenly broken up; something *has been extinguished. The two men have now grown mutually indifferent, useless to each other; they can go their own ways. Accordingly, the policeman turns around and begins to walk heavily back toward his post, while the man on the edge of the crowd stands there looking at his vanishing enemy.*

Ryszard Kapuscinski, Shah of Shahs, 1989

most important Achaemenian and Sassanian sites in Iran. It is here, in the rock face of the Kuh-e Hossein, that Darius I and three of his successors had their **tombs** dug, using as models the tombs of the two Artaxerxes at Persepolis. Their outer façade, in the shape of a cross, has an opening in the centre which leads to the funerary chamber. The lower part of the façade is plain, while the central section is decorated with columns and capitals, and the upper part with representations of the king beside a fire altar, held up by the vassal nations. Only one of the tombs, the right-hand one on the main cliff, bears an inscription which attributes it to Darius I (521–485 BC). The single tomb on the far right is generally attributed to Darius II (425–405 BC), while the remaining two tombs (from left to right) are thought to be those of Artaxerxes I (465–424 BC) and Xerxes I (485–465 BC).

Opposite the Achaemenian tombs is a square stone structure, known as the **Kaabah-e Zardusht**, or Kaaba of Zoroaster, and usually considered to be an Achaemenian fire temple. The walls on three sides have niches set in them which resemble windows while, on the fourth side, a door leads into the building. This tower, probably built during the reign of Darius I, is one of only very few of its type still standing. It would probably have held the sacred fire of the Achaemenians. In 1936, while the base of the tower was being excavated, inscriptions were discovered on the outer wall. The first one, written in Middle Persian, is one of the four versions of the priest Kartir's text (a longer version of this appears at this same site on the carving of Shâpur's victory over the Romans). The second inscription, written in Parthian Arsacid Pehlevi, in Sassanian Pehlevi and in Greek, tells of Shâpur's campaigns against Rome which ended in one case in the death of Cesar Gordian, in another in the defeat of a Roman army 60,000 strong and in the capture of Antiochus, and in the last case in the capture of the Roman emperor Valerian in 260 AD. The importance of these inscriptions for the understanding of Sassanian history is vital: indeed, without Kartir's inscriptions his very name and the role he played in the development of Zoroastrianism would be completely unknown to us. As for Shâpur's text on his Roman campaigns, it is the direct equivalent of Darius' Achaemenian text at Bisotun.

On the same rock face as the Achaemenian tombs are eight **Sassanian bas-reliefs**. The choice of this site by the Sassanian rulers was hardly a chance one and they most probably hoped to benefit from the divine emanations, or *xvarnah*, of their predecessors at this spot which had become sacred for the Achaemenians. To the far left of the site, beside the road, are two small Sassanian fire altars carved into the rock. They are pyramidal in shape, with small columns at the corners and a hollow in the top in which the fire was lit.

The first bas-reliefs are on the far left of the rock face, before the Achaemenian tombs. The first carving shows the investiture of Ardeshir I (224–241 AD), the founder of the dynasty. The king and the god Ahura Mazda handing him the beribboned crown are both represented on horseback. Under the hoofs of the horses are the bodies of their enemies, Artabanus V, the last Parthian king, and Ahriman, the God of Evil. Inscriptions in Middle Persian and Greek give the identity of the four figures. The scene is carved in very high relief, with the horses almost free-standing, and is considered by many to be the finest example of Sassanian carving.

The second scene shows Bahram II (276–293) with members of his family and dignitaries. Its most interesting feature is that it was carved over a much earlier Elamite bas-relief, dated between the ninth and seventh centuries BC. Only the two figures at each end of the carving remain. This, along with the carving at Kurangun near Bishapur, is one of the rare examples of Elamite rock carving to have survived in Iran.

The third bas-relief, under the furthest tomb on the left, shows Bahram II on horseback and in combat. Next are two carvings set one above the other. The top one, which is badly damaged, represents Shâpur II (309–379) leaning on his sword; the lower one shows Hormizd II (303–309) unseating an enemy with his spear. The sixth relief commemorates Shâpur's (241–272) victories against the Romans: the figure kneeling before Shâpur's horse is believed to be Emperor Philip the Arab, while standing behind him is Emperor Valerian, who was captured at the battle of Edessa in 260. Note the billowing and heavily pleated clothes which are characteristic of Shâpur's reign, a sharp contrast to the more austere style of Ardeshir seen in the first bas-relief. The next carving, dated to the reign of Bahram II, shows a fight on horseback set in two registers separated by a horizontal line. The last carving represents the investiture of Narseh (293–302) receiving the crown from the hands of the goddess Anahita.

Pasargadae

On the road to Isfahan and Yazd, about 70 kilometres (43 miles) from Persepolis, are the ruins of another Achaemenian city, **Pasargadae** (Pâsârgâd). It was here, in the Murghab Plain, that Cyrus II (559–530 BC) decided to build his capital, on the same spot, according to legend, where he defeated the Median army lead by Astyages in 550 BC. This decisive battle marked the beginning of the years of conquest which lead to the formation of the Achaemenian Empire. It has been suggested that the city was built on the site of earlier constructions which could date back to the very first Achaemenian rulers of the seventh century BC. Although this theory has yet to be verified by further excavations, the ruins of Pasargadae nonetheless represent the earliest known examples of Achaemenian architecture.

Many fundamental questions concerning the role of Pasargadae still remain un-

(above) *The cliff at Naqsh-e Rostam with the tombs of the Achaemenian kings;*
(below) *victory of Shâpur I over the Romans*

answered because of the lack of detailed documentation and the state of the ruins. Was the city an administrative or religious centre, or was there a sharing of these functions between Pasargadae and Ecbatana, the old Median capital which Cyrus had taken over? In any event, it appears that the construction work at Pasargadae, like at Persepolis, was never completed, perhaps because of Cyrus' untimely death in battle in 530 BC.

With the accession to the throne of Darius I in 522 BC, who belonged to a different branch of the Achaemenian family, Pasargadae was relegated to a secondary role and the new ruler quickly began building other cities, first Susa and then Persepolis. Pasargadae was used mainly for the investiture ceremonies of the Achaemenian kings.

The ruins of Pasargadae are much less well preserved than those of Persepolis and are dispersed over a wide area across the plain. The first building that one comes to, a small gabled structure set on a stepped platform, is generally identified as the **tomb of Cyrus**, and known locally as the tomb of Solomon's mother. Set apart from the other ruins, the mausoleum, which is built of white limestone, is simple and austere. Around the tomb are the remains of the columns of a temple built at a later date. Classical historians recorded how distressed Alexander the Great was when he arrived in front of the tomb in the spring of 324 BC, only to find that it had been desecrated: the bones of the body were scattered on the ground and there was no trace of the king's clothes and jewellery, his gold sarcophagus, or the rich draperies which Alexander's soldiers had described when they had visited the tomb some years previously. The Macedonian, who considered himself to be the heir of Cyrus, ordered that the tomb should be repaired and sealed to prevent further profanations.

A path leads from the tomb to the ruins of Pasargadae. Although the buildings appear at first sight to be haphazardly placed in relation to one another, they were in fact originally carefully integrated into extensive landscaped gardens, of which only the water canals now remain. The largest of the buildings, known as Cyrus' royal residence, is composed of a central hall of five rows of six columns, flanked on two sides by long porticos. This hall illustrates well one of the characteristic building techniques seen at Pasargadae, the use of alternating blocks of black and white limestone for the column bases. Fragments of carvings are still visible on the openings of some of the doors and the large corner pillar carries a short inscription in three languages, bearing the name of Cyrus. A second, slightly smaller building, surrounded by porticos on all four sides, can be seen a few hundred metres to the south. Near it, stands a gatehouse which is notable for the decoration of one of the door jambs (now under cover). This unique sculpture, 2.7 metres high (8.9 feet), representing a winged genie, is the oldest intact Achaemenian carving to have been found.

From these ruins one can see the remains of a square tower in the distance, known as Solomon's Prison, and thought to have been a fire temple similar to the one at Naqsh-e Rostam.

About 200 kilometres (124 miles) further along the same road that leads to Isfahan, one comes to the small but very picturesque village of **Izad Khâst** (between Adâdeh and Amin Abâd). Above the modern village which spreads out at the foot of a cliff, are the ruins of an ancient fortified settlement, perched on a rocky outcrop.

EXCURSIONS FROM SHIRAZ

The road which leaves Shiraz towards Bandar-e Bushehr, on the Persian Gulf, and Ahvâz, in Khuzestân, passes by the site of **Bishâpur**, known for its bas-reliefs and the ruins of a Sassanian city. The trip through some superb mountain scenery with grandiose gorges and wooded valleys can easily be done as a day's excursion from Shiraz (130 kilometres [81 miles] one way). The site of Bishâpur itself is very attractive: the bas-reliefs are carved on the rock face overlooking the Shâpur River and are surrounded by trees which provide welcome shade in summer.

The first two **carvings** are on the left bank of the river (on the right-hand side as one enters the gorge). Both represent Shâpur I's victories over the Romans. The subject matter here is the same as at Naqsh-e Rostam but is treated slightly differently. The first bas-relief is badly damaged and the details no longer visible; the second one, however, shows the king receiving the crown not from Ahura Mazda but from a putto, an element borrowed from Western iconography. Unusually, this scene is not restricted to the main protagonists but is accompanied on either side by several registers of figures in an overall design reminiscent of many Roman scenes of triumph.

To reach the carvings on the other bank, cross the river by the road bridge and follow the path which leads into the woods. The third bas-relief once again shows Shâpur's victory over the Romans: here, the two horses are trampling the bodies of Emperor Gordian III and the god Ahriman underfoot, while Philip the Arab kneels before the king. The absence of Valerian from this scene suggests that it was carved before the year 260 and that it therefore predates the two bas-reliefs on the other bank.

The fourth carving shows Bahram II (276–293 AD) accepting the submission of Arab nomads who have come with their horses and camels. This carving has been damaged by a later irrigation channel which was once attached to the rock face. The fifth bas-relief shows the investiture of Bahram I (273–276) in the now familiar composition, similar to the investitures at Naqsh-e Rostam and Naqsh-e Rajab.

The last relief is treated in a slightly different manner: the king, in the centre, is shown from the front, leaning on his sword. On the left are two registers of court dignitaries and soldiers, while on the right stand prisoners and servants carrying booty. This scene, dated to the reign of Shâpur II (309–379) is the latest one at the site.

On the heights above the river are the ruins of the ancient Sassanian **royal city** of Bishâpur built from 266 AD by Shâpur I. The excavations here were carried out by French archaeologists under the direction of Georges Salles and Roman Ghirshman in the 1930s and 1940s and then taken over by Iranian archaeologists.

On approaching the city, one notices first of all the old stone walls with their semicircular towers. Behind them is the palatial complex and, below, a fire temple. The temple is composed of a central square room surrounded by tall walls which were originally over 14 metres (46 feet) high. Each wall has a single door in it which leads to a dark covered corridor. At the top of the stairs, on the right, is the door to a long hall where mosaic fragments, strongly influenced by Roman styles, were found during the excavations (they are now in the Archaeological Museum in Tehran and the Louvre in Paris). At the back of this hall another corridor leads to the palace. The walls of this cross-shaped room were divided into 64 niches decorated with carved and painted stucco, still visible in a few places.

About 500 metres (1,640 feet) to the west of the temple is another series of buildings of unknown purpose as well as a votive monument made up of two columns topped with Corinthian capitals. In front of them a third base originally held a statue of Shâpur I. An inscription in Sassanian and in Arsacid Pehlevi dates the monument to 266 AD.

Another interesting visit to be made in the area, which could be combined with a trip to Bishâpur (about 70 kilometres [43 miles] from Bishâpur), is to the bas-relief at **Kurangun**, one of the rare examples of Elamite carving to be seen in Iran. It is dated between the 15th and the 11th century BC and represents a seated god and goddess surrounded by priests or worshippers. It is thought to be an older version of the Elamite relief at Naqsh-e Rostam, damaged by a Sassanian carving. From Bishâpur, continue on the Nur Abâd and Yâsuj road. Kurangun is near Sih-Talu, 15 kilometres (9.3 miles) to the northwest of Fahliyân.

Further Sassanian ruins and bas-reliefs can be seen at **Firuz Abâd**, 120 kilometres (75 miles) south of Shiraz, an excursion which takes just over half a day there and back. About 20 kilometres (12 miles) from Firuz Abâd, the road enters the impressive Tangâb gorge, overlooked by the fortifications of a Sassanian castle, the Qala-ye Dokhtar (Maiden's Castle), built about 100 metres (328 feet) above the road by Ardeshir I (224–242 AD). A bit further on, after the remains of a Sassanian bridge, one comes to the first of two bas-reliefs carved in the rock face, a representation of the investiture of Ardeshir I, accompanied by his son Shâpur. The second relief is carved two kilometres away. Its subject matter is classic and represents once again Ardeshir's victory over the Parthian king Artabanus V; its composition, however, is highly original and shows the decisive moment in battle when Ardeshir (in the lead) killed Arta-

*Dried rose petals are
used to make rose water,
an essential ingredient
in Iranian cuisine,
particularly for
sweets*

banus (depicted falling from his horse). Unlike the other stereotyped and rather
static Sassanian bas-reliefs, this one is full of vigour and movement.

The ruins of the ancient Sassanian city of Gur are a few kilometres further on, at
Firuz Abâd. The city was circular and surrounded by walls and a moat. In the centre are the remains of a large building, perhaps a fire temple. Ardeshir's palace was
located outside the town; today there is very little left of the great vaulted halls and
enormous walls of this edifice.

THE ZURKHÂNEH

Outside Iran, the *zurkhâneh*, or 'Houses of Strength', are little known and yet they perpetuate one of the country's most distinctive cultural expressions. The *zurkhâneh* itself is a small, spartan gymnasium, basically a shallow octagonal hollow about a metre deep, with a beaten-earth floor in which the young men of the neighbourhood meet to exercise and train. Unlike Western gymnastics, the exercises in the *zurkhâneh* are a collective sport with specific rituals, formal competitions, and strict moral and ethical rules. The athletes, or *pahlevân*, work together to the sound of a beaten drum played by the *morshed* (the 'guide') from a raised seat in a corner of the room. The precise movements of each exercise are carried out by all the participants in the same order and at the same rhythm. The equipment used is very simple, based on ancient weapons and adapted to the restricted space of the *zurkhâneh*. Small planks of wood and heavy clubs, weighing between four and 40 kilos (88 pounds), are used for the loosening-up exercises while the more advanced athletes use large wooden shields which can weigh 60 kilos (132 pounds) each. Another exercise consists of turning around on the spot, arms stretched out, a bit like the whirling dervishes.

But the *zurkhâneh* is much more than a demonstration of strength and skill. Its origins go back to the pre-Islamic period; after the Arab conquest it was forced underground and became a symbol of national resistance. Little by little, with the Islamisation of the population, the target of this resistance changed and came to represent the support of Shi'ite values against Sunni governments. The *zurkhâneh* became the meeting place of opponents to the Sunni regimes. Certain moral qualities (courage, abnegation) were required of the *pahlevân* as well as absolute fidelity to the Prophet and the Imams. The *zurkhâneh* reached its zenith during the Safavid Dynasty when Shi'ism became the state religion, but it declined afterwards and was artificially revived by the government in the 20th century, not so much for its religious aspects as for its ancient Iranian origins and the nationalism that accompanies it. For a while the *zurkhâneh* was seen as manipulated by the government, but this ended after the 1968 assassination by the secret police of a well-known *pahlevân* who had become a national hero. Today, the *zurkhâneh* is still frequented in the popular quarters of Tehran and Isfahan, even if it does have fewer supporters than the other national sport of football.

The Southeast: the Desert and the Straits of Hormuz

The southeast of Iran, which includes the provinces of Kermân, Sistân and Baluchestân, and Hormuzgân, is dominated by large areas of desert, which are difficult to cultivate, and by high mountains chains which occasionally reach over 4,000 metres (12,000 feet) in height. To the south, the desert and the mountains open out onto a narrow coastal plain along the Straits of Hormuz and the Sea of Oman and onto the main port of the region, Bandar-e Abbâs. The province of Yazd, located between Isfahan and Kermân provinces and geographically similar to the latter, will also be dealt with in this section.

Yazd

The geographical location of **Yazd** (1,230 metres [4,035 feet]), surrounded by salt lakes and built in the middle of an apparent wilderness between two deserts—the

Traditional village houses are centred around an inner courtyard, Fahraj village near Yazd

Henna mill near Yazd

Dasht-e Kevir to the north and the Dasht-e Lut to the east—may seem an unlikely
one for the development of a large settlement. But Yazd has made the most of its
position half-way between Isfahan and Kermân, on the main route that leads to Pakistan and Afghanistan. The early history of the town is unclear but the site would
appear to have been occupied by the Sassanian period. In 642 AD it was conquered
by the Arabs. Unlike so many other Iranian towns, Yazd was spared by the invading
Mongol armies of Genghis Khân (12th century) and by those of Tamerlane (14th
century), although the period of great prosperity it enjoyed after this date, when it
was famous for its carpets and its weaving, was brought to an abrupt end by the
Afghan invasion in the 18th century. Today, Yazd is the main provincial town and an
important centre with some 260,000 inhabitants. The building of a university just
outside town should contribute further to its future development.

 As in all the towns of the region, buildings in Yazd are traditionally of brick and
pisé and have flat or domed roofs, on top of which are low rectangular towers, the
walls of which are pierced at intervals to catch the wind. These are the wind towers
(*bâdgir*), a very efficient ventilation system which allows air to circulate within the
houses. Traditionally, the most important room in the house was the coolest one, a
covered patio with a fountain in the centre. The entrance to the house often gave

directly onto this room, and from it one had access to the bedrooms, a communal room and the terrace. The wind tower, placed above the water basin, created a draught which kept the room at a comfortable temperature.

The wind towers serve not only as ventilation shafts in the houses but also to cool water. Yazd is built at the foot of the Shir Mountains and for centuries the town's water has been brought down from these hills by a complex system of *qanâts*. In the desert around the town, large brick domes flanked by two wind towers indicate the presence of an underground reservoir, some of which are very deep, in which the water is cooled by the draft created between the towers. Once a commonplace feature of Iranian architecture, the windtower is unfortunately gradually disappearing. Old, eroded towers are no longer systematically replaced or repaired as more highly-prized, electrically operated methods of cooling and ventilation are slowly reaching even the smallest villages.

The most interesting buildings in Yazd are the Islamic ones, built within the town, and the Zoroastrian ones, mainly located outside it. In the centre of town is the **gateway to the Chahâr Suq Bazaar**, built in the 19th century, and easily recognizable by its three rows of arcades, one above the other, and its two tall minarets. Opposite it, on the other side of the square, is the **Mir Chakhmâq Mosque** (1437), named after a well-known Timurid governor of the town (it contains a very fine marble *mehrab*). Near the bazaar stood the complex of the **Vaght-o-Sa'at Mosque** (Mosque of Time and Hour) which included a *madresseh*, a library and an observatory. Today only the mosque itself, built in 1325, is still standing. Its most interesting feature is the stucco and tile decoration of the dome chamber and *mehrab*.

In the northern part of town (take Imam Khomeini Avenue from Dr. Beheshti Square) is the entrance *pishtaq* of the **Friday Mosque** (masjed-e Jomeh) which was built in the 14th century. The gateway, topped by two minarets, has an unusually tall and narrow *eivân* covered on the inner surface with stalactites. The dome of the main hall and the stalactite *mehrab* (1375), which are entirely decorated in glazed tilework, are very fine. Near the mosque is the **Tomb of the Twelve Imams** (boqe-ye Davâzde Imâm), a small 11th-century Seljuq building with carved stucco decoration around the *mehrab*.

THE ZOROASTRIAN COMMUNITY

Although Zoroastrians were recognized as *ahl al-dhimma*—People of the Book—after the Arab conquest and were therefore free to worship their own gods (see page 67), a large number nevertheless converted to the Islamic faith. Conversion brought with it a number of important financial and social advantages, including the avoidance of the capitation paid by non-Muslims and the opportunity of holding an administrative post. Periodic toughening of the Islamic position towards Zoroastrianism caused mass conversions and large-scale emigration to India from the eighth century on. Zoroastrian communities in Iran and India have remained in contact since this time, and in the 20th century the Parsis (the Indian Zoroastrians) have given considerable financial support to their fellow Zoroastrians in Iran.

The Zoroastrians, despite their relatively large numbers, have experienced a certain amount of discrimination, generally in the form of confiscation of belongings or property, arbitrary taxation or profanation of their sanctuaries. However, in the rural areas well removed from the large Muslim centres, and particularly in the Yazd region which was considered strategically unimportant, Zoroastrian traditions were kept alive. The Zoroastrian community in Yazd is currently estimated at slightly over 10,000, making it the largest in the country.

There is still a **Zoroastrian fire temple** (*âteshgâh*) in Yazd where the sacred fire is kept burning permanently. Worshippers and visitors can watch the fire through a glass window, as entry into the hall is forbidden except for the guardians of the fire. The fire was brought to Yazd around 1940 and is said to have burned without interruption for 1,500 years since *c.* 400 AD. The temple itself is a modern building, built especially to house the holy flame, and includes a small exhibition of Zoroastrian writings; on the wall hang the portraits of two of the donors who provided funds for the construction of the temple. Above the door on the outside is the winged symbol of Ahura Mazda in blue and yellow glazed tiles, the same emblem that appears in Acheamenian architecture. The temple is located on Ayatollah Kâshâni Avenue, near the centre of town.

According to Zoroastrian beliefs, Earth is one of the elements associated with the divinities known as Amesa Spenta, and it cannot be soiled by contact with a dead human body, as death is an evil brought about by Ahriman, the spirit of Evil. For the same reason, Fire, the most holy of the elements, must not come into contact with dead bodies either. As burial in the ground and cremation were prohibited, Zoroastrians adopted the practice of exposing the bodies of their dead in large open-air circular constructions, known as **towers of silence**, or *dakhma*. A few hours after a death, the body would be brought to the foot of the tower where a ritual ceremony would be held in the presence of relatives and friends of the deceased. The body was then carried by the priests into the tower where it was laid out on flat stones on the ground—thus avoiding any contact with the earth. In a short time the body would be torn apart by vultures and crows; the bones were then thrown into a circular pit in the centre of the tower.

At Yazd, the towers of silence are built on the hilltops outside the town. At the foot of the towers stand the remains of the buildings which once served for the funerary ceremonies. When the towers were still used for Zoroastrian burials, only the priests were allowed into them. Nowadays, however, some of them have been opened

to the public. In the 1970s, the custom of exposing bodies in the towers was gradually replaced by burial in the ground (to avoid all contamination of the earth, the graves were lined with an 'inert' substance such as cement). The towers were used until about 1978, after which all Zoroastrian dead were buried in the cemetery at the foot of the towers.

The road from Yazd to Taft and Shiraz passes through the small oasis of **Abarkuh**, located in a desert depression of the same name. Once a prosperous centre along the trade routes that linked the Persian Gulf, Central Asia and Turkey, Abarkuh has a half-abandoned air about it today. Its Friday Mosque, in the centre of the town dates back to the 13th or 14th century. Although relatively badly preserved, it does contain a carved stucco *mehrab* (14th century) with a fine interlaced decor. On a hill just outside town stands the **Gonbad-e Ali**, an octagonal funerary tower built in 1056 for Hezârasp ibn Nasr, the ruler of a local dynasty. Unlike most funerary towers which are built of brick, this one is of stone and is in very good condition. Its *muqarna* cornice is the oldest example of this type of exterior cornice and probably originally held up a pyramidal roof. Except for the inscription under the cornice, the walls are plain.

Ark-e Ban, one of the most important castles, last inhabited around 150 years ago, Kermân

Kermân Province

Kermân is the third largest province in the country but has only just over a million and a half inhabitants, and has always been considered one of the poorest regions of Iran. Its climate and topography certainly do not encourage dense human settlement: the Dasht-e Lut encroaches onto the north of the province, while the centre is taken up by a huge mountainous massif, of which several summits reach over 4,000 metres (12,000 feet) high. Here in particular, the survival of the villages and towns depends heavily on the *qanât* system dug into the mountains, which provides water even in the hottest of summers. Thanks to this, each year the oases of Kermân produce large crops of cereals, dates, oranges and pistachios (the pistachios of Rafsanjân are said to be the best in the country).

Despite being located away from the main political centres, which has enabled it to maintain a certain political autonomy, Kermân Province has not escaped the successive invasions that have swept into Iran. It was first pillaged in the 12th century by the Oghuzz Turks, then by the Mongols and more recently by the Afghans and Baluch. Because overland travel into Kermân from the interior of the country is difficult, the province has had close links with the south and Bandar-e Abbâs, the main port on the Sea of Oman in the Straits of Hormuz. Two important caravan routes linked this port to the towns of Sirjan and Sabzvârân, and trade between India and the Persian Gulf, which was encouraged by the Safavids, ensured a constant movement of travellers and merchants through Kermân. In the last hundred years, the province has benefited considerably from being joined up to the national railway network and from improvements in the road system, especially those sections between Yazd and Zahedan which pass through Kermân and Bam, and continue on to Pakistan.

At the beginning of the Islamic period, and until the tenth century, the provincial capital was **Sirjân**, a town located at a strategic point on the roads east to Shiraz and south to Bandar-e Abbâs. Besieged from 1393 to 1396 by Tamerlane's army, the castle of Sirjân—of which a few remains are still visible—finally fell, and its inhabitants were deported. Partially occupied again in the 14th century, the site was then abandoned; the modern town of Sirjân is built very near the old one.

The present capital of the province is the city of **Kermân** (250,000 inhabitants), located in a valley to the north of the mountains, at an altitude of 1,800 metres (5,905 feet) which gives it a relatively cool climate even in summer. Kermân is thought to be a very ancient city and to have been founded by the Sassanian king Ardeshir I in the third century. The town was governed successively by Arabs, Turks, and Mongols, and became quite prosperous under the Safavids thanks to trade with India. However, it suffered in the 18th century during Nâder Shah's military campaigns and from the devastation caused by the Qâjâr ruler Aghâ Mohammed (1794). Kermân's most interesting monument is its **Friday Mosque** (masjed-e Jomeh), built in 1348 by the local Mozzaferid Dynasty and considerably rebuilt during the Safavids, in the 16th century. The entrance *pishtaq* and the tall and narrow *eivân* are decorated with blue and white floral motifs. Unlike Isfahan where the twisted columns around the arch are a monochrome turquoise, here they are decorated in polychrome geometric designs.

Near the mosque is the **Vakil Bazaar** (Regent's Bazaar) which dates in large part to the Safavid period. South of it, is the **Imam Mosque** (ex-masjed-e Malek), a Seljuq mosque of the late 11th century which has been restored several times since. To the north of Dr Shari'ati Avenue, stands a third mosque, the masjed-e Pâ Menâr, which is of interest for the decoration of its entrance gate (14th century). Also to the north of the main avenue, near Falastin Street, are the ruins of the Gonbad-e Sabz, or Green Dome, a mausoleum of the Qarakhitay princes (13th century) badly damaged by an earthquake in 1896.

About 40 kilometres (25 miles) southeast of Kermân in the small town of **Mâhân**, is the mausoleum of Shâh Nematollâh Vali (died in 1431), a Muslim Indian king who founded a dervish order. Built in the 15th century, the tomb was restored under the Safavids (dome and main gate) and enlarged by the Qâjârs, who added the minarets.

One of the most interesting sites in the province is the **citadel of Bam** (200 kilometres [124 miles] from Kermân), built on a rocky outcrop overlooking the modern village nestling at the foot of the walls. Although there was a settlement at Bam as early as the beginning of the Islamic era, the present buildings are Safavid and have been since restored. Bam was besieged several times in its history. The last time was when the Zend ruler, Loft Ali Khân, took refuge there in 1794. The fortress was eventually captured by the Qâjâr king, Aghâ Mohammed, who ordered the massacre of all its inhabitants.

Today, the fortifications shelter a ghost town of half-collapsed houses. Once past the first set of walls, one climbs up through the old bazaar—the mosque is off to the right of the path—towards a second enclosure which surrounds the citadel itself, with its fortified residences, stables and armoury. The impressive view from the top of the citadel over the maze of abandoned streets and the oasis below makes the climb well worthwhile.

For those interested in the early development of mosques in Iran, a visit to the Friday Mosque at **Fahraj**, 50 kilometres (31 miles) east of Bam, is recommended. Although relatively little known, this mosque is nevertheless important as it was probably built in the second half of the ninth century, making it one of the oldest in the country. Similar to the Tarik Khâneh in Dâmghân, this is a hypostyle mosque with no *eivân*, but with a deep portico along the *qebla* wall. The columns are rectangular with half-columns at each corner, and, like most mosques of this period, the building is almost completely unadorned.

Hormuzgân Province

Hormuzgân Province is the coastal province that faces the Sultanate of Oman and the United Arab Emirates across the Straits of Hormuz, only 53 kilometres (33 miles) away. Because of a very hot and humid climate and an average annual precipitation level below 100 millimetres, the province is almost entirely a desert. Easy communication between the coast and the hinterland is hampered by the presence of a mountain chain, which for centuries has been difficult and hazardous to cross. Even today, the provinces of Kermân and Fârs are linked to Hormuzgân only by three main roads, of which two lead to Bandar-e Abbâs, the main port of the region.

At the beginning of the 14th century, the prince of Hormuz, in flight from advancing Mongol troops, founded a town on a small island 18 kilometres (11 miles) offshore, opposite the modern port of Bandar-e Abbâs. The town and the island, both named **Hormuz**, quickly became a prosperous trading post. In 1514, Hormuz was conquered by the Portuguese navigator Alfonse of Albuquerque and became one of the main Portuguese bases along their sea route to India and the Far East. The French merchant Jean-Baptiste Tavernier, who visited the island in 1665, described it in the following terms: 'There grows here neither tree nor grass, and the land is everywhere covered in salt which is good and as white as snow, so that it is absolutely sterile. There is no fresh water either except that which falls from the sky and is collected in tanks.' Thanks to its strategic position in the straits, Hormuz controlled all shipping entering and leaving the Persian Gulf. This Portuguese monopoly on trade in the region inevitably aroused the jealousy of the other great powers and, in 1622, Shâh Abbâs succeeded, with help from British ships, in landing on the

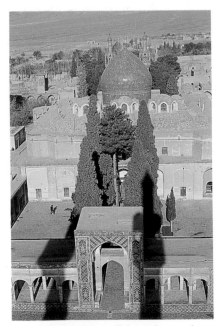

Dome of Shâh Ne'mat ollâh-e-Vali mausoleum in Mâhân, Kermân

island and capturing the fort. In return for this help, the Safavid ruler granted the British East India Company trading rights in Persia.

From this time on, Hormuz lost its economic importance and a new settlement, **Bandar-e Abbâs**, built opposite the island on the mainland, rapidly emerged as the main port of the Safavid Empire. At the end of the dynasty, however, the port declined and was abandoned by the European trading companies who preferred to move further west along the coast, to Bushher. From 1793 to 1868, Bandar-e Abbâs belonged to the territory of the Sultan of Mucat (Oman). Today it is once again the main port of Iran (accounting for 52 per cent of maritime commercial traffic in 1988), largely as a result of the war with Iraq which temporarily closed down its main rival, Bushehr, in Khuzestân.

The islands in the Persian Gulf and the Straits of Hormuz may be visited by boat from Bandar-e Abbâs. The first of these islands is **Hormuz** itself (42 kilometres^2 [16 miles^2]) where the castle built by the Portuguese in 1515 still stands. The castle, and its well preserved ramparts, can be reached on foot from the town of Hormuz. **Qeshm**, on the west coast of the Straits, is the largest of the Iranian islands; although still very underdeveloped at the moment, it will soon undergo quite drastic changes if the plans to transform it into a tourist centre and an economic investment area are ever implemented. The main town, Qeshm, is on the northeast point of the island.

Further west in the Persian Gulf is the island of **Kish**, the only free port in Iran. In the 12th and 13th centuries, Kish was an important Arab port, known for the quality of its pearls. Supplanted by Hormuz, it fell into oblivion until the 1960s when the last Shâh turned it into a luxury holiday resort complete with a casino and an international airport. Since the Revolution, Kish has become a popular destination with Iranians who come here for duty-free shopping, in particular for electronic goods which are much cheaper than on the mainland. The hotels and restaurants, however, are very expensive on Kish and most visitors stay only a short while. In addition to the boat links with Bandar-e Abbâs and Bushehr, there are flights from Kish to Tehran and Shiraz. Tickets, however, are difficult to buy at short notice because of high demand.

Sistân and Baluchestân Province

Because of the harshness of its climate and its geographical isolation, this province of the far southeast of Iran is one of the poorest in the country and the most underdeveloped. The road which runs south along the Afghan border from Mashhad (1,000 kilometres [621 miles] away from Zahedan) was only built after World War II; until then the only link with the rest of the country had been the road that goes to Kermân.

The province of Sistân and Baluchestân owes its name to its two main regions. Sistân is a deep basin in the north which extends into Afghanistan as far as Kandahâr. It has an average altitude of 500 metres (1,640 feet) above sea level and is surrounded in the east by the Palangan chain of mountains. In the centre, several lakes collect the waters of the Hirmand-rud, the main river of the basin which springs up in the Kuh-e Bâbâ Mountains of Afghanistan. This region is the ancient Drangia, the country of Rostam, hero of the epic *Shâhnâmeh*. Once extremely fertile due to an efficient irrigation system, it turned into a desert after Tamerlane's invasion in 1383 when the dams and *qanât* were deliberately destroyed. Entire towns had to be abandoned and even today only the area around Zâbol is inhabited. The problem of obtaining water is still an important one in Sistân: the construction of a dam on the Hirmand in Afghanistan has considerably reduced the volume of water in the river to the extent that the largest of the lakes, the Hâmun-e Sâberi (or Lake Sistân) was almost dry during the winter of 1976 and has still not fully recovered.

The proximity of the Afghan border makes travel in Sistân difficult for foreigners. Drug trafficking across the border is a major problem and consequently the police and the locals are wary of outsiders. The atmosphere in the main town, **Zâbol**, is frankly unpleasant and it is not advisable to stay there any longer than is strictly needed. It may be necessary, however, to pass through to reach **Kuh-e Khâje**, a Parthian site a few kilometres southwest near the village of Divâneh. This ancient citadel dates back to the first century AD and was built on a basalt outcrop in the centre of a lake. In winter, when the water level is low, it is usually possible to walk out to the island, but in spring one has to take a *tuten*, the local form of punt made of reeds. The frescoes on the walls of the citadel for which this site is famous were taken away long ago, but the ruins of the palace and a fire temple can still be visited.

Baluchestân, in the south of the province, is an arid and mountainous region with occasional large basins. A first chain of mountains stretches from Khorâssân along the Pakistani border. Its highest points are Mount Taftân (4,042 metres, 13,258 feet), an active volcano just south of Zâhedân, and Mount Bazmân (3,503 metres, 11,490 feet). A second, lower chain, the Makran Mountains (rising 1,000–2,100 metres, 3,000–6,800 feet) stretches from east to west, separating the coastal basin from the Bampur River and the large salt lake of Jâzmuriân. It is in this basin, linked by road to Kermân and Zâhedân, that the old provincial capital, **Irân Shahr**, is located. From Irân Shahr, one can drive to the small port of **Châbahâr** on the Sea of Oman, on the other side of the Makrân Range. This whole coastal region is very underdeveloped and until the recent construction of an airport at Châbahâr, the port was almost completely isolated. Its only real link with the rest of the country was the main road to Irân Shahr. Even today there is no proper road along the coast either towards Pakistan or towards Hormuzgân and Bandar-e Abbâs.

Thanks to the presence of underground rivers and extensive irrigation, crops such as sugar cane, cereals, tobacco, banana trees and citrus fruit can be grown in oases in the valleys of central Baluchestân, despite very low rainfall (85 millimetres [3.5 inches] a year on average in Zâhedân). The coast, on the other hand, is extremely arid, and the local economy is heavily dependant on sea fishing. In antiquity, the inhabitants of this area, known as Gedrosia, were called the Ichtyophages by classical authors because of their habit of eating the fish they caught raw. No story illustrates better the harshness of the coastal climate than that of the return of Alexander the Great from the Indus in the autumn of 325 AD. Two months after setting out, suffering desperately from thirst and the heat, his army managed to reach Kermân; almost two-thirds of the men perished on the way. The troops who had taken a northern route along the Hirmand Valley and through Sistân, however, hardly lost a single man.

The main ethnic minority in the province are the Baluch who live principally in Sistân and in the southwest, around Irân Shahr and Sarâvân, although isolated pockets of Baluch are still found further west, even as far as Hormuzgân and Kermân provinces. Chased out of northern Khorâssân by the Turko-Mongol invasions in the 12th century, the Baluch settled in southeastern Iran and in western Pakistan where they lived a nomadic life. They mixed with the local population, including the Brahui, a Dravidian people who are thought to have formed part of the Indo-European waves that swept down into India in the third millennium BC. The absorption of the Brahui by the Baluch has been so complete that it is difficult today to tell them apart. However, a few pockets of Brahui are thought to exist still between Sarâvân and the coast. As for the Baluch, they were forced into a more settled life style in the second half of the twentieth century, and now work in the main urban centres such as Zâhedân and Irân Shahr.

Zâhedân, the provincial capital, is of little interest other than being located about 100 kilometres (62 miles) away from the Pakistani border. It is here that the train from Quetta (Pakistan) arrives. The frontier post is located at Taftan (Pakistani side) and Mirjâve (Iranian side). There are also bus services between Zâhedân and Mirjâve, and between Taftan and Quetta. At Zâhedân it is possible to get visas both for India and Pakistan at the consulates of those countries (the Pakistani Consulate is on Shahid Moqadam Avenue, tel 23389; and the Indian Consulate is on Imam Khomeini Avenue, tel 2337).

Although Zâhedân is not yet linked to the Iranian railway system—which begins only at Kermân, 541 kilometres (336 miles) away—it does have an airport with regular flights to other cities in Iran, including Tehran, Isfahan and Mashhad. These might prove useful to those travellers who want to avoid crossing the desert by road.

(following pages) *Tile panel from one of the royal pavilions in the gardens at Isfahan, c. 1600, courtesy of the Board of Trustees of the Victoria and Albert Museum.*

Hotels

Most hotels in Iran now have room prices in US$ for foreign tourists (and expect to be paid in dollars). These prices are much higher than those paid in rial by Iranian nationals. With the development of tourism, it is likely that there will be price increases in the near future. For this reason, the hotels below are placed in three categories: superior (US$50–US$200 for a double room); moderate (US$50–US$30); and budget (less than US$30). As a general rule, hotels in Tehran and Isfahan are more expensive than those in other cities. See the section on accommodation page 22.

Tehran

SUPERIOR
Azâdi Grand Hotel (ex-Hyatt), Chamrân Highway, at Evin. Tel 808 3021/9; fax 808 3039; telex 212 845, 214 302. Restaurants, coffee shop, shops, bank. Rather a long way from the centre of town but convenient for the International Fair Centre.

Esteghlâl Hotel (ex-Hilton), Chamrân Highway, at the corner of Vali-e Asr Avenue. Tel 290 011/5; fax 292 760, 297 045; telex 212 510. In the same area as the Azâdi Grand. Offers similar services.

Homâ Hotel (ex-Sheraton), Vali-e Asr Avenue, Vanak Square, Shahid Khodâmi Street. Tel 657 860; fax 653 509. Also a long way from the city centre.

Lâleh Hotel, Dr Fatemi Avenue. Tel 655 021, 656 021/9. Located in a corner of Lâleh Park near the Carpet Museum and the University.

Kiyân Hotel, Vali-e Asr Avenue, Zartosht Street. Tel 650 237.

MODERATE
Tehran Grand Hotel (Bozorg-e Tehrân), Ostâd Motahari Avenue, at the corner of Vali-e Asr Avenue. Tel 624 383, 623 857. Still quite far from the centre but a very decent hotel.

Kosar Hotel, Vali-e Asr Avenue, Khosro Khâvar Street. Tel 898 121/4; fax 898 374. A comfortable hotel located near the city centre with restaurant.

Evin Hotel, Chamran Highway, Evin intersection. Tel 291 036/9; fax 291 039. Next door to the Azâdi Grand. Comfortable and the staff is friendly. Restaurant.

Hotel Bozorg-e Ferdosi (Ferdowsi Grand), at the corner of Ferdusi Avenue and Mesri Street. Tel 645 9991; fax 645 1449. A new hotel very well situated in the centre of town, near the Archaeological Museum.

BUDGET

Râmâtiâ Hotel, Vali-e Asr Avenue, Hejdahom Street. Tel 627 856, 626 377. A bit far from the centre but good.

Marmar Hotel, 49 Sepahbod Qarani Avenue, Somayyeh Street. Tel 830 083/7. A few minutes on foot from Enqelâb Avenue.

Irân Hotel, Vali-e Asr Avenue, Kâryâbi Street. Tel 893 161. A comfortable hotel near the city centre.

Irânshahr Hotel, Irânshahr Avenue, by Mahzâd Street. Tel 820 518. Near the Marmar Hotel.

Bolvâr Hotel, Keshâvary Boulevard. Tel 658 546. Located between Lâleh Park and the University.

Châlus

SUPERIOR

Caspian Enghelab Hotel (Enghelab Khazar Hotel), 12 kilometres (00 miles) on the road to Ramsar, Châlus. Tel 22001/11, fax 220 12. Although it was built about 20 years ago, this is still one of the best hotels in the country. Very comfortable but quite expensive.

Hamedân

SUPERIOR

Bu Ali Hotel, Bu Ali Avenue, just north of Azâdi Square. Tel 33070-2; fax 33072. Good rooms but a bit expensive.

Khâju Bridge, built around 1650, is a popular place for an evening stroll

Isfahan

SUPERIOR

Abbâssi Hotel (ex-Shâh Abbâs hotel), Shahid Ayatollâh Madani Avenue. Tel 26014. The most famous hotel in town, located in an old caravansarai to which a modern wing has been added. Unfortunately not quite up to standard now and very expensive. The garden and teahouse are well worth visiting.

Kowsar Hotel, Bustan-e Mellat, near the Si-o-Se Bridge. Tel 40236. On the south bank of the river. Restaurants, shops. Comfortable but quite expensive.

Ali Qâpu Hotel, Chahâr Bâgh Avenue, five minutes away from the Si-o-Se Bridge. Tel 31283. Very central, friendly, and very comfortable. Restaurant, shops.

Suit Hotel, Bustan-e Aemieh, near the Si-o-Se Bridge. Tel 43872. Next door to the Kowsar. Less well kept up and more expensive than the Kowsar.

Azâdi Hotel, Chahâr Bâgh Avenue, near Jamal Abdolrazzâq Avenue. Tel 35056, 39011. A comfortable hotel.

MODERATE
Aryâ Hotel, Shahid Ayatollâh Madani Avenue. Tel 27242. Very central location near the Abbâssi hotel.

BUDGET
Mehmânsarâ-ye Piruzi, Chahâr Bâgh Avenue. Tel 61043. Good but a bit expensive.

Mashhad

SUPERIOR
Homâ Hotel, Tâleqâni Square, Feyziyeh Avenue. Tel 32001. The best hotel in town, with shops and restaurants, but a bit far from the centre and quite expensive.

Atrak Hotel, Beit ol-Moqadas Square. Tel 22044. A comfortable hotel, well situated.

MODERATE
Asia Hotel, Pâsdârân Street. Tel 20074; 58876; fax 58030. A comfortable, central hotel, with a teahouse.

Jam Hotel, Pâsdârân Street. Tel 90045. Opposite the Asia hotel.

BUDGET
Irân Hotel, Andarzgu Avenue. Tel 28020. Near the bazaar.

Azâdi Hotel, Azâdi Avenue. Tel 51927.

Atlas Hotel, Beit ol-Moqadas Square. Tel 45022. Good and well priced.

Shiraz

SUPERIOR
Homâ Hotel, Azâdi Park, Meshkinfâm Street. Tel 28000/14. Currently the best hotel in town, with restaurants, a coffee shop, and shops. Opposite Azâdi Park, on the north bank of the river.

Pârk Hotel, Shohadâ Square. Nearer the centre of town than the Homâ Hotel above. Comfortable.

MODERATE

Arg Hotel, Shahnaz Avenue. Tel 228 891; fax 21931. Good rooms but the food in the restaurant is uninteresting.

BUDGET

Atlas Hotel, Atlas Avenue. Tel 29225, 47748. On the north bank of the river, near the Hâfez mausoleum.

Kosar Hotel, on Zend Boulevard, west of Shohadâ Square. Tel 35724/5.

Tabriz

SUPERIOR

Tabriz Hotel (ex-International), Abressan Crossroads. Tel 341 082; fax 341 081. The best hotel in town. Comfortable but a bit far from the centre.

MODERATE

Daryâ Hotel, 22 Bahman Avenue. Tel 44464. Comfortable. Near the train station, to the west of the town centre.

Irân Hotel, 22 Bahman Avenue. Tel 49516. Comfortable. Close to Hotel Daryâ.

BUDGET

Morvârid Hotel, Bâgh Golestân Square. Tel 60520. A fairly decent hotel, near the centre and Golestân Park.

Language Guide

PRONUNCIATION

Except for a few letters, the pronunciation of the Persian language does not present any great difficulties for English-speakers.

■ VOWELS

a	as in 'hat' or 'map'
â	a long 'a', akin to that of 'wash' or 'what', somewhat like the 'o' in 'on'; in the spoken language, this letter has a tendency to be pronounced like an 'oo' before the letter 'n'; so *Irâni* (Iranian) often becomes 'Irooni'
e	as in 'get' or 'end'
i	ee, as in 'speed'
o	as in 'bone'
u	always 'oo' as in 'who', not as in 'use'

All the vowels are pronounced separately; thus 'ai' is pronounced 'a-i' and 'ei' is pronounced as in 'raid'.

■ CONSONANTS

b, p, t, l, m, n, v, z	are pronounced as in English.
gh	like a thickly pronounced French 'r'
kh	like the Scottish 'ch' of 'loch' or the German 'ich'
ch	as in 'rich' or French 'chat'
sh	as in 'show'
q	pronounced like a 'g' from the back of the throat
r	trilled
g	hard as in 'get', never as in 'page'
s	always as in 'sand', never as in 'rise',
h	always pronounced

VOCABULARY

■ USEFUL PHRASES

Hello	*salâm, salâm aleikum*
Good morning	*sobh bekheir*
Good evening	*shab bekheir*
Goodbye	*khodâ hâfez*
How are you?	*hâle shomâ chetor-e ?*
Well, good	*khub*

Thank you	*mersi*
Thank you very much	*kheili mamnun*
Please	*lotfân, befarmâyid*
Excuse me	*bebakhshid*
Have a nice trip	*safar bekheir*
Yes	*bale*
No	*na, nakheir*
My name is...	*esmam ...e*
I am English	*man Engelestâni am*
I am a tourist	*man turist / jahângard am*
student	*dâneshju am*
Do you speak English?	*shomâ engelisi baladid ?*
I do not speak Persian	*fârsi balad nistam*
What is that?	*ân chist ?*
Do you have... ?	*shomâ ... dârid ?*
Where is... / are... ?	*... kojâst ?*
Where are the toilets?	*tualet kojâst ?*

■ TRAVEL

Car	*mâshin*	West	*maghreb*
Coach	*otobus*	Far	*dur*
Train	*qetâr*	Near	*nazdik*
Station	*istgâh*		
Airplane	*havâ peimâ*	**■ TIME**	
Airport	*furudgâh*	Day	*ruz*
Taxi	*tâksi*	Today	*emruz*
Ticket	*bilit*	Yesterday	*diruz*
Town	*shahr*	Tomorrow	*fardâ*
Village	*dehkadeh*	Morning	*sobh*
		Midday	*zohr*
■ DIRECTIONS		Evening / night	*shab*
Right	*dast-e râst*	Week	*hafte*
Left	*dast-e chap*	Month	*mâh*
Straight	*mostaqim*	Year	*sâl*
There	*ânjâ*	Date	*târikh*
Here	*injâ*	Hour	*sâ'at*
North	*shomâl*		
South	*djonub*	**■ THE DAYS OF THE WEEK**	
East	*mashreq*	Friday	*jomeh*

Saturday	*shambeh*
Sunday	*yek shambeh*
Monday	*do shambeh*
Tuesday	*se shambeh*
Wednesday	*chahâr shambeh*
Thursday	*panj shambeh*

■ ACCOMMODATION

Hotel	*hotel*
	mehmânkhâneh
Guesthouse	*mosaferkhâneh*
Single room	*otâq-e yek nafari*
Double room	*otâq-e do nafari*
With shower/bath	*bâ hammâm*
Bed	*takht*
Blanket	*patu*
Towel	*hule*
Soap	*sâbun*
Clean	*tamiz*
Dirty	*kasif*

■ SHOPPING

Market	*bâzâr*
Open	*bâz*
Closed	*tatil*
Money	*pul*
How much?	*chand e?*
Expensive	*gerân*
Cheap	*arzân*
Big	*bozorg*
Small	*kuchek*
Pretty	*qashang*
Very	*kheili*
Carpet	*farsh, ghâli*
Wood inlay	*khâtam*
Caviar	*khâviâr*

■ MEALS

| Restaurant | *restorân* |

Tea house	*châi khâneh*
Breakfast	*sobhâneh*
Lunch	*nahâr*
Dinner	*shâm*
Hot	*garm*
Cold	*sard*
Knife	*kârd*
Fork	*changâl*
Spoon	*qâshoq*
Plate	*boshqâbe*
Glass	*livân*
Water	*âb*
Coffee	*qahve*
Tea	*châi*
Non-alcoholic drinks	*nushabeh*
Bread	*nân*
Butter	*kareh*
Jam	*morabbâ*
Honey	*asal*
Soup	*sup*
Yoghurt	*mâst*
Cheese	*panir*
Meat	*gusht*
Chicken	*juje*
Lamb	*barreh*
Vegetables	*sabzi*
Salad	*sâlâd*
Fruit	*miveh*
Fruit juice	*âbmiveh*
Apple	*sib*
Pomegranate	*ânâr*
Orange	*portaqâl*
Water melon	*hendevâneh*
Pistachios	*pesteh*

■ HEALTH

| Doctor | *doktor, pezeshk* |
| Ill | *bimâr, mariz* |

Hospital	*bimârestân, marizkhâneh*	■ IN TOWN	
Dentist	*dandânsâz*	Mosque	*masjed*
Chemist	*farmasi, dârusazi*	Bank	*bânk*
Medication	*dâru, davâ*	Police	*shahrbâni*
Diarrhoea	*es-hâl*	Town hall	*shahrdâri*
Cold	*zokâm*	Museum	*muzeh*
Fever	*tab*	Bridge	*pol*
Flu	*ânfluânzâ, grip*	Avenue, street	*khiâbân*
		Side street	*kucheh*
■ NUMBERS		Motorway	*bozorgrâh, otobân*
One	*yek*	Square	*meidân*
Two	*do*	Port	*bandar*
Three	*seh*	Church	*kelisâ*
Four	*chahâr*	Consulate	*konsulgâri*
Five	*panj*	Centre	*markaz*
Six	*shesh*	River	*rud, rud khâneh*
Seven	*haft*		
Eight	*hasht*		
Nine	*noh*		
Ten	*dah*		
Eleven	*yâzdah*		
Twelve	*davâzdah*		
Twenty	*bist*		
Twenty-one	*bist o yek*		
Thirty	*si*		
Forty	*chehel*		
Fifty	*panjâh*		
Sixty	*shast*		
Seventy	*haftâd*		
Eighty	*hashtâd*		
Ninety	*navad*		
One hundred	*sad*		
Two hundred	*divist*		
Two hundred and thirty-one	*divist o si o yek*		
Thousand	*hezâr*		
Two thousand	*do hezâr*		

Glossary

Arg	bazaar, centre of town
apadana	audience hall or throne room
ârâmgâh	tomb
âteshgâh	Zoroastrian fire altar
bâdgir	wind tower, traditional ventilation system in houses
borj	tower
boqe	mausoleum
châdor	'tent'; long cloth worn by women in public and which covers them from head to foot
dakhma	tower of silence
eivân or *iwan*	vaulted room open on one side
gach	carved stucco, often used as decoration in mosques
gonbad	dome
haft rangi	'seven colours'; polychrome painted tiles not formed of mosaic
hejâb	'veil'; term used for the correct dress worn by women in Iran, either a *châdor*, or a scarf covering the head.
Hejira	day of the flight of Mahommed from Mecca to Medina in 622; date with which the Islamic calendar begins
hypostyle	area with a roof supported by pillars
Imam, emâm	Shi'ism: descendants of the Prophet and of Ali, are authorized to interpret the Koran; Sunni: leader of prayer in the mosque
imâmzâdch	'son of the Imam'; used for the tombs of the descendants of the Shi'ite Imams
Ka'aba	sacred edifice at Mecca which contains the venerated Black Stone
khân	caravanserai
khâtam	marquetry
madresseh	theological college
maqsura	reserved enclosure in the *qebla* wall
masjed	mosque
masshad	place of martyrdom
mehrab	niche in the *qebla* wall
menâr	minaret
mimbar	pulpit of a mosque
minai	12th century overglaze enamelled ware from Kâshân
Moharram	first month of the Islamic lunar calendar; month of mourning in the Shi'ite faith for the commemoration of the death of Imam Hussein

muqarna	corner squinches which form the transition from a square plan to a circular one in Islamic architecture
nizâmiyeh	*madresseh* founded by Vizier Nizâm al-Mulk
pishtaq	tall, formal gateway at the entrance of mosques or bazaars
pol	bridge
qaliân	water pipe
qanât	underground water canals
qebla	direction of Mecca
sahn	courtyard in a mosque
sayyed	descendant of the Prophet
talâr	covered terrace
tappeh	artificial hill
taziyeh	religious plays performed during the month of Moharram
tell	artificial hill, also tappeh

Recommended Reading

An excellent reference book on all aspects of Iranian history, geography and culture is the English-language *Encyclopaedia Iranica* (Routledge & Kegan Paul, ten volumes published to date, A–Coffee, 1985 continuing)

PHOTOGRAPHIC BOOKS
Good photographic books on present-day Iran are rare. One photographer in particular, Nasrollâh Kasrâiân, stands out for the very high quality of his work. His books on the Turkomans and the Kurds are particularly interesting for the insight they provide into the daily lives of these people.

Kasrâiân, Nasrollâh et Arshi, *Zibâ Torkman-e Irân* or *Turkomans of Iran* in Persian and English (Sekeh Press, Tehran, 1991)

Kasrâiân, Nasrollâh et Arshi, *Zibâ Sarzamin-e mâ Irân* or *Our Homeland Iran*. Persian and English text. (Sekeh Press, Tehran, 1992)

Arshi, Ziba and Kasraian, Nasrolah, *Kurdistan* (Kegan Paul, 1992)

HISTORY
Cambridge History of Iran, 1983. For those who want a detailed and precise account of Iranian History.

Roy Mottahedeh, *The Mantle of the Prophet, religion and politics in Iran* (Peregrine, Penguin, 1985). A fascinating glimpse of the world of the Shi'ite clergy and of the training of a young *mollah*.

Ferrier, R W, *A Journey to Persia* (Tauris, 1994). A description of the Perisan court and empire in the seventeeth century as seen through the eyes of the French traveller Jean Chardin.

Frye, Richard, *The Heritage of Persia*, (Cardinal 1976). A scholarly study of pre-Islamic Persia.

Frye, Richard, *The Golden Age of Persia, Arabs in the East*, (Weidenfeld & Nicholson, 1975). A very detailed cultural history of Persia from the Arab conquest in the ninth century to the Turkish invasions in the eleventh century.

Ghirshman, Roman, *Iran*, (Penguin, 1978). An archaeological history of Iran from Neolithic times to the Arab conquest, written by one of the greatest archaeologists to have worked in Iran.

Lewis, Bernard, *The Assassins*, (Al Saqi Books, 1985). A very readable history of the Assassin movement in Iran and other regions of the Middle East.

Daftary, Farhad, *The Assassin Legends*, (Tauris, 1994). A more recent and detailed work concentrating on the stories that have developed around the Assassins.

Savory, Roger, *Iran under the Savafids*, (Cambridge UP, 1983)

TRAVEL WRITING
Bird, Isabella, *Journeys in Persia and Kurdistan* 2 vols, (Virago, 1989)
Byron, Robert, *The Road to Oxiana*, (Pan, 1981)
Morier, James, *The Adventures of Hajji Baba of Ispahan*, 2 vols, (Tynron, 1990, facsim ile of the 1897 edition)
Smith, Anthony, *Blind White Fish in Persia*, (Penguin, 1990)
Freya Stark, *Valley of the Assassins*, (Century Travellers, Arrow, 1991). This is per- haps Freya Stark's best-known book in which she recounts her travels on horse back through the wilds of Luristân and Mazanderân in the early 1930s.
Freya Stark, *Beyond Euphrates*, (Century Hutchinson, London 1989)

RELIGION AND PHILOSOPHY
Boyce, M, *Zoroastrians, their Religious Beliefs and Practices*, (London, 1979)
Gibb, H A R, *Islam*, (Oxford paperbacks, 1987). A short, general introduction to Islam.

LITERATURE
Attar, Farid ud-din, *The Conference of the Birds*, (Penguin Classics, 1984). A wonder ful allegorical tale, one of the greatest works of Sufi mysticism.
Khayyam, Omar, *The Ruba'iyat of Omar Khayyam*, (Penguin Classics, 1988). A good translation, closer to the original than that of Fitzgerlad. Illustrated edition, with useful appendices.
Kordi, Gohar, *An Iranian Odyssey*, (Serpents's Tail, London, 1991)
An compelling autobiography told by a blind Kurdish woman who beats all the odds and becomes a student at Tehran University.
Melville, Charles, ed, *History and Literature in Iran*, (Tauris, 1993)

ART, ARCHITECTURE AND CRAFTS
Ettinghausen, Richard & Grabar, Oleg, *The Art and Architecture of Islam 650-1250*, (Pelican History of Art, Penguin Books, 1991). A detailed account of the early development of art and architecture throughout the Islamic world. Useful for placing Iranian Islamic culture in a wider context. Well illustrated.
Ferrier, R W, *The Arts of Persia*, (Yale, 1989). Comprehensive introduction to all aspects of Persian art and architecture, both pre-Islamic and Islamic. Well illus- trated.
Housego, Jenny, *Tribal rugs, an Introduction to the Weaving of the Tribes of Iran*, (London, 1978)
Wulff, Hans, *The Traditional Crafts of Persia*, (Massuchusetts Institute of Technology Press, 1966). Deals with all aspects of traditional technology, from building *qanât* to weaving and marquetry.

(following pages); *Dasht-e Kevir desert between Tehran and Qom*

SOCIOLOGY

Beck, Lois, *Nomad—a Year in the Life of a Qashqa'i Tribesman in Iran*, (Tauris, 1991). A fascinating description of the daily life of a nomadic tribe and the breakdown of traditional ways in the modern period.

Haeri, Shahla, *Law of desire—Temporary Marriage in Iran*, (Tauris, 1989). A very revealing account of a little-known Shi'ite institution: that of the temporary marriage, a contratual agreement which may last from several hours to several years.

LANGUAGE

Elwell-Sutton, L, *Elementary Persian Grammar*, (Cambridge UP, 1974)

Mace, John, *Teach Yourself Modern Persian*, (Hodder & Stoughton, 1989)

Moshiri, Leila, *Colloquial Persian*, with cassette (Routledge, 1991)

Pocket dictionaries, as well as larger ones, can easily be bought in Tehran bookshops, including the following:

Farzenegi, Kh, *Djadid English-Persian Dictionary*, (Golshaie, Tehran, 1989)

Haim, S, *Shorter Persian-English Dictionary*, (Farhang Moaser, Tehran, 1991)

COOKERY

For those interested in discovering for themselves the unusual but delicate flavours of Iranian cuisine, the following cookbooks in English are recommended:-

Hekmat, Forough, *The Art of Persian cooking*, (Ebn-e- Sina Publishers, Tehran, 1970)

Mazda, Maideh, *In a Persian Kitchen*, (Tuttle, 1987)

Simmons, Shirin, *Entertaining the Persian Way*, (Lennard Publishing, 1991)

Index